Air Power Supremo

Dedication

For Air Commodore Peter Gray (retd) who introduced me to the achievements of MRAF Sir John Slessor and sparked my interest in researching and writing more about this great air power thinker and strategist.

Air Power Supremo

A Biography of
Marshal of the Royal Air Force
Sir John Slessor GCB, DSO, MC

William Pyke

Foreword by
Andrew Roberts

Pen & Sword
AVIATION

AN IMPRINT OF PEN & SWORD BOOKS LTD
YORKSHIRE – PHILADELPHIA

First published in Great Britain in 2022 by
PEN & SWORD AVIATION
an imprint of Pen & Sword Books Ltd
Yorkshire – Philadelphia

ISBN 978-1-39909-552-5

Typeset by Concept, Huddersfield, West Yorkshire, HD4 5JL.
Printed and bound in England by CPI Group (UK) Ltd, Croydon CR0 4YY.

Pen & Sword Books Ltd incorporates the Imprints of Aviation, Atlas, Family
History, Fiction, Maritime, Military, Discovery, Politics, History, Archaeology,
Select, Wharncliffe Local History, Wharncliffe True Crime, Military Classics,
Wharncliffe Transport, Leo Cooper, The Praetorian Press, Remember When,
White Owl, Seaforth Publishing and Frontline Books.

For a complete list of Pen & Sword titles please contact
PEN & SWORD BOOKS LTD
47 Church Street, Barnsley, South Yorkshire, S70 2AS, England
E-mail: enquiries@pen-and-sword.co.uk
Website: www.pen-and-sword.co.uk
or
PEN & SWORD BOOKS
1950 Lawrence Rd, Havertown, PA 19083, USA
E-mail: uspen-and-sword@casematepublishers.com
Website: www.penandswordbooks.com

Contents

Acknowledgements

In March 2020, and only a few days before the first Covid-19 lockdown, I gave a talk to the British Modern Military History Society at their venue at Woodcote in South Oxfordshire. The subject of my talk was Sir John Slessor and his role as Chief of the Air Staff during the early 1950s.

Among the attendees was Robin Brodhurst, who introduced himself to me. He had served with Sir John's grandson, Anthony, in the Royal Green Jackets and had maintained contact with Anthony, who at the time was travelling through the Balkans. Robin told me that he had always been an admirer of Sir John and his qualities as an air power thinker, and he thought that a new biography was long overdue. He asked if I had considered writing one. More importantly, Robin – himself a military historian who in 2000 had published an impressive biography of Sir Dudley Pound, entitled *Churchill's Anchor* – put me in touch with Anthony. This serendipitous meeting was the seed from which this book has germinated, and I am deeply indebted to Robin for encouraging me to embark on this endeavour.

From then on it was Anthony who encouraged me to write this new biography of his grandfather. He holds a comprehensive collection of Sir John's material that includes personal letters and papers, flight logbooks, photographs, sketch books and other memorabilia; he also pointed me towards other historical sources. Sir John was a keen observer of military characters and the human figure, and his many serious drawings and cartoons provide ample evidence of his innate skill. Anthony also provided me with several amusing anecdotes which are included in the book. Together, that material and the family stories have helped to provide a much deeper understanding of Sir John Slessor's character and nature.

It took me eleven months to complete the first draft of the book. During that time Anthony and his family returned to the UK in August to live in the Moray area of northern Scotland. From that time we had numerous phone conversations and correspondence via email. He provided great support to the book project, read my completed chapters and provided extremely useful advice for improvements to some of the text. His enthusiasm was infectious. He developed contacts with several key individuals in the military publishing world, and in January 2021 Anthony was instrumental in securing a contract with Pen & Sword with a plan to publish the book in early 2022.

I am also deeply grateful to my sister, Belinda Pyke, and our friend, Marion Doyen. They both proofread drafts of my first eight chapters, made helpful comments and gave me great encouragement.

In writing the narrative of various military events I recognized the important need for several maps that would enable the reader to have a fuller understanding of military dispositions. Stephen Alport is an accomplished artist and graphic designer. He is a near neighbour here in Cardiff and he willingly undertook to draft the maps to a high standard. But he also had another string to his bow. He was expert at enhancing and retouching the old photographs required for the book, using a variety of software programs. He spent many patient hours improving those images and I was fortunate to have his help.

Finally, and critically, I am extremely grateful to Peter Gray, who was my tutor at the University of Birmingham and encouraged me to write my Master's dissertation on Slessor, particularly focusing on his time as Chief of the Air Staff in the early 1950s. I realized early on that Slessor was an unsung British Cold War strategist who was instrumental in establishing the policy of strategic airborne nuclear deterrence through the build-up of the V-force effected during the mid- to late 1950s. This book is dedicated to Peter.

Beyond this preamble of acknowledgements, I would be remiss if I did not mention the one person without whose support none of this would have been possible. My wife, Mary, has been patient and supportive, and without her tolerance and encouragement this book would never have left the starting blocks. Behind every throne . . .

William Pyke
Pontcanna,
Cardiff
June 2021

Foreword

It is remarkable that despite his fascinating, exciting life and his tremendous importance in twentieth-century history, Marshal of the Royal Air Force Sir John ('Jack') Slessor has not been the subject of a really first-class biography, until now. We are thus hugely in William Pyke's debt for filling a significant historiographical lacuna, and for doing it with such élan and scholarship. 'Although he would himself have hotly denied it,' Professor Sir Michael Howard wrote of Slessor, 'he was indeed a truly great man. His contribution to the winning of the war had been outstanding. No less was his contribution to the subsequent keeping of the peace.' This book brilliantly explains how Slessor did both, earning the implicit trust of Sir Winston Churchill into the bargain.

In retrospect, it redounded greatly to the lasting advantage of the Royal Air Force and Great Britain and its Empire that Jack Slessor contracted polio at the age of three. He survived with a debilitating weakness in both legs and always had to walk with a cane. On the outbreak of war in 1914, therefore, he was formally certified as 'unfit for any form of military service'. If he was to fight for King and Country – which he was determined to do – he would have to do it sitting down. The newly created Royal Flying Corps provided just such an opportunity.

Slessor's career, and his thinking and writing about air power, spans almost the whole story of flight in the first half of the twentieth century, from the painful birth-pangs of industrialized warfare right up to the strategic complexities that are familiar to us even today. A formative military thinker, and in many ways a successor to his contemporaries Major General J.F.C. Fuller and Basil Liddell Hart, Slessor took theories and put them into actual practice on the ground and in the air. He fearlessly came up with the geopolitical strategies of deterrence and addressed the terrifying contentions of the atomic and nuclear age, in a way that has successfully kept the peace between the Great Powers for three-quarters of a century.

This well-researched and well-written book is being published at a critical time for Western democracy. Russia's revanchist expansionism and guileless disregard for international probity, combined with China's burgeoning economic global role, coupled with her blatant geopolitical ambitions to push against US hegemony both in the South China Sea and worldwide, suggest that we are being reluctantly forced into a new Cold War. Cyber warfare and an increasing focus on the Space battlefield (satellites, Hypersonic Glide Vehicles, 'Star Wars', et al.) have added poignancy to considerations of deterrence, conflict escalation, and First Strike capabilities.

Fortunately, Slessor's thoughts and writings provide a useful guide in our present dilemmas. Pyke's book takes us through the declensions in Slessor's thinking as it evolved, encompassing many aspects of the phenomenon of air power. Slessor's vital contributions to the Battle of the Atlantic, the Mediterranean, Italian and Balkan campaigns, the Special Relationship and postwar geopolitical developments are all covered with masterly analysis.

Born into a military family in 1897 in India, Slessor returned to England three years later. After an idyllic childhood in Oxford, he joined the RFC and within a year had won the Military Cross for air operations in the Sudan, before serving on the Western Front in 1917 and 1918. He was the first pilot to engage an enemy aircraft over Britain (a Zeppelin). At the time of the Armistice – aged only 21 – Slessor was a major and had received the two Croix de guerre of France and Belgium.

During the interwar years, Slessor crystallized his ideas on the application of air power. He also commanded a squadron on India's troubled North-West Frontier, lectured at the Army's staff college at Camberley on the changing role of air power in support of ground forces, and commanded the air wing of no fewer than three squadrons in Waziristan. In 1936 he wrote the seminal work *Air Power and Armies*, which is still used in the US Air Force to this day. Many of the theories to be found in the book, such as that of Air Interdiction, would be put into practice during the Second World War and beyond.

Recognizing that he had an important contribution to make, the self-confident Slessor was never far from the centre of power, and, as Pyke demonstrates, he was instrumental in bringing about significant changes. His participation in secret, civilianized ABC (American British Conversations) staff talks in early 1941 helped to prepare for America's entry into the war. Readers will recognize Slessor as key to the forging of strong links between the Royal Air Force and the United States Army Air Forces, subsequently to become the United States Air Force.

Slessor held three commands during the war: of 5 Group, Bomber Command; of Coastal Command; and as Deputy Commander-in-Chief of the Mediterranean Allied Air Forces (MAAF). He arrived at Coastal Command just as the Atlantic Gap was being closed, and deployed aircraft into 'the vital ground' of the Bay of Biscay. It was on his watch in 1943 that the U-boats suffered their heaviest losses, turning the tide of the war for the Western Allies and allowing Operation Overlord to be undertaken the following year. As Deputy Commander of the MAAF – the largest coalition air force ever assembled at that time – he brought to bear his diplomatic skills, both internationally and in inter-service relationships. These helped him make a critical contribution to the campaigns in Italy and the Balkans.

As a Cold War strategist, Slessor made a seminal contribution to British defence policy, one that placed nuclear deterrence at the centre of defence strategy, which represented a fundamental shift in policy. Through persistence and persuasion, he ensured that Britain's independent airborne nuclear deterrent would effectively come under her tutelage, albeit transmuting subsequently to the submarine-based systems of today. As this ground-breaking book proves, Slessor's influence was much more than a mere contribution: he led the way, especially amongst fellow service chiefs, and guided his political masters. Slessor was a prodigious writer of books and articles, publishing widely on a range of air power issues throughout his career in the RAF and in retirement, and much of what he wrote in the early period of the Cold War correctly predicted its eventual outcome.

In 1991 General the Lord Ramsbotham was asked by a senior colleague why the RAF had never produced a thinker. 'They have,' the general replied, 'Slessor.' This excellent book will leave readers in no doubt that Ramsbotham was right.

Andrew Roberts
April 2021

Introduction

Marshal of the Royal Air Force Sir John Slessor stands out as one of the greatest air power thinkers of the twentieth century. But, in addition, he was also a world-class military and political strategist. He lived a rich, adventurous and varied life in far-off lands as well as on European battlefields, and was amongst the first generation of military airmen, rising in the Second World War to command appointments critical to the success of Britain's military endeavour. His air force career of thirty-seven years spanned the period that saw the inception of air power, from flying the fragile wood and canvas biplanes of the First World War evolving through to the atomic air power era of the four-engined, high-altitude jet bombers that appeared in the 1950s.

I came to write this biography for several reasons. A thorough literature search revealed that many of the leading military and political historians, and other academics, have underestimated, ignored or often dismissed Slessor's important contributions. *The Times*'s anonymous obituarist wrote in 1979 that 'Slessor did not come out of the last war as one of the great popular figures. He was not a commander whose attributes caught the attention of the man in the street, nor of wartime servicemen for that matter'.[1] This misses the mark. That Slessor was not well-known by the man in the street is down to his key role in the hard grind of vital campaigns in the Atlantic and Mediterranean, where his contribution was, with no hint of hyperbole, campaign-winning. As for the attention of wartime servicemen, you would be hard pushed to find an enlisted man who knew him whose admiration was anything other than unstinting. But those written remarks finally compelled me to challenge these prevalent assumptions by setting the record straight and writing a biography that demonstrated, with clear historical evidence, his many achievements throughout his career. Additionally, Slessor was certainly not without admirers both in Britain and the United States during his lifetime. Those who came to recognize Slessor's qualities have included British military historians Sir Michael Howard, Sir Max Hastings, Anthony Seldon, John Baylis, Henry Probert, Noble Frankland and Andrew Roberts, and the American military historians Phillip Meilinger, Clayton Chun and Andrew Pierre.

Jack Slessor came from a distinguished line of military officers whose exploits have been recorded in minute detail in Alethea Hayter's deeply researched book, *The Backbone*.[2] Jack's great-great-grandfather was Major General John Slessor, who served in both the British and Portuguese armies, ending his career as Governor of Oporto and dying in 1800. John Slessor had seven children, one of whom – Royal Naval Lieutenant Henry Slessor – was killed in action in 1806, while two others served in the army. Of those two, Captain William Slessor, commissioned into the East India Company, was killed in a hunting accident at Kishanganj, India in 1810. The other was Jack's great-grandfather, Major General John Henry Slessor. John Henry commanded a battalion of the 35th in General Sir Charles Colville's 4th Division at Waterloo. His division saw no fighting on the day but was held in reserve by Wellington, sitting astride the road to Brussels in anticipation of Bonaparte's flanking manoeuvre to turn the British right flank and achieve a clear road on to the Belgian capital. This did not materialize, and the division was duly accorded the privilege of storming Cambrai six days later. John Henry finished his military career as Governor of Zante, off the west coast of Greece.

Jack's father, Arthur, continued the family military tradition, seeing extensive service in India, where Jack was born in 1897 at Ranikhet on the southern edge of the Himalayas. By the time of his death Jack's family had amassed an eclectic family of cousins: French, Portuguese, Spanish, Italian, American and Australian.

In his formative years the young Jack Slessor grew up in Oxford during the first decade of the twentieth century. But he had a difficult start in life, contracting poliomyelitis at the age of 3. But none of this deterred Jack from participating in most sports, even though the disease left him with lameness in both legs. He was to spend the rest of his life walking with a cane. He attended the Dragon preparatory school (then known as Lynam's) on the Bardwell Road in Oxford and at the age of 13 he transferred to Haileybury College in Hertfordshire. Jack enjoyed his time at Haileybury despite the spartan conditions in the dormitories and washrooms. He described himself as an average student who was more interested in the Classics and Humanities rather than scientific subjects. He continued to be active in sports, including cricket, which he loved – demonstrating a deft skill with the bat by all accounts – although his lameness meant that he always needed the services of a 'runner'. The declaration of war in August 1914 changed Jack Slessor's plan to stay on at Haileybury. Perhaps, if war had not intervened, he might well have followed his father to read Classics at Oxford. But at the end of the autumn term he travelled to London aged 17 to enlist with the Army. He was to be thoroughly disappointed when the Medical Board rejected his application on the basis of his being 'totally unfit for any form of military service'.[3] But Jack was always a persistent character. Using family connections, he managed to get an interview with the Royal Flying Corps (RFC). He made a favourable impression, and the interviewers said that if he obtained permission from his father and headmaster, and passed the Medical Board examination, he would be accepted on his 18th birthday. The true story of how Jack managed all that in one day stretches credibility, involving train journeys and hijacking his father's horse in the midst of a parade. But achieve it he did.

A year later, having seen action against Zeppelins over southern England and attacked Turkish positions in the Sinai, Slessor and three fellow air officers were deployed to Darfur, in western Sudan, where the campaign focused on an uprising of rebel tribes. Flying their BE2c aircraft, they found themselves supporting a large force of Sudanese and Egyptian troops. Slessor became actively involved in bombing and strafing the rebel force. In the course of one solo attack, aged only 18, he was struck in the leg by a stray .450 Remington bullet. Despite the injury, and losing a worrying quantity of blood, he managed to steer his aircraft back to its desert airstrip. He was operated on immediately – with the congenial anaesthetic of hot champagne and brandy – and was invalided back to England, arriving in early June 1916. For his bravery in Darfur he was awarded a Military Cross. While convalescing in London, and dressed in a suit rather than his customary uniform, he found himself aboard a bus when two ladies climbed aboard and moved along the aisle; one of them pinned the coward's badge of a white feather to his lapel. He saw further action over the Western Front between May 1917 and early 1918.

Between 1919 and 1939 Slessor undertook two tours of duty in India and commanded the Army Cooperation Squadron based at Farnborough. He was posted to the Air Ministry initially in 1925 and later between 1928 and 1930 when he reported to the Chief of the Air Staff, Lord Trenchard. 'Boom' Trenchard was to have a considerable influence on Slessor's career. They remained colleagues and friends for the rest of their lives. By the early 1930s Slessor was evolving ideas for tactics to be used by the RAF in joint operations with the Army. Slessor subscribed to most, but not all, of Trenchard's ideas on strategic air bombardment. Slessor wrote later 'our belief in the bomber was intuitive, a matter of faith'.[4] However, he was never keen on the idea of morale bombardment in order to break the will of the people, for reasons of both morality and strategic effect.

Between 1931 and 1934 Slessor lectured at the Army Staff College, Camberley. His course was to propose, review and analyse the ways in which the Army and the Air Force could cooperate in the context of an air/ground battlefield setting. His lectures delivered over the four-year period were published subsequently in his first book, *Air Power and Armies.* It was a seminal work that was well received in Britain and America. Whereas other air power theorists concentrated on the primacy of the bomber in offensive operations, Slessor stressed the importance of air/ground cooperation on the battlefield, which until then had been largely, although not entirely, ignored at the higher levels.

In 1937 Slessor returned to the Air Ministry for a third time to be appointed as Deputy Director of Plans. With Germany rearming rapidly and making increasingly belligerent threats, war was starting to look ever more inevitable. It was a frustrating period for Slessor, who was sensibly looking to build an air force that could effectively counter the Nazi threat. Until 1939 budget restraints led to delays in delivering a heavy bomber force into squadron service. The only redeeming feature under Scheme 'M' of the air rearmament programme (see Appendix B) was an increase in the number of Fighter Command's newest models, the Hawker Hurricane and the Supermarine Spitfire, that were essential to winning the Battle of Britain in 1940.

When war came in September 1939 Slessor was part of a Joint Services planning group. The Anglo-French alliance provided the only effective force capable of preventing an invasion of Northern France and the Low Countries. But in May 1940 the Germans simultaneously invaded Holland, Belgium, Luxembourg and finally northern France. Within six weeks the French armies had been defeated, the RAF had lost a thousand aircraft to enemy action and the British Expeditionary Force (BEF) was becoming surrounded; only with the help of the Royal Navy and 'the little ships' did they manage to pull off a miraculous evacuation from Dunkirk. These were dark moments as Britain's survival as a sovereign nation hung in the balance.

During the summer of 1940 Roosevelt sent his personal emissaries and United States Army Air Forces specialists to Britain to assess Britain's chances of survival. Slessor was detailed to escort the Americans around RAF airfields and to take the opportunity to discuss with key individuals the imports of American military aircraft. Among Slessor's great strengths were his personal charm, affability and an incorrigible determination to achieve positive outcomes. He got on well with most Americans, who liked and respected him because of his clear, straight-talking manner, which he used with both wisdom and authority (in stark contrast, it must be said, to the British penchant for understatement and social obfuscation). He gained their trust and several of them, including Carl Spaatz and Ira Eaker, became close personal friends. In late 1940, after the Battle of Britain, Sir Charles Portal, Chief of the Air

Staff, assigned Slessor to be his representative at the secret ABC staff conversations that were held between senior military American and British officers. It was a clear sign of how much trust Portal had in the young Air Commodore Slessor. These talks took place in Washington eight months before the Japanese attack on Pearl Harbor; the British representatives routed through neutral Lisbon, Portugal, and wore only civilian clothes. The ABC discussions centred on two key issues: the position America would take if it entered the war in Europe, and the aircraft allocations to be made available to the British. The talks were a success and ensured that a future Anglo-American strategy was mapped out. Portal was impressed with Slessor's achievements, and it was no surprise that he requested Slessor to accompany him to the Casablanca Conference in 1943. His contributions there were invaluable in resolving outstanding difficulties relating to differences of opinion between the American and British chiefs of staff, particularly in finding a form of words to describe Allied priorities that would soothe American sensibilities, most poignantly in regard to their worries over the Pacific theatre of operations. Once again Slessor's (in this case, prandial) wordsmithing did the trick and Portal signed off the memo with scarcely an amendment.

Slessor held three operational commands during the Second World War. In April 1941 he was Air Officer Commanding (AOC) 5 Group, Bomber Command. It was a low point in Bomber Command's performance. Not only were the aircraft underpowered or obsolescent, but the aircrews did not yet have the necessary navigation aids and often failed to find and bomb key targets. It was a frustrating time for Slessor, who was always committed to carrying the war to Germany through a sustained bombing offensive. Bomber Command's best days still lay in the future.

In February 1943 Slessor took over as AOC-in-C Coastal Command, at a critical moment in the Battle of the Atlantic. Early 1943 saw a critical loss of Allied shipping to U-boat attacks. At Coastal Command Slessor controlled 850 aircraft of all types, 456 of which were dedicated to antisubmarine warfare. Slessor deployed his aircraft effectively in two critical areas: the Bay of Biscay and the North Atlantic Air Gap, south of Greenland.

To understand the reason for Coastal Command's Bay of Biscay campaign and the danger of the U-boat threat it is important to consider the Kriegmarine's strategy. Location had given the Germans a distinct geographical advantage. In June 1940 Admiral Dönitz had visited Lorient after the German occupation of Western France. As commander of the Kriegsmarine's U-boat fleet, he was convinced he could destroy marine cargoes destined for Britain, thereby leading ultimately to its defeat. Lorient together with four other sites on the Biscay coast were ideal for much shorter transit routes to the mid-Atlantic. He authorized the construction of reinforced concrete bunkers (U-boat pens) that were completed by late 1941. Between that time and early 1943 Allied shipping losses had become a critical issue. But by June 1943 the tide had turned. Although the U-boat menace had not been eliminated, and for some months would continue to pose a significant threat to Allied shipping, vital to the build-up of men and supplies preparing for the invasion of Europe in 1944, the survival of the UK no longer hung in the balance.

During his time at Coastal Command eighty-four U-boats were destroyed by Slessor's aircraft. His strategy for the Bay of Biscay and also the Atlantic Air Gap had been vindicated. Slessor was well-respected by his aircrews, and many considered him to be the best commander of Coastal Command during the war.

In January 1944 Slessor was appointed as Deputy Commander of the Anglo-American Mediterranean Air Forces, which at that time was the largest and most international of the Allied air forces. Between March and May Operation Strangle was put into effect. It was a test of Slessor's as yet untried theory of air interdiction. The operation was a resounding success and seriously restrained the movement of the German forces north of the Gustav line. Elsewhere, Slessor was actively involved in forming the Balkan Air Force, which supported Tito's Yugoslavian partisans fighting the Germans. He also became involved in an attempt to support the Warsaw uprising by airlifting arms and supplies to the Polish home army, but the mission ended in failure. He never forgave the Russians for their cynical disregard for the Polish forces being crushed by the Germans in central Warsaw and within a short distance of Soviet forces massing on the outskirts of the city; they were waiting for the Germans to annihilate the Polish forces, thus ridding Stalin of the future opposition to his own plans for occupation. Slessor had foreseen the impending difficulties and reluctantly argued against the operation. His forebodings were realized: there were very heavy aircrew losses and most of the matériel fell into German hands.

During more than six years of war Slessor had taken charge of three demanding commands. He now needed time to plan and think about the future of the RAF and he was appointed as the Air Member for Personnel (AMP) for three years with responsibility for demobilizing a large number of service personnel, and reshaping a smaller air force relevant for the post-war world. Between 1948 and 1949 he was appointed as Commandant of the Imperial Defence College. This gave him valuable time to think about key strategic and military issues. As World War tumbled into Cold War the emergent threat of the Soviet Union as a potential adversary was one of the key issues. During that time he also travelled to America to deliver lectures to military staff colleges and to visit senior Pentagon officials.

When Jack Slessor became Chief of the Air Staff he was confronted with considerable challenges. First, the Soviet Union had tested its first atomic bomb in 1949, thereby presenting a realistic threat to Britain. The USAF's Strategic Air Command (SAC) had started deploying nuclear-capable B-29s at five airfields in eastern England that would make the area a prime target for a nuclear attack in time of war. Second, in 1950 Bomber Command had a small and obsolescent fleet of Lincolns and Lancasters. These did not have the range, speed and altitude to reach Soviet targets and would have been easy prey for the Soviet MiG-15 fighters then entering service in large numbers. Slessor impressed on his political masters the urgent need to build up the complement of four-engined jet bombers that would eventually be capable of delivering Britain's atomic deterrent. Despite the crippling restrictions of post-war austerity, he received approval from Attlee's government to proceed with the production of twenty-five Valiants, which had now been given 'super-priority'.

In June the North Korean army invaded South Korea. Western experts tried to decipher whether the orders to do so came directly from Stalin, or whether the newly installed Chinese Communist government was orchestrating the installation of Communist governments throughout Southeast Asia. From Slessor's perspective, he was concerned that if general war broke out, Britain would become a prime target for Soviet air attack. During the ensuing months the Americans regained the initiative and executed an ambitious invasion plan near the Korean coastal city of Inchon. The invasion was a success. It emboldened General MacArthur to invade North Korea as far north as the Yalu river and the Chinese border. Slessor considered that this provocative advance in North Korea would bring in the Chinese Army and Air Force. He duly warned both Clement Attlee and Ernest Bevin, the foreign secretary.

In early December 1950 matters came to a head when Truman did not rule out the use of atomic weapons in a widening conflict.

All of this alarmed Slessor. The British did not have information about America's war plans. The Americans, wary of a socialist British government, simply acknowledged that the British would be consulted in a time of acute crisis. Without clarity, such a crisis might well put Britain under threat of atomic attack. Slessor briefed Attlee, who immediately flew to Washington. Fortunately, the moment of crisis passed. But the Korean War continued for a further thirty months, until an armistice was signed in 1953.

Winston Churchill was elected prime minister in October 1951. He called on the British Chiefs of Staff to prepare a paper that looked at a fundamental reappraisal of British defence policy. With regards to the defence of Europe, a NATO agreement in Lisbon would require the Europeans to provide ninety-six army divisions and 9,000 aircraft, all to be completed within a two-year time frame. It was an unrealistic ambition. Most European nations were in various states of post-war recovery and would be unable to reach the so-called 'force goals'.

Slessor and his Chief of Staff colleagues, Field Marshal Sir William Slim and Admiral Sir Rhoderick McGrigor, took time away from their offices and spent several days at the Royal Naval College at Greenwich. Slessor took a dominant role in writing the draft paper. In essence, it placed nuclear deterrence at the centre of the British strategic defence policy. It was a revolutionary move. It comprehensively rejected the requirement to build up large conventional forces in Europe that would, in any event, cripple several of the recovering European economies.

The paper, known simply as the 'Global Strategy Paper, 1952' (GSP), was presented to the Cabinet in June 1952. In truth, the paper was written as much for the Joint Chiefs of Staff (JCS) in Washington as for the British Cabinet. The message was clear, and Slessor was sent to Washington to sell the idea. The JCS were unimpressed, although ironically the British paper inevitably influenced Eisenhower's 'New Look' defence policy that was adopted in 1954.

In the quest to develop a credible deterrence programme, air reconnaissance of the Soviet Union's key strategic sites was required. President Truman forbade clandestine 'spy flights' over the western Soviet Union. However, if British pilots flew American reconnaissance jets with RAF insignia, this would circumvent Truman's restriction. British pilots were trained to fly the RB-45c Tornados based in at RAF Sculthorpe in Norfolk. The overflights occurred in April 1952 with three planes manned by six RAF crew. Each aircraft took a different route with the intention of locating the Soviet long-range air bases. The operation was a success, and twenty out of thirty-five long-range Soviet airfields were identified by radar scope photographic images.

But Slessor's biggest challenge was to ensure that, despite budgetary restraints, plans stayed on track to produce the 240 V-force bombers that were now set to enter service during the 1950s. He faced criticisms and objections from both military theorists, such as his friend, Basil Liddell-Hart, and Labour and Conservative MPs who preferred 'to leave atomic air power to the Americans'. His great achievement as Chief of the Air Staff was to ensure that the V-force project continued. Britain would have an independent nuclear deterrent.

Slessor retired on 31 December 1952 after thirty-seven years of service to the Air Force. He had ensured that the development and production of the V-force would proceed. But retirement did not diminish his enthusiasm for writing about strategies to deal with the challenges of the Cold War. He wrote numerous articles during the 1950s. He also wrote three books between 1953 and 1957, gave lectures in both Britain and America, and appeared on BBC and ITV television, in addition to radio programmes. The discussion of deterrence and the use of atomic (and later hydrogen) weapons had entered the national consciousness. His publications during the 1950s demonstrated his qualities as a first-rate strategic thinker. John Baylis wrote in 1977 that 'Slessor's post-war publications laid the foundations for further study ... which are now the main organizing concepts of contemporary strategic thought.'[5] Slessor continued to make a strong plea to his readers that the great deterrent had abolished total, general war.

Chapter 1

Twilight, La Belle Époque

The Last Rays of the Golden Edwardian Age, Halcyon Days in Oxford and Haileybury

John Cotesworth Slessor was born on 3 June 1897 in Ranikhet, a small town located 160 miles northeast of Delhi in the Himalayan foothills. During the 1890s Ranikhet was also a military cantonment and hill station for the army at the time of the British Raj. John's father, Arthur Kerr Slessor, was a major in the Sherwood Foresters regiment, who had served in postings to the West Indies, the Gold Coast (now Ghana) and latterly in India. The family background and history on both John's father's and mother's sides was predominantly military, with his antecedents serving in both the Army and Royal Navy.[1] His great-grandfather, Major General John Slessor, commanded a battalion at the Battle of Waterloo.[2]

John Slessor was better known as 'Jack' to his family and friends. He was the first born in a family of three boys and a girl.[3] Jack recalled his earliest experience as follows:

> My first memory in life was standing on the little low brick wall between our front garden (I suppose 100 ft by 100), being supported by Nanny, and watching the battalion marching to the barracks headed, of course, by the band, on the way from the [Folkestone] docks. I think the first time I remember hearing the Regimental March 'on the first of May or March away, and what would all the ladies say'. Shortly after this, Father, realizing that he had little hope of a career in the Army having lost 3 years by the existing system of university entry, which meant you did three years at Oxford and <u>then</u> went to Sandhurst, and having missed the great SA [South African] war – put in for the job as bursar of his old college, Christ Church, of which he had been a scholar, and got it. So, we went to Oxford and lived in a little house in the Woodstock Road.[4]

In the Edwardian era Oxbridge college stewards were often recruited from the senior ranks of the Army, being valued for their traditions of strong leadership, discipline and organizational skills. The role of Christ Church's

Steward is equivalent to that of the more commonly titled college bursar, being responsible primarily for the handling of accounts, but also supervising the organization and allocation of students; the management of college staff, who included the cleaners, cooks and gardeners, amongst other trades; and the booking of dinners and other social events. Jack Slessor recalled that his father was 'a good scholar, an excellent gardener, and a sound judge of vintage port'.[5]

The 6-year-old Jack was enrolled in the Dragon Preparatory School in central Oxford, which he attended for seven years until 1910. He had many happy memories of growing up in central Oxford. Their second home in the Iffley Road had idyllic views to the west, 'across the expanse of smooth turf and beyond to the trees of Christ Church meadows – hardly another building in sight'.[6] The early years of his upbringing in the beautiful surroundings of central Oxford made a lasting impression on young Jack. To be growing up in Edwardian England in a prosperous home was a special time. Historians have also referred to the period as the final years of the 'gilded age' of peace and prosperity that was brought to an abrupt end by the start of the First World War in August 1914.[7] In 'Recollections' held in Haileybury's school archive, Jack Slessor recalled Edwardian Oxford with 'horse trams still clanking down the High and hansom cabs waited for fares at St. Aldate's, their horses wore straw hats in high summer and tossed their nose-bags, scattering grain on the cobbles of the cab-stand to the delight of the Oxford sparrows. Winter was fun. There was skating on the flooded meadows downstream of the Barges.'[8] However, not all was perfect for Jack. At the age of 3 he suffered from infantile paralysis, now better known as poliomyelitis. This illness left him with lameness in his legs for the rest of his life, usually walking with the aid of a cane. But this did not prevent him from enjoying sports, notably cricket. The Christ Church cricket field was just beyond the rear garden in the Iffley Road, and he would have watched the college team play on numerous occasions.

In September 1910 Jack was enrolled as a boarder at Haileybury School near Hoddesdon in Hertfordshire, some 20 miles north of London. The school was originally founded as a training establishment in 1806 for administrators of the East India Company (EIC). It would have been the equivalent of the present-day executive management school. However, following the Indian mutiny of 1857–1858, the EIC became insolvent, and the establishment was closed. It was reopened as a public school in 1862, but still maintained strong links during the time of the British Raj. Many of the early attendees were the sons of the military and civil servants who were serving in India.

Over the years the school has produced more than its fair share of famous alumni with diverse talents; they include Clement Attlee, the prime minister between 1945 and 1951, several senior air commanders in addition to Slessor, notably Air Chief Marshals Sir Trafford Leigh-Mallory and Sir Henry Robert Brooke-Popham; the racing driver Stirling Moss; the artist Rex Whistler; and the playwright Alan Ayckbourn.

Attlee's biographer, John Bew, gave a further insight into Haileybury during the late Victorian era. Attlee was at Haileybury fourteen years before Slessor. Bew described the school in the 1890s as being 'more Etonian than Eton itself, though a bit cheaper'.[9] The school of 520 boys had a strong work ethos, stressing the virtues of military-style discipline, and a commitment to service in the Empire. Little would have been different by the time Jack Slessor arrived at Haileybury.

Perhaps Jack underestimated the value of his time at Haileybury. In *Central Blue*, an autobiographical account of his life, together with his thoughts, opinions and impressions until the end of the Second World War, he recalls, 'my career at Haileybury was entirely undistinguished', adding 'I was a rather idle boy with a capacity for making friends and getting a good deal of fun out of life, but with a marked distaste for hard work.'[10] During his time there he preferred the arts to scientific subjects. He had a particular love of the classics, believing 'an education in the classics is as good a basic training for the military as for any other career'.[11] But he surely understated the benefit of the sound education he received during his school years. In his adult life Slessor demonstrated time and again his proficiency in writing. Lord Trenchard relied on Slessor to write many of his speeches, referring to him as one of his 'English merchants'. Archival material has repeatedly demonstrated his talent for comprehensive yet concise analysis in his many reports.

His time at Haileybury was also a period of deeply held patriotism for King, Country, Empire and Church. These values were reinforced in the public school environment and moulded his thinking throughout his adult life. Entry into the military might have seemed a natural progression for the young Slessor. It must have. However, as he recalled, 'Though I came of a service family, a couple of lame legs resulting from an attack of infantile paralysis as a small boy had put paid to my hopes of a military career of any sort.'[12]

Chapter 2

The Kaiser's War

Unfit for Duty, Flying Training, the Sudan, the Western Front, and a White Feather

In his books and articles Slessor referred to the First World War as the 'Kaiser's War'. To the reader this may appear a little odd. Why did he not refer to it as 'the Great War' or 'the First World War'? Undoubtedly, like perhaps many of his contemporaries who lived and fought through the period, he held Kaiser Wilhelm II uniquely responsible for its cause.[1]

Over a period of three years Slessor would see action over England, the Sinai, Sudan and finally the Western Front. Those experiences would give him much to think about in forming his views on air power theory, practice and policy during the interwar years. In his own words he reflected on the period thus: 'I rather enjoyed the first war. One made a lot of friends, had a lot of fun, fell in love once or twice and generally behaved in the manner of most healthy young air force officers.'[2] However, he was incredibly lucky to survive the war. Over the Western Front in 1917 the average life expectancy for pilots in combat while flying was placed at just sixteen hours, and far shorter for new, inexperienced pilots. Some 70 per cent of all pilots flying over the Western Front were either killed, wounded or went missing in action between 1914 and 1918.[3]

Slessor was just 17 when war came in August 1914. He was still at Haileybury and perhaps had war not intervened he may well have followed in his father's footsteps to read Classics at Oxford. Instead, he wasted no time in planning to enlist in the Army. He left Haileybury and his studies in the Lower Sixth Classics group at the end of the autumn term and moved to London in the new year. During this time he stayed at Haileybury House in Stepney. In previous years Old Haileyburians had raised funds to establish Haileybury House as a charitable foundation to help in tackling extreme poverty in the East End of London.[4] It was also used to give underprivileged boys an opportunity to join the army cadets and had been a route for some to eventually becoming NCOs.

Slessor enlists in the Royal Flying Corps, 14 June 1915

At Haileybury House Slessor made his contribution in the evenings at the 'Boys' Club' as the cadet officer for A Company of the 1st Cadet Battalion of the Queen's Royal Regiment. But ultimately he was in London to enlist in the Army. He was to be disappointed. He failed his army medical, being instantly regarded as 'totally unfit for any form of military service' – a legacy of the polio he had contracted as a child. This had left him with lameness in his legs. But Slessor was always persistent and, in his own words, 'made himself a nuisance to a lot of busy people who had other things to do'. One of those 'busy people' was Lieutenant Colonel W.W. ('Willie') Warner, who was responsible for recruiting officers for the new Royal Flying Corps (RFC), formed in 1912 as the aviation section of the Army. It was no coincidence that Warner had served in India with Slessor's uncle. He would reflect later that he never had reservations about 'pulling strings', affirming a 'lifelong conviction that the best methods for the selection of officers are by selective and controlled nepotism'.[5] In addition, Slessor's enthusiasm and confidence would certainly have helped in the interview. Turning to his colleague, Warner asked, 'I don't see why this boy shouldn't be perfectly able to fly, do you?'

'Yes,' came the reply, 'I should think he would fly all right, let's see you walk across the room!'[6] However, the offer came with a critical requirement: his application had to be signed by both his father and the Master of Hailey-bury School that same day, and he had to attend the medical board at the War Office at 5pm. Young Jack was now under immense time pressure to fulfil the requirements. But by an amazing coincidence Jack's father had been called into service as a commanding officer at an army camp only 3 miles from Haileybury. Jack rushed to get the first available train to Broxbourne station, 20 miles north of central London. As the train pulled into the station, 'by the longest of long odds' a marching column of troops and a band were being followed by Jack's father riding on the commanding officer's charger. Not only did Jack get his father's signature, but he also took the charger, leaving his father in a bemused state in the middle of the road, and galloped off to Haileybury, where he also got the Master's signature. Jack returned to London and was ushered into the Medical Board 'damp with sweat and pink with excitement'.[7] And that was it; he was accepted for air duties with the RFC, and was to start in June, the month of his eighteenth birthday. Slessor's initial interest in flying had been sparked at the age of 15 after he had attended a school careers talk on the RFC[8] given by an old Haileyburian, Robert Brooke-Popham, who at that time was the commander of 3 Squadron. Perhaps at that moment Slessor did not hold out much hope on account of his medical history. He was not to be disappointed.

Flight Training, Brooklands and Fort Grange, Gosport, Hampshire, June–September 1915

Slessor started his flight training programme at Fort Grange near Gosport in Hampshire. He received his FAI flight certificate as a pilot after flying solo for only ninety minutes.[9] During his time at Brooklands and Fort Grange Slessor amassed a further thirty hours of flying, but not before pranging four aircraft. In his autobiography, *Central Blue*, he wrote, 'I had flown a number of queer old aeroplanes', including one called 'the Caudron, with the gliding angle of a brick'.[10] This was hardly surprising, for in those early years of aviation, flying and an understanding of aerodynamics were still in their infancy.

Despite these mishaps Slessor was considered 'a good pilot'; he made the grade and was commissioned during the summer as a second lieutenant and finally received his 'wings' at the Central Flying School at Upavon in Wiltshire in August.[11] One of his first duties was to deliver one of the new BE2c biplanes from Coventry to St Omer on the Western Front.[12] While there he made a cheeky, and failed, attempt to join 13 Squadron, which at that time was deeply involved in the Battle of Loos.

Slessor and the Zeppelin raid, 23 Squadron, September–October 1915

In September Slessor and some of his fellow officers from Fort Grange were selected to train in 23 Squadron for night flying. These young pilots were responsible for defending southeast England, and particularly London, from Zeppelin raids. In early October he took delivery of a new BE2c and flew to Sutton's Farm near Hornchurch in Essex.[13] The airfield at that time was basic: level ground with stubble left from a recent harvest providing the landing strip, canvas hangars for the aircraft, and a gun crew that had a 13-pounder and one searchlight. On 13 October Slessor was on standby duty alone at the airfield. It was a cold, clear evening when he received an urgent phone call from the War Office. Of all people, it was Willie Warner informing him that he had received information of four or five Zeppelins over Thetford and travelling south-westwards towards London. He was ordered to patrol as long as his fuel supply would allow. The following day he wrote a long letter to his mother describing the entire experience in detail, part of which reads:

> The fog was a bit clearer and I decided to go up. I was carrying four 8lb powder bombs in a rack under the machine [a BE2c] ... and six inflammable bombs. I cleared the mist at about 500 feet – it was a lovely night. I could see London and all the suburbs, a maze of subdued lights, through the ground fog to the West. I had not been up 10 minutes, and

was about 3,000 high, still climbing, when I saw the Zep. over the Thames somewhere with a searchlight on him. He looked like the other side of a salmon, and I judged he was about 8–9,000 feet up. I climbed on as fast as I could, but lost him after about 3 minutes, and the searchlight got off him and I never saw him again.[14]

However, his sortie finished ignominiously with a crash landing in extremely poor visibility back at the Sutton airstrip. It resulted in damage to a wing tip, an aileron and an undercarriage support strut. That October night five Zeppelins went on to drop bombs that caused thirty-one civilian deaths and damage to buildings in central London and the suburbs.[15]

The following day Slessor and a few of the groundcrew used a truck to take the damaged parts of the aircraft over to Farnborough. As they passed down the Mile End Road in the East End of London they were accosted by an angry mob, only to be guided through eventually by a police escort. Mile End Road was close to the area that had been bombed the night before. The experience stayed with Slessor throughout the interwar period: that civilians might be terrorized by 'the few puny raids of the first World War'.[16] However, it is possible that he mistook anger for fear – the anger, totally unjustified, that this very young RFC pilot had not been able to prevent the Zeppelin raid.

Action in the Sinai, 17 Squadron, January–March 1916

In October Slessor joined the troopship *Scotia* at Avonmouth for deployment to Mudros on the east side of the Greek island of Lemnos in the eastern Aegean. The Mudros air base was within flying range of the Dardanelles peninsula. However, when he arrived, he learnt that the campaign was going badly with evacuation in progress.[17]

Consequently, Slessor was redeployed to Egypt and he disembarked at Alexandria in January 1916. From there he was transferred to 17 Squadron and for nearly three months he was based in the Sinai. He flew numerous reconnaissance sorties in a BE2c over Turkish positions, culminating in a successful bombing raid on the supply base at El Gabbara. But there were also pleasant breaks from front-line squadron duty. He enjoyed hunting trips to the 'big *jheel*', a large area of wetlands, and the shallows of Lake Mariut, south of Alexandria.[18]

The Darfur rebellion and 'the Flying Chariots', C Flight, 17 Squadron, March–May 1916

However, Slessor was about to be redeployed once more, this time to Darfur province in western Sudan. This area had suddenly become an unexpected flashpoint in this area of Africa. Both Egypt and Sudan were designated as British protectorates. In the historic scramble for Africa, the British had taken control of Egypt after invasion and a decisive military victory in September 1882. After the Battle of Omdurman in Sudan in 1898, the British reasserted Egypt's historic claim to sovereignty over Sudan.

In 1899 the governor-general in Khartoum, Sir Reginald Wingate, had installed a deeply unpopular Dervish leader, Ali Dinar. Sultan Ali Dinar had established his cruel, tyrannical and rapacious authority from his seat of power in El Fasher, the largest town in the province.[19] But the coming of the First World War led Ali Dinar to question his continuing allegiance to the British. He was courted by both the Turks and the Germans, who were eager to foment uprisings in any areas under British control. In addition, the Senussi people based in neighbouring Libya gave their support to this anti-British stance. The tipping point occurred in April 1915 when Wingate received a letter from Ali Dinar renouncing his allegiance to the Khartoum government and proclaiming a *jihad* in the name of the Sultan of Turkey. This attempt at secession would not be tolerated. The insurrection had to be dealt with, but weather and logistics were a challenge. The rainy season that occurs between July and September slowed down any advance on Ali Dinar's rebel army. It would be twelve months before military action was taken.

Wingate ordered the mobilization of 2,000 loyal Egyptian and Sudanese troops under the command of Lieutenant Colonel Phillip Kelly to restore control over Darfur. He also requested the inclusion of aircraft in the attacking force for reconnaissance and, when necessary, selective bombing and strafing sorties. As the war historian H.E. Jones noted in *War in the Air*, 'not only because of the help they would afford him by reconnoitring and bombing Ali Dinar's positions ... but also the sudden appearance, out of the blue, of "flying chariots" such as no-one in Darfur had seen before was calculated to impress upon Ali Dinar's followers the futility of resistance'.[20]

The decision was taken on 30 March to mobilize C Flight of 17 Squadron, then based in Sinai and led by Captain E.S. Bannatyne, with two other pilot officers: Lieutenants Slessor and Bellamy. The entire air component comprised the three pilot officers, fifteen support groundcrew, four dismantled BE2c aircraft, spares, petrol supplies, ammunition, and portable canvas hangars. At each stage of the journey great care had to be taken to avoid any damage to the fragile wood and fabric airframes. This became a major logistic operation that would involve a 2,000-mile journey over twenty-two days, first by ship from Suez to Port Sudan, then by train to the railhead at Er Rahad in the neighbouring Kordofan province, where the planes were reassembled.

The planes were then flown the final 300 miles to their landing strip at Jebel El Hilla on 11 May.[21]

Operating in this harsh desert environment posed numerous challenges. Sandstorms and dust devils were a recurring problem. Keeping fine sand and dust out of the aircraft's engine parts and the Lewis guns presented a constant challenge for the groundcrew. Temperatures during the day could reach up to 50°C, the heat having a deleterious effect on airframe control surfaces (ailerons and rudder) and engine performance. For that reason Slessor and his fellow pilots flew many of their reconnaissance sorties in the early mornings. Navigation was always a major challenge over the featureless and barren landscape. Radio communications either between ground controllers and aircraft or between aircraft were non-existent. Their sorties were long, hot and very tiring. Slessor wrote, 'pilots always used to fly alone on the long sorties with a large petrol bucket tank fitted in the [front] observer's seat. Bannantyne, on one occasion, did a total of eight and a half hours, which was pretty creditable, not only to the pilot but to the engine.'[22] Slessor made light of the dangers of becoming disoriented over the vast area, or of engine failure during their long sorties. The chances of survival in this desert environment would have been slim. It was very fortunate that their 90hp Royal Aircraft Factory aeroengines performed extraordinarily well under those adverse conditions.

The critical moment in the Darfur campaign came on 22 May when Kelly's force was advancing westward in a square formation that made contact with Ali Dinar's Fur forces near the village of Beringia, 12 miles north of El Fasher. Even though Ali Dinar's forces outnumbered Kelly's troops, training, discipline and modern weaponry made the difference. During that day Ali Dinar's brave but ill-disciplined troops repeatedly threw themselves against the rifles, machine guns and field artillery of Kelly's forces. Eventually Fur casualties amounted to well over a thousand and the broken force retreated towards El Fasher.

The following morning Slessor flew over El Fasher and came across the remainder of Ali Dinar's army of approximately two thousand men in open country, south of the town. He strafed the 'disorganised rabble' with his Lewis gun and threw out three of his 20lb Hales bombs. After which, in his own words, 'I had bad luck with Ali Dinar himself identifying his splendid white Bisharren camel; and sure enough there he was in the midst of this milling crowd of demoralized Dervishes. Much more by luck than good judgement I made a remarkably good shot with my last bomb and blew his camel to pieces, but Ali Dinar had got away with it.'[23] It was credibly reported that the bomb only just missed the Sultan as he was dismounting the camel to

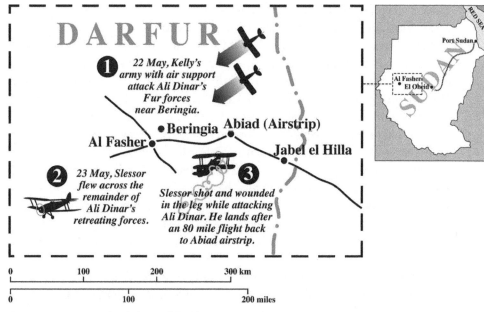

Operations against the Sultan of Darfur, May 1916.

get on a donkey. However, the remnants of his Fur army had one last trick in the game. A bullet hit Slessor in the thigh. The injured pilot then had to get back to safety steering the aircraft by hand against strong headwinds and poor visibility for the 80 miles to the Abiad airstrip. He had been airborne for five and a half hours.[24] It was alleged that Ali Dinar himself shot at the aircraft with a Remington hunting rifle purportedly given to him by Wingate.[25]

An Egyptian army doctor decided that the bullet needed to be extracted immediately. However, since no anaesthetic medication was available, Captain Ballantyne decided to give the wounded Slessor two half bottles of champagne together with some brandy. Through 'the pearly mists of inebriation' the doctor cut into the back of Slessor's thigh and extracted the bullet.[26] He kept the bullet – identified as being a .450 calibre of the type used for Remington rifles – as a souvenir and conversation piece. Over the following six weeks he was evacuated back to England as a 'cot case' on the hospital ship *Delta* and arrived at Southampton in early July.

Back to Blighty, July 1916, and 58 Squadron, Cramlington, Northumberland, January–May 1917

In August 1916, and after the appalling carnage suffered on the opening of the battle of the Somme, *The Times* editor decided to print the account of

Slessor's exploits at El Fasher.[27] The public desperately needed good news, albeit from an infinitesimally small sideshow in the war.

Slessor was approaching his 19th birthday at the time of the El Fasher action that had involved taking his 'flying chariot' into battle and experiencing the realities of war in the third dimension only twelve years after the Wright brothers' Kittyhawk maiden flight. A century later the author and war historian Brigadier Andrew Roe wrote that 'the brilliant work of the Royal Flying Corps during operations in Darfur will rank as one of the finest efforts of our Army airmen in the war'.[28] For his actions and bravery Slessor received the Military Cross in January 1917. One of the Slessor family stories relates to Jack's convalescence, whilst he was recovering from his wound and wearing civilian clothes: 'He was on a bus in London when two women climbed on board. They approached every man of fighting age, not in uniform, with their fistfuls of white feathers. Jack was awarded his badge of cowardice.'[29]

Now back in England Slessor made a full recovery. For a short period he was assigned to Northolt, northwest of London, as a flying instructor on Farman MF.11 Shorthorn aircraft.

In January 1918 the 20-year-old Slessor was sent as a flight commander to form up the new 58 Squadron based at Cramlington, north of Newcastle, in Northumberland. There they were re-equipping with the new Armstrong-Whitworth FK-8, powered by the impressive 140hp Napier engine. However, his time there was short-lived.

The Western Front, Acq airfield, Arras, 5 Squadron, May 1917–April 1918

The appalling losses of aircraft and pilots on the Western Front led to an urgent requirement for replacement pilots to be put in the line – and these would include Slessor. 58 Squadron had originally been forming up to go out to France as a reinforcement but instead the squadron was broken up in order to supply replacements for multiple squadrons in France. In what came to be known as 'Bloody April', April 1917, the RFC lost 250 aircraft, with 400 aircrew killed, missing in action, or taken prisoner. Ironically, although the battle was being won on the ground along the British section of the front, the RFC was losing control of the air. The reason for this reversal was the appearance of new, superior, well-armed and highly manoeuvrable German fighters. Two types in particular, the Albatros D.111 and the Halberstadt, dominated the skies over the front in early 1917. In groups, known as *jastas*, they hunted down British reconnaissance aircraft.

Slessor arrived in May and was posted to 5 Squadron based at Acq, near Arras, as a flight commander. The squadron had re-equipped with the RE8. Known affectionately in Cockney rhyming slang as the 'Harry Tate', after the famous music-hall comedian, it was considered by many as a difficult plane to fly, and by some as downright dangerous.[30] However, Slessor mastered its shortcomings. He became notably proficient in the air at directing British and Canadian ground artillery fire on to German targets.[31] Photo reconnaissance was still in its infancy, but Slessor and his observer Frank Tymms earned special mention when they completed 'a successful shoot in continuous rain that revealed enemy batteries located up to 4,000yds behind the German line'.[32]

However, there was always the constant danger of being attacked by the German *jastas*, or of being hit by ground fire, especially ack-ack, or 'Archie' as it was nicknamed. On one occasion his RE8 was hit by friendly fire that tore a hole in the wing, fortunately without exploding and causing terminal damage.[33]

Air superiority over the battle space ebbed and flowed throughout the war. The German Fokker monoplane had dominated until May 1916, only then to be outclassed by the Nieuports and Bristol Scouts. In the autumn the appearance of the aforementioned Albatros and Halberstadt heralded a period of German dominance in the air. But it was not to last. From July 1917 the Sopwith Camel, the RAF SE5 and the Bristol F2 regained superiority.[34] This was a time of rapid advances in engine performance, armaments and manoeuvrability that were achieved in a matter of months.[35]

Slessor spent eight months with 5 Squadron on the Western Front before transferring to Headquarters 28 Wing as an artillery and infantry cooperation officer. Throughout the last eighteen months of the war the air fighting was hard and bitterly contested.[36] But Slessor found time to socialize with friends to the rear of the line and to drink good port and smoke good cigars.[37]

Instructor at the RAF Central Flying School, Upavon, Wiltshire, June–November 1918

In April 1918 the RFC and the Royal Naval Air Service (RNAS) were merged to form the Royal Air Force. In June Temporary Major Slessor – he received the rank on 3 July, one month after his 21st birthday (the RAF having not yet sorted out its own discrete ranks) – was posted to the Central Flying School to command A Squadron, which was now equipped with SE5s. He was promoted to assistant Commandant in August. In a very real sense he had come full circle from receiving his 'wings' three years previously. The standard of training had improved immensely in that time. Pilots were trained thoroughly during those closing months of the war with new ideas in technique, training and fighter tactics.

Thus, by the war's end Jack Slessor, aged only 21, had reached Field rank (major) and been awarded three crosses for gallantry: the British Military Cross, and the Croix de Guerre of both France and Belgium.

Chapter 3

Amanuensis

Disciple to the Founding Father:
Trenchard and Slessor

There was never any doubt that Slessor idolized Lord Trenchard and, as he wrote in *Central Blue*, 'There are some rare people whose presence one indistinctively and immediately feels: Here is a great man. Not a great soldier or airman or statesman, but a great man. They are very rare, but when one meets them, they are unmistakable. Smuts was one of them, Trenchard was another.'[1] However, that is not to say that the two men did not have their differences of opinion and sometimes disagreements on key points of policy. They first met during 1917 when Trenchard was visiting 5 Squadron, in which Captain Slessor was a flight commander, then based at Acq, near Arras in northern France. At the time Trenchard was the General Officer Commanding the RFC in France. His abilities for organizing and creating an excellent esprit de corps amongst the young airmen, and his strong and clear leadership qualities marked him out as a future top air commander. He had already achieved a senior rank at the relatively young age of 44.

Trenchard was a larger-than-life character with immense drive and confidence. He got the nickname 'Boom' on account of his deep, loud and penetrating voice. Slessor recalled his admiration when he was a young staff officer at the Air Ministry that Trenchard:

> was never a clear thinker. His racing brain was always a length or two ahead of his hesitant tongue. He'd send for you and talk away and off you'd go and produce a paper you thought he wanted ... and there would be your paper covered in Boom's writing which was more or less illegible. He had a wonderful capacity for getting people's names mixed up. I was never sure whether I was going to be addressed as Slessor, Leigh-Mallory, or Collier. One had to be ready for anything. He was a man of strong views – almost violent sometimes. Many people did not agree with him – I did not always – but everyone recognised and admired

his sincerity and single-mindedness. He was incapable of a petty thought and however much one might disagree with him, one could not help loving him and respecting him.[2]

As Russell Miller, Trenchard's biographer, wrote: 'Yet he was the driving force in successfully establishing the Royal Air Force as a separate service in the face of savage and persistent opposition from the Royal Navy and the Army, both of whom wanted to control their services.'[3] Slessor got to know Trenchard more when he was in the plans section of the Air Ministry between 1928 and 1930. It developed into a lifelong friendship. Slessor corresponded with his old mentor during his time in operational wartime commands. He recalled 'and even when I was CAS I never disobeyed a summons to lunch or dine with him at Brook's club, where he had a little room on the right of the hall which came to be recognised tacitly as Boom's room.

Hugh Trenchard

Trenchard was born in Taunton in 1873 into a military family. As a young student he struggled with his academic studies. Nevertheless, he had always set his sights on joining the Army. He only just succeeded in meeting the minimum standards of entry for an officer's commission. During an initial posting in India, he met Churchill when playing in a polo match.[4] That initial contact would eventually have a significant effect on Trenchard's career in future years. Like Churchill, his was a restless soul with a spirit for adventure. In 1900 he volunteered to join his old battalion, the Royal Scots Fusiliers, then deployed to South Africa during the Second Boer War. He was seriously wounded in action in the Transvaal and, after an extended period of convalescence in Europe, predictably elected to return to Africa. With the Second Boer War over, Trenchard transferred to the Southern Nigerian Regiment. There he spent ten years leading expeditions into the unexplored interior, cutting tracks and building bridges. He returned to Britain in 1912 and was persuaded by a friend to join the new Royal Flying Corps (RFC). He finally convinced his commanding officer to permit him to enrol in a flight training course at Brooklands. After spending thirteen days there, over which time he had logged a dangerously slim seventy-four minutes flying a Maurice Farman, he qualified to 'wings' standard and was sent to the Central Flying School at Upavon where he passed, despite being rated as an 'indifferent flyer'.[5] However, he was an exceptionally good organizer, issuing numerous orders to junior staff. Trenchard was a born leader and his military experience led to his promotion to command the military wing at Farnborough. By November 1914 he was sent to lead No. 1 Wing in France. In July 1915 he succeeded

General Henderson as the General Officer Commanding RFC, for all British air operations in support of the British Army on the Western Front.

War's end: demobilization and rationalization

By 1918, at the end of the First World War, Britain's global economic health and strategic hegemony had deteriorated significantly. The war had turned Britain from a creditor nation to a debtor nation. She now faced three apparently irresolvable challenges. The first was to demobilize 3.5 million men in the Armed Services in a period of less than two years, and the second was to rebuild its peacetime economy. Within that period the Armed Services were reduced by two-thirds and in 1920 the figure had fallen to 370,000. The defence budget had been reduced from £604 million to £100 million in the same period. Nevertheless, for Winston Churchill, as both War and Air Minister, juggling economic realities combined with rapid demobilization was proving to be an administrative headache of mammoth proportions.

The third challenge was the country's ravaged economy. David Lloyd George's Liberal Government was now under pressure to nurture a war-weary public under conditions of austerity, satisfying the laudable aspiration 'to provide a fit country for heroes to live in', at a time of national penury, relative to pre-war prosperity.

Britain's significantly increased number of global responsibilities, after the Treaty of Versailles in 1919, contributed to the third challenge. Not only did it retain its former imperial duties, it now also inherited responsibilities for the administration and control of other parts of the globe. With the cut in the number of troops in the Army, how would Britain administer and control not only the Empire but also the newly acquired mandates and protectorates in Africa and the Middle East?

Churchill recognized that the use of the Royal Air Force in a policing and administrative role throughout the Empire might prove to be a cost-effective solution. But Chief of the Air Staff Frederick Sykes appeared to be oblivious to the realities of the economic situation. Sykes had grandiose plans for a post-war air force with 340 squadrons. It was an unrealistic programme. Churchill was looking for cost-cutting measures and was deeply unimpressed. In 1919 he promptly replaced Sykes with Trenchard, who had a more realistic proposal that would realize a more modest total of eighty-two squadrons. It helped that he already had a good rapport with Churchill.

The threat to the future of the RAF

The threat to the very survival of the Royal Air Force as an autonomous service continued during those early post-war years. During ongoing service budget rationalization discussions, it was suggested that the Army and Royal Navy should supply all the RAF's support services, leaving the RAF solely responsible for flight training. But Trenchard was tenacious and sought all means possible to ensure the Royal Air Force's survival. In his 1919 memorandum entitled 'The Permanent Organisation of the Royal Air Force', he outlined his vision for the development of the RAF throughout the 1920s and beyond. Central to his proposal was the development of an 'Air Force Spirit' and the establishment of institutions and structures that included the Cadet College at Cranwell, the Air Force Staff College at Andover and the Technical Training College for aircraft engineering apprentices at Halton.[6]

The origin of Air Control

In the midst of inter-service arguments during 1919, an ideal opportunity for the RAF presented itself: tribal issues in Somaliland. Trenchard proposed using the Air Force to quell riots and insurrection amongst Dervish tribesmen. It was a test of what would later come to be described as 'Air Control'. Churchill authorized the RAF to carry out a bombing campaign against Dervish forces led by Abdullah Hassan, also known as the 'Mad Mullah'. The operation was a success. In Parliament, Churchill announced that the RAF had achieved a 'decisive result'. Moreover, 'for a cost of about £30,000 [it] achieved much more than we could do with one ground expedition of up to £7 million in present currency'.[7]

Later that year a single Handley Page V. 1500 bomber attacked Kabul with four 112lb bombs and a further sixteen 20lb bombs. This one raid was a 'watershed moment' for the Air Ministry, with General Sir Charles Munro, Commander-in-Chief India, believing the raid 'was an important factor in producing a [Afghan] desire for peace'.[8]

Those Air Control operations came at an opportune moment. Their success staved off any immediate threat of dismemberment of the RAF. Air Control had now gained wide acceptance. In 1921 the Cairo Conference decided in favour of Air Control in Iraq (Mesopotamia) as a substitution for the Imperial Army.

Slessor wrote: 'Trenchard was Chief of the Air Staff for ten years between 1919 and 1929. It was a long tenure but, in his case, it was amply justified.' Though Trenchard disliked the term 'Father of the Royal Air Force', he was indispensable at a time when the fledgling Service could have easily been subsumed back into its Army and Navy roots. Slessor recalled, 'as a young staff officer in 1923 I had seen something of his almost single-handed struggle against the forces of military conservatism to preserve the infant RAF and that victory was not yet really secured. When I came back [to the Air Ministry] in

1928 I believe that if he had failed, if the RAF had been split up again between the older Services after the last war … we should have lost the Battle of Britain.'[9]

Lord Trenchard was a very effective operator both with politicians and civil servants. Churchill had appointed Trenchard because of his headstrong approach. Moreover, his total commitment to developing a distinctive 'Air Force Spirit' was gaining ground.

Trenchard's vision for the future of the RAF

Trenchard had three main beliefs that he had held since the end of the First World War: first, that air superiority was an essential prerequisite to military success; second, that air power was an inherently offensive weapon; and third, that although the material effects of aerial bombardment were great, the psychological effects (morale) would be far greater. In July 1922 the RAF published its first doctrine manual, CD-22, which was simply entitled 'Operations'.[10] The doctrine may have provided a sound strategy for directly attacking the enemy's war-making potential, but it was vague in several areas and came to be criticized by the other service chiefs. What targets were being considered: airfields, munitions factories? Furthermore, Trenchard could not demonstrate how the morale of the enemy and its people would be broken. Would the public rise up against its government demanding that it sue for peace? Inevitably, any air bombardment would lead to the deaths of civilians. Whereas Douhet, the Italian air power theorist, proposed deliberately targeting the civilian population, Trenchard retorted 'I emphatically do not advocate indiscriminate bombing', but at the same time added that 'attacking legitimate targets in populated areas was inevitable'.[11] Interestingly, Slessor lent only tepid support to morale bombing, preferring to emphasize the use of industrial intelligence which would ensure 'effective' rather than 'indiscriminate' targeting.[12] This dilemma was never truly resolved before the Second World War and it was Slessor, as Director of Plans at the Air Ministry in 1939, who was tasked with getting a ruling from the Air Council (see Chapter 5).

During Trenchard's last year as Chief of the Air Staff his 'English Merchants', Slessor and Peck, produced, under their Chief's direction, a paper entitled, 'The Fuller Employment of Air Power in Imperial Defence'. This became known informally as 'Boom's last will and testament'. In simple terms it was a declaration that 'fairly took the gloves off',[13] unequivocally reinforcing the Air Staff's beliefs and ambitions, which would have far-reaching effects for a vast Empire with heterogeneous cultures and a diversity of terrains from the arid desert landscapes of the Middle East to the densely forested areas of West Africa. It was a bold move, and it irritated both the

Army and the Navy. The RAF now had ten years' worth of experience of Air Control in various parts of the world and had proved itself more than capable of fulfilling its responsibilities and expectations. The Air Staff belief that real economic savings, with at least no less efficacy, could be secured by the substitution of the Air Force for other arms over a very wide area looked to be vindicated. The term 'substitution' became a highly emotive term for the two other services, the Army and the Royal Navy. As Slessor wrote, 'the proposals were drastic and far-reaching, covering India, the Sudan, East and West Africa, the Red Sea, the Persian Gulf, and Coastal Defence throughout the Empire'. Slessor and the other members of the Air Staff did not expect that these bold recommendations would be instantly endorsed by the Committee of Imperial Defence. Slessor never bought in to the idea that substitution through Air Control would be a universal panacea in all areas. It was one of the few occasions when Slessor disagreed with his mentor.

He wrote further:

> Trenchard as CAS was a master of interdepartmental tactics and there were two occasions on which I think his judgement was at fault in this respect – when he was betrayed by his enthusiasm and the force of his vision into actions which were in fact ill-served by his perfectly sound purpose. Both these occasions had to do with what became known as 'Substitution' – the substitution of airpower for the traditional methods of force on the ground. Substitution became a highly controversial subject and led to no little unproductive bickering, which undeniably marred, to some extent, inter-Service relations in the years between the wars.[14]

But it would be incorrect to assume that the RAF's *raison d'être* between the wars owed its existence solely to Air Control. Aircraft were in action, in co-operation with land forces, in all the small wars on the wild fringes of the Empire. Other activities included anti-slavery patrols, photographic surveys and map-making, humanitarian aid, the evacuation of civilians from war zones, and famine relief.[15]

Chapter 4

Educating the Army

The Army Staff College and the Publication of
Air Power and Armies

By early 1930, and allowing for a six-month break in service, Squadron Leader Slessor had now completed fourteen years with the Air Force, initially with the RFC and later with the RAF. During that time he had flown with eight squadrons and had seen wartime action in England, Sinai, Sudan and finally over the Western Front in France. During the early 1920s he was involved as an instructor at the Central Flying School at Upavon and later flew Bristol Fighters in India. Between 1925 and 1928 he had taken command of 4 (Army Cooperation) Squadron based at Farnborough. Between 1928 and 1930 Slessor was working in the plans department at the Air Ministry, where he reported directly to Lord Trenchard, Chief of the Air Staff. Trenchard had a high regard for young Jack Slessor and when Field Marshal George Milne – then Chief of the Imperial General Staff – told Trenchard that the RAF officer detailed to teach at Camberley was unable to discuss the broader aspects of air power, Trenchard assured him that the next officer holding the post would be a fine tactician, a strategic thinker and someone well-connected to the Air Staff and would be conversant with current policy. That officer would be Jack Slessor[1]. Milne was ahead of his time in thinking about twentieth-century innovations and, as CIGS, he threw his weight behind changing attitudes embracing developments in warfare's equipment and tactics. Under his watch the study *Mechanised and Armoured Formations* was published in 1929.

A close call

Slessor was always keen on any sport associated with horses and in March 1930 he visited Aintree racecourse with his wife, Hermione, to watch the annual Grand National steeplechase. Walking around the course in a pair of new shoes before the race, Slessor rubbed his foot slightly and unfortunately he picked up an infection. This developed into a serious case of septicaemia that nearly cost him his life. He was lucky to survive. Slessor himself put it down to having a tough constitution that he had inherited from his father, who had survived both yellow and blackwater fevers. The doctors had given up and were surprised when he pulled through at all. All this put an abrupt end to Slessor's tour of duty at the Air Ministry and he was granted a period of sick leave. After such a close call he would need an extended period of rest and recuperation.

But Slessor was never one to be idle, and as soon as he had recovered enough to travel, he decided to take a lengthy trip with Hermione through continental Europe. They had no set plan or itinerary and they went where the spirit took them. They visited Paris, Venice, several resorts along the Dalmatian coast of Yugoslavia, the Danube and Budapest. Hermione and Jack were both exceptional artists, Hermione especially so – by the age of 18 she was an accomplished classical oil painter and bronze sculptor specializing in portraits of horses and figures. But this trip provided Jack with an inexhaustible supply of colourful characters on whom to hone his drawing and caricature skill, one of Batemanesque quality, developed since boyhood and polished on the Western Front. His sketch books from this journey reveal Parisian waiters with droopy moustaches, Venetian gondolieri, Austrian mountain guides, Carabinieri in dress uniform, and Balkan gentlemen of a certain age dressed in their Ottoman garb, puffing away on pipes. To these, he would come to add, within only a few years, fierce Pashtun tribesmen, muskets in hand, and turbaned Sikhs in their opulent *dastārs*.

Returning to England fully recovered at the end of his sick leave, Slessor knew that he would be on the Directing Staff of the Army Staff College, Camberley at the start of 1931. He was told to start work on a new Army co-operation project resulting in a manual that would set forth the ways in which the RAF would cooperate and coordinate its activities with the Army in future land campaigns. In effect, this gave Slessor a six-month period, and thus plenty of time, to complete the draft manual for approval in December. At that moment Jack and Hermione had already sold their house in Sandwell for family reasons and were staying *pro-tem* with Hermione's parents at their home in Dorton, near Thame in the Bicester hunting country of South Oxfordshire. With so much spare time on his hands, Slessor took part in foxhunting wherever and whenever he could. He developed a real love for the sport, and particularly when hacking home by himself in the Oxfordshire countryside. He remembered 'the smell of autumn fires, bare elms against the gleam of the western sky, little owls hooting, the light from cottage doors'.[2] One may wonder at how a man with two gammy legs (Jack's self-description) could possibly stay atop a horse jumping over hedgerow, fence and ditch. In fact, he had a custom-made handle, akin to a suitcase handle, stitched onto the pommels of his saddles, thereby allowing him to grasp said handle with one hand as he led the charge over hill and dale, leaving the other hand for the reins.

With the peace and solitude of Dorton, Slessor had ample time to give considerable thought to overhauling the way his new manual would be written. He brought in many of his own ideas. In a very real sense, the manual that Slessor wrote was revolutionary. Always original in his thinking, he recast the way that in future campaigns the organization, inter-Service roles and relationships should operate with close cooperation and coordination between the Army and Air Force commanders. In this co-equal alliance, the Air commander would be responsible for the air component, but he would also serve as an adviser to the Army commander. But how would this operate in practice? As Phillip Meilinger wrote, 'the importance of this thorny issue of command and control would be raised again and again in the years ahead'.[3]

Camberley Army Staff College

On arrival at Camberley, Hermione had an immediate duty to take tea with the Commandant's wife along with the wives of all the other directing staff. Sitting on a sofa, the wife of a Guards officer turned to Hermione and, by way of opening small talk, asked her which regiment her husband belonged to. Hermione explained that her husband was not in a regiment but was, in fact, the RAF officer attached to the College. 'Well, don't worry, dear,' Hermione's interlocutor reassured her, 'it's one better than the Tank Corps.'[4]

In December Slessor turned in his draft manual to the Director of Staff Duties at Camberley and for one term he sat in on lectures as a student to get the feel of the teaching environment. In March 1931 he replaced Trafford Leigh-Mallory as the Air Force member of the Directing Staff.

Slessor recalled that '1931–1934 were four happy years and life at Camberley had all the ingredients of content, interesting and constructive work, and congenial company in pleasant surroundings, regular holidays and many opportunities for sport of all kinds.'[5] Camberley's Commandant in those years was Major General John J. Dill. Slessor would continue to work with Dill during the wartime years, and particularly at the time of the Casablanca Conference in January 1943.

The Camberley Staff College was established in 1858 to address the obvious deficiencies in the way the British Army had handled its campaigns during the recent Crimean War.[6] The objective was to produce highly educated officers who would then provide capable administration for the needs of a modern army. The Passed Staff College qualification (psc) was considered the pinnacle of an Army officer's education and the recipients were then expected to perform all future command and staff duties to a professional level of excellence.

The course for army officers lasted two years, with an annual intake of sixty student officers. Over his four years at Camberley, Slessor taught several hundred officers, some of whom he would be reacquainted with during the wartime years. However, Slessor had real concerns about various aspects of the course, and he recognized significant shortcomings in the way army officers were selected and trained.

Slessor's primary role at Camberley was to discuss, analyse and explain to his cohorts of students the role of air power in cooperation with the army. Apart from being an excellent communicator, Slessor was ideally qualified. Not only did he have the valuable experience he had gained in his flight operations over the battle zones in France between 1917 and 1918, he had recently completed three years with No. 4 Army Cooperation Squadron that had kept him up to date with current technological advances, ordnance and flight manoeuvres.

Slessor emphasized that 'the war of 1914–1918 in the air was, for obvious and natural reasons, an Army cooperation war in the narrowest technical sense of the term. At the outset, and for many months afterwards, the only important use of aircraft appeared to men's minds to be that of reconnaissance and artillery [spotting] aircraft to carry on their work of close co-operation.'[7]

The methods of teaching included individual written work, group work in student syndicates during map-based exercises, war games, lectures and First World War battlefield tours. During their programme the students were set exercises in which they were required to review, examine and recommend counterforce action to be taken by Britain's army and air force assets.

When discussing the possibility of future conflicts on the continent of Europe, amongst numerous other scenarios that were examined, Slessor had already posed the threat of a resurgent Germany. 'It has been suggested, for instance, that the first stage of an air war against this country may be a struggle on the ground for the possession of airbases in the Low Countries, from which an effective air invasion of England could be sustained.' In such circumstances Slessor considered that the primary solution for this exercise was for his army students (in 1934!) to identify the air bases as the 'vital ground' upon which victory was dependent, or at least defeat to be avoided, and therefore for ground forces to counterattack, defeat the enemy army in the field, and retake the air bases. This exercise was the culmination of his tour at Camberley and was viewed by Slessor with great satisfaction. How prescient it was that Slessor had thought through an invasion scenario that became reality only six years later during the German *Fall Gelb* (Case Yellow) campaign in which they overran the Low Countries in addition to Northern France. In his 1934 exercise Slessor had planned on the Air Force achieving air superiority early in the campaign and to have a committed and clear plan for a ground counterattack. But, as Slessor was to witness, neither of those aspirations proved possible in May 1940. The British and French air forces never achieved air superiority over the Luftwaffe. They simply did not have the aircraft numbers. Furthermore, many British aircraft types were obsolescent. The Luftwaffe maintained air superiority over the battlespace throughout the invasion of France. In addition, the Anglo-French allies were not fighting to a coherent plan.

But did this invalidate Slessor's 1934 battle plan? The answer was no. When the roles were reversed in 1944, with Allied air superiority carrying out tactical operations and a clear battle plan, the German army was defeated in Normandy.

Air Interdiction: a new concept

Slessor introduced an entirely new concept in his new Army Cooperation Manual. He wrote, 'Valuable results may be achieved by carefully organised air attacks on the enemy's system of supply, maintenance and transportation. The more highly organised the enemy the more vulnerable he will be to actual interference with his supply.'[8] It was a clear definition of what would later be called Air Interdiction. The manual went on further to state that when the enemy did begin to retreat, owing to the combined efforts of air and ground attack, aircraft could become even more effective, turning a withdrawal into a rout and crushing the enemy's power of resistance. Slessor stressed that air attacks on the enemy's communications would depend on the proper use of all available intelligence supplemented by expert technical advice, adding 'air action in this sphere depends for its effect far more on dislocation and disorganisation than upon actual material damage'.[9]

Slessor believed that modern and mechanized land warfare would require 'ever increasing amounts of matériel especially of petroleum products and ammunition and would need resupply by rail transport'. This, Slessor declared, would be the enemy's 'Achilles heel'. Based on his examination of air attacks on railway networks in 1918, he considered that targeting junctions and mainline stations would not achieve the objective. First, they could often be repaired rapidly (because engineering repair sections would always be close by) and second, there were too many alternative lines through big stations which made it practically impossible to cut them all. Better targets were presented by signal boxes, telephone networks and marshalling yards, indeed anywhere where targets were less well defended and further away from repair resources. Slessor concluded, 'So, in this battle – as indeed in any battle – the objective of the Air Force should be *to isolate the battlefield from enemy reinforcements and supply.*'[10]

But Slessor did not ignore the importance of strategic bombing. In Part II of *Air Power and Armies* he devoted twenty-four pages to 'Strategic Concentration', emphasizing that such bombing must be planned in conjunction with the air and ground tactics, situation and mission in the theatre of operations. Slessor quoted Lord Trenchard:

> All bombing even when carried out on very distant and apparently independent objectives, must be coordinated with the efforts that are being made by the land or the sea forces ... It is utterly wrong and wasteful to look upon them as entirely separate duties.[11]

Slessor saw a natural continuum of operations ranging from tactical air support in the theatre of operations through to the strategic bombing of the enemy's vital centres so bringing about the dislocation and restriction of output from the war industry. Indeed, he openly acknowledged that the primary role of air power in any future major war would be the use of strategic bombing to assail the enemy's vital centres. However, it should be noted that when lecturing to his army students at Camberley, he was examining several scenarios where the army was already involved in a land campaign. In truth, Slessor was always a strong advocate of Lord Trenchard's thinking and by mid-1934 he seemed to have convinced his army colleagues at Camberley that he was an 'air power zealot'.[12]

This was the birth of the concepts of air superiority and air supremacy, until then poorly understood and not widely appreciated. Within only six years armies and their commanders would subordinate almost all their plans to considerations vis-à-vis control of the air. On the other hand, to some of his Air Force colleagues Slessor had gone 'too khaki'.[13] In an atmosphere in which the army staff would often question the Air Force's role, Slessor was careful to emphasize to his Camberley students, and later to readers of *Air Power and Armies*, that 'no attitude could be more irritating in its effects than to claim that the next great war – if, and when it comes – will be decided in the air, and the air alone'.[14] But with mechanized warfare, driven by the tank and aircraft, Slessor posited 'Can it really be supposed that we shall ever again in the face of air action, see the millions of men, the thousands of tons of ammunition, the network of trenches stretching halfway across Europe?'[15]

The Army's cult of administration

If Slessor had one particular criticism of the army mindset it would be its obsessive approach to the concept of administration. There was an army slogan, applied as the acid test of any operational plan – 'is it administratively sound?' Slessor thought all plans should be administratively practical, but that the Army regularly took this to an extreme. He considered that the Army had become too hamstrung by administrative procedures which would allow 'the administrative tail to wag the operational dog'. This mindset continued both during and after the Second World War. Slessor considered that this approach inhibited the Army from grasping the initiative, taking bold but calculated risks at short notice. Slessor wrote 'we lost opportunities and made unnecessary difficulties for ourselves at Anzio for that reason. The General Staff were told by the 'Q' [matériel supply] side that we could not advance because we had not yet got three days' supplies with the troops and five days' supplies on the beaches. The initiative to break out of the beachhead was lost and for four months they were hemmed into an enclave around Anzio. If we there had matched our enemy in his quality of tactical flexibility and instantaneous exploitation of opportunity, the subsequent history of the campaign in Italy might have been very different.'[16]

Slessor also had concerns about the calibre of officers and their ability to think innovatively: 'We were pretty good at teaching them how to do things; we were not so successful in teaching them to think what to do.'[17] But Slessor was not alone in holding those views. Early in the Western desert campaign General Erwin Rommel was impressed by the toughness and fighting spirit of the British tommy. He remarked that British commanders suffered from a 'rigid inability to move'. Things were to change, as evidenced by General Morshead's hard-fought and manoeuvrist defence of Tobruk and Montgomery's victory at the second Battle of El Alamein (notwithstanding the Allied advantages in intelligence, and men and matériel).

Nearly eighty years later, in 2015 the military historian Edward Smalley published a paper entitled 'Qualified, but unprepared: Training for War at the Staff College in the 1930s', in which he concluded that 'the inter-war Staff College graduate was not perfectly trained, nor was he properly prepared for a first class war ... Camberley never replicated the pressures of the combat environment, either in exercises, or its unwillingness to reject underperformance, this influenced both student work ethic and the directing staff's approach to risk taking'.[18]

Slessor's view on sport and the Camberley Drag Hunt

Slessor emphasized the importance of sports and the building of team esprit. He felt this was often lacking amongst the students during his time at Camberley. One of the great sporting traditions at Camberley was the twice-weekly drag hunt. (Whereas foxes were the quarry in foxhunting, drag hunting involved the hounds following an artificial scent traditionally laid by a runner dragging a bag soaked with 'the smell'. Nothing is chased and nothing caught.) The runner could set up a challenging trail that would entail jumping hedgerows and other difficult obstacles. The whole idea was to test the student's strength of character by sending him on horseback. Slessor wanted the students to encounter the danger and uncertainty inherent in the drag hunt and to develop both initiative and courage. He wrote, 'I believe that hunting and steeplechasing are first-class training for an officer of any Service. But it is manifestly absurd to pretend that there have not been excellent officers to whom the horse is anathema.'[19] But he did point out that Naval and RAF officers were constantly tested simply by flying aircraft and commanding ships, two activities that had inherent dangers and were part of an officer's experience, whereas Army officers in peacetime encountered little by way of danger. That said: 'There was a slight tendency for the Drag to assume undue importance in the curriculum at Camberley.'[20] In spite of his enthusiasm, Slessor was not in favour of making it compulsory, as it was for many years.

Family tragedy

The only blight on Jack and Hermione's happiness was the death of Jack's young brother in Burma. Of the four siblings, Anthony was the baby. Devilishly good looking and immensely talented at every sport with or without bat and ball, notably polo, Tony, or 'Bud' as he was affectionately known in the Regiment, was hugely popular. An artist with skills comparable to those of Jack, Anthony was a regular illustrator for his regimental magazine – the *Oxfordshire & Buckinghamshire Light Infantry*. Unmarried, he was a catch eyed up by regimental wives for their sisters and cousins. In December 1932, aged 28, he had a fatal accident while out shooting snipe. Ironically, it was a repetition of the fatal shooting accident suffered by his great-great-uncle, William, in India aged 31 in 1810, shot through the head whilst recharging his muzzle-loader. For Jack it was a devastating blow.

Air Power and Armies; Slessor's contribution to joint Army/Air Force operations

As the end of 1934 approached, Slessor was asked to state his preferences for his next appointment. He had always been sceptical about expressing such wishes in the belief that, if things did not go well, you'd only have yourself to blame. However, he half succumbed to persuasion and simply remarked that he had been born in India and served there, that he was just finishing four years at the Staff College, Camberley, and that he had served in Army Cooperation Squadrons, and commanded one, so perhaps something totally different could be found for him. The RAF posted him to command the Army Cooperation No. 3 (Indian) Wing in Quetta (then India, now Pakistan), based next door to the Quetta staff college. Slessor left for Quetta at the end of 1934. While there he had the opportunity to refine the lectures he had given at Camberley over the previous four years and was able to add further material from his flight operations in the Waziristan Campaign. His collection of lectures, notes and maps was published in 1936 as *Air Power and Armies*. The book was well received and reached a wide readership in Britain and America. It stands out as a seminal piece of work that demonstrated how air power and land forces could work closely together to bring about successful outcomes in campaigns.

On the first page of his Introduction, Slessor wrote that military history's prime function was to enable commanders and staff officers of the future to be wise *before* the event, and to learn not only from the successes, but also from the failures of their predecessors. He felt 'there is a great deal in the history of the war in the air which may serve as a model for the future'.[21]

Throughout the book Slessor stressed the constant need to achieve air superiority (control of the air) that would then enable air forces to strike critical lines of communication behind the enemy's front line, attacking bridges, canals, rail networks and motor transport – in other words, to paralyse movement and to create maximum disruption amongst his troops and his supplies. But for all the well-thought-out theories on tactical support, the British aircraft industry had not yet produced a specialized type for close air support.[22] In any event he did not favour close air support unless it could be carefully controlled by air and ground controllers.

Slessor was to implement the air interdiction campaign in central Italy during 1944. It was to be the testing ground for previously untried interdiction operations. He was not disappointed. The initial operation, Strangle, and the follow-up operation, Diadem, demonstrated dramatic and successful effect (see Chapter 12). Air interdiction continued as an extraordinarily successful tactic in Normandy, and later in the Battle of the Bulge when clearing weather finally allowed Allied air power to rescue the stretched defenders just as General Patton arrived with his counterstroke.

When Slessor wrote *Air Power and Armies* he was not just focusing on an army readership; he was also addressing his Air Force colleagues. His contemporaries in air power theory – Douhet, Mitchell and Trenchard – had paid scant attention to tactical operations, preferring to advocate the role of the bomber in strategic offensive operations. However, the book did not confine itself solely to a discourse on air interdiction; it covered a wide collection of issues ranging from the role of strategic bombing to the use of reconnaissance, and the role of the fighter. He emphasized the unique advantage of air power: agility in the third dimension, in that it was not limited to any one course of action. It can switch, literally almost at a moment's notice, from one objective to another several hundred miles away, all from the same air base.[23]

Slessor remained convinced that the heavy bomber should not be used simply as a battlefield weapon – in a sense, as airborne heavy artillery. Unless the plan was coordinated with a rapid follow-up by ground troops it rarely, if ever, succeeded. Slessor was proved right on this issue in the bombing of Monte Cassino in central Italy and later at Caen in Normandy. Both operations failed to dislodge the German defenders and only led to extensive collateral damage both in lives and property.

One method that Slessor favoured after achieving air superiority would be to use the bombers as bait to attack the enemy's vital targets, thereby compelling enemy fighters into the air where they would be destroyed. This tactic was employed by the US Eighth Air Force during Operation Argument in the spring of 1944.

However, Slessor did have some 'blind spots' in his assessment of tactical air power. Phillip S. Meilinger noted that Slessor did not address the dangers of anti-aircraft artillery, a subject which merited more than silence. Certainly he was not oblivious to the threat and had earlier commented on its dangers in his letters home from the Western Front. Furthermore, like the American theorists at their think-tank, the Air Corps Training School (ACTS), Slessor considered that while escort fighters might be technically desirable, they were impractical. But no one could see the future, most especially the development of the long-range fighter (notably the Merlin-powered P-51 Mustang) and the increasing use of fuel drop-tanks that would allow them to protect deep missions by the USAAF into Germany. Nevertheless, few would disagree with Phillip Meilinger's opinion that 'Jack Slessor was perhaps the most prescient thinker in the RAF regarding the form future war would take.'[24]

Air Power and Armies: an appraisal

Air Power and Armies has long been a prescribed textbook at the USAF's academies on tactical operations in conjunction with ground forces. Some sixty-five years after Slessor wrote *Air Power and Armies*, in 2001 Clayton

Chun, an air historian at the USAF's academy, concluded his remarks on the book thus:

> Jack Slessor was an air power visionary. He advanced the ideas of using air power to support ground and joint operations between armies and air forces, but also saw the value of strategic bombardment against a nation's war fighting capability. Slessor also was the first air power theorist to recognise that joint cooperation and coordination were necessary among the air and ground forces in order to succeed with close air support and interdiction. Slessor provided a more practical and balanced view of air power than did Douhet, Mitchell, or Trenchard, his mentor.[25]

Chapter 5

Rearming for War

The Struggle to Prepare and the Inexorable March to War

In May 1937 Group Captain Slessor was appointed as the Deputy Director of Plans at Adastral House, home of the Air Ministry, situated in central London. It was now eight years since he had previously worked in the Ministry. At that time he was head of a small planning group that reported directly to Lord Trenchard. Much had changed since those apparently carefree years of the late 1920s. The 1930s had ushered in an era of global depression, considerable uncertainty and emerging threats to world peace.

The deteriorating world situation, 1931–1936

The threat of future confrontations and war had emerged in three areas: the Far East, Germany and East Africa. In September 1931 Japan invaded Southern Manchuria, signifying the beginning of Japanese imperial ambitions. Britain became concerned that continuing Japanese imperial expansion might eventually threaten its own colonial interests in large areas of the Far East, notably in Malaya, Burma, Singapore, Hong Kong and ultimately India. In Germany, Hitler became Chancellor in January 1933, denouncing the punitive treatment which Germany had received from the Versailles Treaty. He proclaimed the Third Reich and embarked on a comprehensive rearmament programme. In March 1936 Hitler sanctioned the remilitarization of the Rhineland and its occupation by 30,000 German troops, in violation of treaty obligations. In October 1935 Italy invaded Abyssinia as part of her own imperial expansion plan for East Africa.

Taken together, these threats meant Britain now had to consider her own position in relation to three potential adversaries. However, the greatest threat was always considered to be Germany's military expansion, and particularly that of its growing air force, the Luftwaffe.

The RAF expansion schemes and the concept of 'parity'

Throughout the early 1930s the government had attempted to meet these emerging threats through a determination to ensure that no adversary would be allowed to get to a position of achieving an aerial 'knockout blow' against Britain. In Parliament Baldwin continued to reassure the House, insisting 'that in our air strength and air power this country shall no longer be in a position inferior to any country within striking distance of our shores'.[1] The watchword for the means by which this could be achieved was 'parity', a way of creating a deterrent to German aggression through the threat of an immediate counterattack by air power equal to its own.

As Germany ramped up its numbers of aircraft, the Air Ministry eventually ended up proposing eight expansion schemes – variously denoted alphabetically between 'A' and 'M'[2] – that had been put forward between 1934 and 1938 (see Appendix B). It was always a case of catch-up to attempt to keep pace with Germany's rapid growth in air power. Parity involved assessing Germany's front line, referred to in plans as 'first line aircraft numbers' and looking to match those numbers in the specific expansion schemes. However, 'parity' was always an illusory concept. Matching mere numbers of aircraft took little account of a comparison of their capabilities. No real consideration was given to replacement aircraft reserves required behind the first line or to a proper examination of comparative aircraft specifications such as bombload, speed, rate of climb, maximum altitude, range and manoeuvrability. As the historian Malcolm Smith wrote, parity was 'the diplomatic factor which sought to make the RAF the political counterpart of the political German Air Force, a running commitment to deterrence which necessitated that at any given time the maximum strength should be concentrated in the front line ... providing defence on the cheap which could only mean a "shop window" force'.[3]

The simple reality was that Baldwin's government (1935–1937) had been too complacent in addressing the Nazi threat. Moreover, in party political terms announcements of rearmament were seen by much of the electorate as a warmongering move, and this was a major vote-losing policy. Less than two decades earlier Britain had seen the devastating results of a major war, with the loss of over 744,000 dead and 1,675,000 injured throughout the three Armed Services.[4] Slessor wrote of that time that 'the people did not want war, didn't believe in the inevitability of war and were not interested in the Services'.[5]

The public perceptions of air bombardment

A further key consideration during the 1930s was a real fear of the possibility of major air bombardment in any future war. Contemporary literature, films and media conveyed apocalyptic visions of aerial warfare. In *War in the Air*, published in 1935, the former RAF officer, L.E.O. Charlton, argued that air defence was essentially futile and that London's railway yards, docks and market centres would be 'drenched in gas' and power stations would be 'attacked with high explosive', with interludes of 'blind panic' – as people sought dark shelter within London Underground's tube system – that would 'beggar description'.[6] H.G. Wells's popular book *The Shape of Things to Come*, published in 1933, was adapted for film release as *Things to Come* three years later in 1936. The film portrayed a fictitious city named 'Everytown' being destroyed by bombs and gas and a surviving population who then lived through a long dystopian future of disease, famine and insurrection. Together with regular fictional articles covering air warfare in magazines and newspapers and the actual accounts of the bombing in Shanghai (1932) and Guernica (1937), this approach would continue to shape the general public's attitude. It is therefore little wonder that in June 1935 a 'Peace Ballot' organized by the League of Nations Union registered 11 million British votes against war. This vote was achieved despite the rise of the Nazi menace in Germany.[7]

Government inaction and the 'locust years'

Baldwin postponed any action on further rearmament expansion schemes until after he was safely re-elected as prime minister in 1935. The chief problem was the delay caused simply by the time taken by politicians in deciding what to do. A chronological account recorded that no action was taken on the RAF expansion schemes in the period between November 1933 and February 1936.[8] In November 1936 Churchill berated Baldwin's administration in a Parliamentary debate, describing this period as the 'locust years': time which should have been spent preparing to face Germany had been fruitlessly eaten up. British aviation companies had been starved of investment, severely restricting important research and development when major advances were being made by other countries in all areas of aeronautical engineering. Churchill addressed the House of Commons thus:

> The Government simply cannot make up their mind. So, they go on in a strange paradox, decided to be undecided, resolved to be irresolute, adamant for drift, solid for fluidity, all-powerful to be impotent. So, we go on preparing for more months and years – precious, perhaps vital to the greatness of Britain – for the locusts to eat.[9]

Slessor and Expansion Scheme 'J'

By the time Slessor appeared on the scene in spring 1937, four expansion schemes had been proposed and then subsequently shelved to be superseded in a vain attempt to keep pace with the ever rising perceived numbers of German aircraft (see Appendix B). Reflecting on that time, Slessor wrote, 'the paramount fact that stared us in the face in Spring 1937 was the phenomenal growth of the German air force'.[10] In the collective mind of the Air Ministry, rearmament was now directed against Germany and Germany alone.[11] Slessor now faced two critical challenges: first, the urgent requirement to build up the RAF's air power with the provision of modern bombers and fighters, and second, to ensure that the growing numbers of aircraft were consolidated with reserves into a coherent force that would be brought to the point of operational effectiveness within the squadrons.[12] In short, to be fit for war.

In May 1937 Slessor wrote, 'our Intelligence estimated that Germany already had 800 bombers technically capable of attacking objectives in this country from bases on German soil'.[13] Furthermore there had been a revolution in aircraft design. By 1934 wooden biplanes were being replaced by single wing models with all metal fuselages and an automatic pilot, retractable undercarriage and variable pitch propellers. The Germans were well ahead not only in aircraft numbers, but also in modern aircraft design in both their bombers and fighters. They were also using them in anger during the Spanish Civil War and gaining valuable combat experience. The depressing reality was summed up by Slessor when he wrote that by September the most that the RAF could mobilize against the Germans at that time comprised:

> Only ninety-six long-range bombers – thirty-six each of Blenheim and Wellesleys and twelve each of Battles and Harrows, pretty poor stuff compared with the Ju-86s, He-111s and Do-17s of which we knew some 250 were mobilizable in Germany. Our nominal bomber strength was 816 in the Metropolitan Air Force, and the remaining 700 odd were mostly obsolete short-range types like Heyfords, Hinds, Audax and Ansons, and in any event over 30 percent of the squadrons would have been rolled-up on mobilization to provide some reserves for the remainder. Here was something to keep one awake at night![14]

During August Slessor enrolled the assistance of the other deputy directors at the Air Ministry covering Operations, Intelligence and Operational Requirements, and wrote a paper to Cyril Newall, the newly installed Chief of the Air Staff (CAS). In the cover note he wrote, 'I am very doubtful whether the Government have any really accurate conception of our weakness in the air; and even the Cabinet to some extent probably share the popular but completely erroneous belief that because we now have 123 squadrons nominally in existence we are capable of taking on all comers.' In the paper itself Slessor pulled no punches. The key part of it read: 'The Air Staff would be failing in their duty not to express their considered opinion that the Metropolitan Air Force in general, and Bomber Command in particular, are at present almost completely unfitted for war.'[15]

As John Terraine wrote, 'Slessor did not let the grass grow under his feet. Newall and Swinton, Secretary of State for Air, were impressed with his forthright language, and the Air Staff was requested to draw up a scheme.'[16] The result was Scheme 'J', which was submitted in October and called for a strike (bomber) force of 1,442 aircraft in ninety squadrons, of which sixty-four squadrons would be heavy bombers and twenty-six medium bombers. The fighter force would be increased to a total of 532 aircraft in thirty-eight squadrons.[17] Completion of the scheme was set for mid-1941. The total cost for the entire Scheme 'J' expansion would amount to £650 million, with expenditures between 1937 and 1942.[18] This would be the first scheme based on *estimates of minimum overall strategic requirements*. John Terraine wrote that 'in many respects it was the best overall of all the schemes submitted'.[19]

The Shadow Factories

However, Slessor had concerns about the ways of achieving the aircraft numbers by the proposed completion date. He commented that 'the Government's dogged adherence to the principle that nothing must interfere with the "normal processes of peacetime industry"' would put the Scheme objective in doubt'.[20] In November Slessor and his Air Staff colleagues expressed the view that the completion date would not be met unless 'shadow factories' were incorporated into the production schedule. The government was now finally listening and from late 1938 those factories were making a significant contribution to production numbers. The shadow factories were newly built manufacturing plants co-located with road vehicle and engine factories. Whereas the aviation companies excelled at research, design and aeronautical engineering, their manufacturing capacity was often low. Shadow plants provided a significant upscaling of capacity, thereby ensuring the mass production of aircraft required to meet the schedule. The key manufacturing plants were located primarily in the Midlands, Oxfordshire and Greater London, and included household names from the automotive industry, such as Rootes, Daimler, Rover and Vauxhall, amongst others.

Sir Thomas Inskip, the 'knockout blow' and his challenge to RAF doctrine

However, Scheme 'J' did not survive scrutiny by Sir Thomas Inskip, the Minister for the Coordination of Defence. Baldwin had appointed Inskip to that position in March 1936. He was given the unenviable task of apportioning limited funding to each of the three Services: Army, Navy and Air Force. By 1937 the Treasury was concerned about the mounting expense as more complex weapon systems were adopted. At the end of June Inskip was asked to review the costs both of rearmament and of maintenance of the enlarged armed forces that would be created by 1942. As the British historian George Peden wrote:

> Inskip was assisted by a panel of senior civil servants including Maurice Hankey; Sir Horace Wilson, the government's chief industrial adviser and confidential adviser to the prime minister; Sir Arthur Robinson, chairman of the Supply Board, which co-ordinated the services' industrial requirements; and Edward Bridges, the head of the Treasury's division dealing with defence expenditure. Each of the chiefs of staff gave evidence to the enquiry regarding his own service, in effect bidding against each other, rather than reporting as a committee, as they normally did.[21]

The result was the 'Inskip Report', completed and presented to the Cabinet in December. In respect of the RAF, the report directly challenged the conventional orthodoxy of the priority being given to the strategic bomber offensive to deliver a knockout blow against the enemy, as was outlined in the RAF's own war manual, *AP 1300*, published in 1928. Inskip rejected some of the assumptions that Slessor and his team had used in proposing Scheme 'J', arguing that 'the role of the RAF had never been to accomplish an early knockout blow ... but to prevent the Germans knocking us out'.[22] It thus followed that there would need to be a focus on fighters for home defence. Inevitably the argument that the best form of defence is a good offence fell out of favour as the German air force became increasingly more powerful. Additionally, there were cost considerations. Three fighters could be built for the equivalent cost of one bomber.[23,24]

The Air Ministry was clearly rattled that a civilian lawyer with no previous experience of air power could dictate the kind of air doctrine that should be adopted by the RAF. Though Inskip had negligible knowledge of air power theory, tactics and strategy, he and his colleagues argued convincingly in Cabinet that there had to be a commonsense approach to Britain's defence. He asserted that Britain had now to adopt a defensive posture in any war with Germany, and over the longer term to prevail with a period of attrition warfare. Malcolm Smith commented that the Inskip Report was the 'single most important document produced on defence matters in the 1930s.[25]

However, Inskip was prepared to give most of the proposed Scheme 'J' priority in his Cabinet report, but to postpone the heavy bomber replacement programme. In an *aide-memoire* written on 9 December Inskip wrote 'my idea is rather [that] to meet our real requirements we need not possess anything like the same number of long-range bombers as the Germans ... the numbers of heavy bombers should be reduced'. Inskip also argued that German aircraft could be better destroyed over Britain by fighters than by an attack on German factories and aerodromes.[26] In summary, Inskip's financial revision to Scheme 'J' put the focus on increasing the number of fighters at the expense of heavy bombers. Increasing the complement of heavy bombers would now be deferred to a later period.

If Inskip was correct on the fighter increases, that was not the case with his proposal for more light and medium bombers. Inevitably when war came the RAF found itself with too many light bombers such as the Blenheims and Hampdens that were of practically no value. As Terraine wrote, 'But Inskip was not really thinking about tactics and strategy; like too many of his Government colleagues, he was thinking above all of expense.'[27] Reflecting on all this sixteen years later, Slessor wrote, 'it is almost impossible to believe the extent to which financial considerations were allowed to exert such an influence in bringing us to the very lip of disaster in the face of the Nazi menace'.[28]

However, Slessor admitted Inskip had made the right call, writing that 'to multiply fighters is the usual refuge of the ignorant about air power, but in this case it was undoubtedly justified'.[29] Only three years later the decision to increase fighter defence in December 1937 was totally vindicated during the Battle of Britain. Slessor was clear in sharing the blame for some of the pre-war proposals for RAF expansion, reflecting that:

> It had always been an article of faith with the Air Staff that the counter offensive was the most important element of our own defence. I think it must be admitted we overstressed that doctrine to the extent of seriously underrating the efficacy of fighter defence ... we did place more reliance on it [the counteroffensive] than we were justified in doing with the bombers of the day.[30]

But in truth no one could predict how future air warfare might develop. The bombing of Guernica and Barcelona during the Spanish Civil War gave some indication of the effects of bombing on urban targets, but not what might be the effects of persistent massive bombardment on major cities. Reflecting on this point, Slessor wrote a memorandum to accompany Scheme 'K', which replaced Scheme 'J' in April 1938, stating that, 'The Air Staff are faced with a peculiar difficulty, the absence of any real experience of air warfare between two first-class powers.'[31] Herein lay the nub of the difficulty in making critical decisions.

But this was also a problem for all the major powers in addressing the future of air warfare. Slessor reflected on this uncertainty, summing it up:

> One fact which it is essential for anyone to realize who wishes to understand the thoughts and pressures that influenced the minds of the Government and their Military advisers in the years before September 1939, *is the war of 1939–1945 was the first air war*. In 1914 to 1918 the Air had been in its too early infancy to have any very significant effect.[32]

No one in December 1937 could foresee the extent of the efficacy that a home defence organization using modern, fast and highly manoeuvrable eight-gun fighters, together with an early warning radar chain with centralized control, might have in future conflict. At the time of the Inskip Report there were development problems with the Spitfire and radar was still in its infancy.

Slessor's proposed purchases of American aircraft: the challenges of the Neutrality and Johnson Acts

In a further initiative Slessor proposed purchasing aircraft from the United States. In November he circulated his 'Plans' document entitled 'American Cooperation with Great Britain in the event of War with Germany'. Then there were the issues of the 'Neutrality Acts and War Debt Settlement'.[33] Although Slessor believed that the American public was generally hostile to Germany's increasingly belligerent behaviour and would be favourable to helping Britain, two hurdles stood in the way of progress on that front. The series of Neutrality Acts between 1935 and 1939 placed a mandatory embargo on the export of military equipment to belligerents. Furthermore, the Johnson Act of 1934 precluded foreign powers from raising capital in American markets if they had any history of defaults. In 1934 the British and French governments had both defaulted on their war loans taken out during the First World War, leaving debts totalling $4 billion.[34]

Despite these constraints the Cabinet approved sending a British Air Mission to both Canada and the United States in February 1938. Canada could not provide the necessary numbers of aircraft owing to the small size of their aircraft manufacturing sector. The United States visit was more promising and resulted in a firm order for 400 aircraft: 200 North American Aviation Harvard intermediate trainers and 200 Lockheed Hudsons, a modified version of the Electra, which could be used in several roles: for navigational training, for reconnaissance or as a light bomber. In addition, agreements were reached in early 1939 with two aero-engine firms, the Wright Aeronautical Corporation and Pratt & Whitney for the provision of engines to be produced to prescribed British specifications. These were not major orders, but they were the forerunner of major imports of American aircraft and components during the war years. The first deliveries of Harvards and Hudsons arrived in Britain between December 1938 and February 1939 and were the only American types to be received by the RAF before the start of the war.[35]

The change of thinking about 'parity'

By the end of 1937 'parity' had become a highly dubious concept. Germany was out-producing Britain in both fighters and bombers. By December German output was estimated at 500 airframes and 1,010 aero engines per month. In that same period Britain was producing 145 airframes and 372 aero engines per month. As Malcolm Smith wrote, these figures seemed to demand drastic solutions, but no short-term remedy was available.[36]

In early 1938 Slessor contributed to the subject: 'On a policy of parity, we are faced with the difficulty that we literally do not know what Germany's air programme is. We think we know with reasonable accuracy that her strength is now about 2,700 aircraft including 1,350 long range bombers. At her ultimate programme we can only make a constructive guess.'[37]

The situation clearly infuriated Slessor. Parity focused on just one metric: the delivery of increasing numbers of aircraft to the first line. Little consideration had been given to any other aspects, such as the need for reserves, aircrew training and the expansion of airfields. New aircraft were now becoming larger, requiring more aircrew and the concomitant need to train personnel. It did not now just involve pilots. It also included navigators, wireless operators and gunners.

As war became inevitable, Slessor believed the window-dressing 'shop-window' policy must go by the board. He wrote, 'if we constantly go on expanding in breadth, we shall never reach the stage when we consolidate, put some depth behind the [parity] façade and put our force on a footing of readiness for war'.[38]

On 11 March 1938, on the eve of the *Anschluss*, Austria's annexation into a Greater Germany, Slessor sent a minute to Newall:

You may think it wise to suggest to the Secretary of State that, instead of proceeding on the basis that we must be prepared for war in the next three years ... we may be forced into war this summer. This means in effect that instead of occupying our time and energies in preparation for further expansion, we should devote them to bringing our *existing* forces up to as high a degree of readiness for war as possible in as short a time as possible.[39]

Bomber Command and the Western Air plans

Slessor wasted no time in examining the operational status of both the Bomber and Fighter Commands. Slessor 'was the central pivot of all this planning, coordinating the information provided by the Intelligence Departments, both inside and outside the Air Ministry, tabulating targets, getting them arranged in some order of priority, and keeping in close touch regarding all tactical appreciations'.[40] For Bomber Command a list of thirteen target sets had been drawn up by Slessor's plans division in October 1937. All were denoted by the prefix WA ('Western Air'). Three of the target sets were prioritized to provide immediate assessments of Bomber Command's ability to complete successful 'raids' once hostilities commenced: WA-1, an attack on the German bomber force and support structures; WA-4, an attack on transportation networks (road, rail, canals) to delay a German invasion of the Low Countries and eastern France; and WA-5, an attack on German war industry – iron and steel, oil refining and storage, and power generation, with priorities being the Ruhr, the Rhineland and Saar. Bomber Command itself carried out the tactical analysis that included what kind of aircraft would be available, what the enemy could use against them, and what kind of bombs would be most effective. Sir Edgar Ludlow-Hewitt, C-in-C Bomber Command, took a highly active involvement in the tactical analysis. In a series of letters to the Air Ministry between 1937 and 1938, Ludlow-Hewitt cast doubt on any chance of success against any of the target sets, and he not only confirmed this view but showed how incapable Bomber Command was of inflicting any blow from British bases without incurring prohibitive losses.[41] Furthermore, 'It was becoming clear that Bomber Command could not do much to counter a German attack either in the air or on land.'[42] Webster and Frankland summed up Ludlow-Hewitt's gloomy assessment succinctly: 'It is surely remarkable that it was less than a year before war broke out that the Air Staff should have realized the limited possibilities of Bomber Command. They now knew that its Commander-in-Chief did not think it was capable of carrying out the operations on which the Air Ministry had based its strategy for the last four years.'[43]

The improvements in Fighter Command

The outlook was better for Fighter Command. In March Slessor had requested a review that would examine the effectiveness of fighters in their role of home defence. His comprehensive questionnaire sought answers to various performance indicators such as the rate of climb, the margin of speed between fighters and bombers, and the likelihood of interception of enemy bombers in varying weather conditions by day and by night.[44] The results were encouraging, with respondents considering that under fair weather conditions a 60 per cent interception rate could be expected during day raids, falling to 40 per cent for night raids. In poor weather conditions the interception rate dropped to 20 per cent and 10 per cent for day and night raids respectively. Although Slessor considered that the fighter's effectiveness was declining because of increasing German bomber speeds, his general view was more accepting of fighter effectiveness than that of many others on the Air Staff. Both Air Vice-Marshal William 'Sholto' Douglas (ACAS) and Sir Hugh Dowding, C-in-C Fighter Command, were even more optimistic. Douglas commented, 'I think in the last few months what with the advent of the 8-gun fighter [Spitfire and Hurricane], RDF [Radar] and the Biggin Hill interception scheme, the pendulum has swung the other way and that as soon as all our fighter squadrons are equipped with Hurricanes and Spitfires – the fighter is on top of the contemporary enemy bombers.' However, Slessor was coming to realize the resistance to communication and cooperation between the two Commands since their formation in 1936. Later that year Slessor had wanted to set up a permanent committee to be attended by representatives of both Fighter and Bomber Commands to review the feasibility of their joint operations, only to receive a sharp rebuke from Douglas. As Webster and Frankland stated, 'this exemplified the separation of the two Commands. The question of whether fighters could assist Bomber Command to solve problems was ignored.'[45] This silo mentality continued to cloud the judgement of the Air Staff until the Americans demonstrated the major success of escort fighters, especially the P-51 Mustangs, in February 1944 as part of Operation Argument[46] Otherwise known as 'Big Week', this was the Allied bombing offensive during the period 20–25 February, deliberately targeting the Luftwaffe's fighter force.

Slessor's report 'The Restriction of Air Warfare': the review of the morality and ethics of bombing

The Spanish Civil War had revealed the horrors of the aerial bombardment of towns and cities, as exemplified with the Guernica raid in April 1937, and later in the Barcelona raids of March 1938. The international condemnation of those attacks concentrated the minds of both senior British politicians and the Air Ministry. How would Britain ensure the accurate bombing of the enemy's military assets and that there would be no collateral civilian deaths?

The Prime Minister, Neville Chamberlain, declared in Parliament in June 1938 that 'it is against international law to carry out deliberate attacks on civilian populations'.[47] In reality, there was no agreed international legislation in place. Chamberlain was only referring to the unratified Hague Rules on Air Warfare that had been drafted in 1923. Earlier that year Slessor and other members of the Air Staff had drafted a report to address this problematic issue, entitled 'The Restriction of Air Warfare'.[48] Having taken note of the indiscriminate bombing in Spain, the central theme of the paper was the restriction of such actions and any wanton assault on civilians. It was summed up in the key message of the paper: 'a direct attack upon an enemy civilian population ... is a course of action which no British Cabinet would sanction'.[49] In drafting the paper Slessor was sensitive to the attitude of neutral countries and particularly American public opinion should Britain, 'be the first to cause casualties to a civilian population and we were impressed with the importance of securing neutral, especially American, public opinion firmly on our side'.[50] However, the reality of bombing with the high likelihood of collateral damage was not thoroughly addressed in the paper, mainly because there was no clear solution. Factories producing armaments in urban areas were usually surrounded by residential housing, often specifically constructed for the workforce. Furthermore, in the late 1930s precision bombing could not be assured. At that time it was difficult enough for the bombers to even find their targets over Germany, given the negligible navigation aids and the likelihood of cloud cover.

Ludlow-Hewitt, C-in-C Bomber Command, grasped the nettle when he wrote, 'in attacking aircraft factories, a proportion of bombs would fall outside the immediate designated area causing serious civilian casualties'.[51] In September the Air Council, while they recognized these operational limitations, stated firmly in their directive: 'it is essential that in the opening stages of a war your action should be rigorously restricted to attack on objectives which are manifestly and unmistakably military on the narrowest interpretation of the term'. Whereas bombers could attack military airfields and army barracks, they were restricted from attacking aircraft factories in urban residential areas. Cyril Newall, CAS, submitted the Air Council directive to Lord Swinton, Secretary of State for Air, concluding that these restrictions were unlikely to last long, but stating 'we obviously cannot be first "to take the gloves off"'.[52] Slessor, who had been directly involved in the development of the policy, concluded, 'it all is a matter not of legality but of expediency ... we never had the least doubt that sooner or later the gloves would come off, but our policy was to gain time'.[53]

After Munich and the Czech crisis: Slessor moves to 'the Citadel of Whitehall'

Alongside all of these challenges was the very real spectre of a war against Germany in late 1938, at a time when the RAF was ill-equipped in both bombers and fighters. Slessor wrote:

> I do not suppose I am alone in looking back upon the Czech crisis of August and September 1938 as the worst period of my life. It weighed like a ton of lead on one's mind and conscience and no-one who went through that time, knowing the facts and feeling their remorseless impact upon his judgement, would be a party to allowing our country ever again to find itself in such an utterly defenceless situation.[54]

The Munich crisis also ensured that the Air Ministry was now put on a war footing and the decision was taken to centralize the key functions of planning, operations and intelligence. To ensure the effective functioning of the government at times of air raids, it was decided to relocate Slessor and other senior members of the Air Staff to the New Public Offices in Whitehall. The building was constructed with a strong steel frame and included a large basement that was adapted to provide accommodation facilities, meeting areas and a map for the War Cabinet, the Chiefs of Staff and their advisers. Slessor called it 'the Citadel of Whitehall'.[55]

The Munich débâcle had only a single redeeming feature. It bought valuable time for the RAF to build up aircraft numbers with reserves. In the last weeks of his life Hitler convinced himself he 'should have gone to war in September 1938 – it was the last chance we had of localizing the conflict' – and that he had been taken for a ride by that 'arch-capitalist bourgeois, Chamberlain, with his deceptive umbrella', adding, 'his one and only object in undertaking the trip was to gain time'.[56]

In truth, British Intelligence had greatly exaggerated both the strength and efficacy of the German air force and the likely casualties from aerial bombardment. Military planners feared up to 200,000 casualties from bombing in the first week of a future war. But Germany was also ill-prepared and would have almost certainly been unable to deal Britain a devastating knockout blow in September 1938.[57] It is worth remembering that many in the German High Command were sceptical of victory even in mid-1939; indeed, some counselled Hitler against his invasion westwards.

In home defence Fighter Command had only twenty-nine front-line squadrons. There were no Spitfires yet in the line, and only five squadrons were equipped with Hurricanes. Furthermore, the Hurricanes – without heating for their guns – could not fight above 15,000ft.[58] The coastal radar chain was only partly complete and the radio links were primitive.[59] Bomber Command had forty-nine front-line squadrons. However, only twenty-five of those squadrons had any effective capability: nine squadrons of Whitley heavy bombers and sixteen squadrons of Blenheim light bombers. The remaining squadrons were operating with obsolescent Battles, Harrows and Wellesleys.[60] Reserves of both aircraft and crews were almost non-existent.[61]

1939: The lead-up to war and the turning point for British aircraft production

The year 1939, Slessor reflected, was a 'foul' one: 'a shattering succession of crises, giant strides towards the inevitable climax of September; the crowning treachery of March 15 when German troops marched into what was left of Czechoslovakia'.[62]

However, British aircraft production was finally turning the corner. As Terraine pointed out, 'in 1938–39 ... the advantages were all in the pipe-line'.[63] The decision to incorporate shadow factories was paying off. The table below illustrates national aircraft production numbers[64]:

Year	German	British
1938	5,235	2,827
1939	8,295	7,940
1940	10,826	15,049

The numbers demonstrated that finally Britain had prepared for war and was now able to confront German aggression when war came in September. However, the numbers do not reveal the poor nature of Bomber Command at the time. Whereas the first-line strength of Fighter Command was in good shape in July 1940, this was far from the case with Bomber Command. Fighter numbers amounted to approximately 700. Forty-eight squadrons were equipped with either Hurricanes or Spitfires. By contrast, Bomber Command had only 280 aircraft in twenty-three squadrons operating with Wellingtons, Whitleys, Blenheims, Battles and Hampdens. As the Official History concluded, 'during the first two years of the war Bomber Command was small, ill equipped and ineffective ... Bomber Command in 1939 was above all an investment in the future'.[65]

That investment was made possible by the submittal and approval of Scheme 'M' in November 1938. The plan called for an 'all-heavy' bomber force of 1,360 aircraft scheduled for completion by March 1942. Slessor, together with Arthur Street, Permanent Under-Secretary of State for Air, and Wilfrid Freeman, the Air Member for Aircraft Development and Production, were instrumental in finally getting the new heavy bomber programme approved. Those bombers – the Stirling, Halifax and Manchester (later Lancaster) – took time to come into operational service and it was only after 1942 that the heavies started to make a real impact in the bomber offensive over Germany. Given all the political prevarication, budget constraints and resistance to ramping up mass production of newly designed aircraft, Slessor summed it up by reflecting that, 'the war came three or four years too early for us'.[66] Scheme 'M' was the last of the pre-war expansion programmes. The final Scheme 'M' approved 800 front-line fighters and 1,360 heavy bombers to be completed by 1942.

Chapter 6

The Curtain Rises

Anglo-French Preparations, Norway, and a Dash to the Front Line, 1940

After Munich

Over a twenty-one month period between the Munich Crisis of September 1938 and the Fall of France in June 1940 Slessor was at the centre of major events as they unfolded. He was a key member of the Anglo-French military discussions until the declaration of war and later he was deeply involved at critical stages during the Norwegian campaign and the Battle of France.

Slessor considered the Munich crisis as 'the climax of misjudgement which was the inevitable culmination of the policies of the preceding years, and from which as inexorably followed the calamities of the years that came after, was the surrender at Munich in September 1938'.[1] Churchill described Munich 'as a defeat without a war', also believing that with the preponderance of French Army divisions located in eastern France, they could have 'rolled forward across the Rhine and into the Ruhr'.[2] On paper this might have looked obvious. To suggest the sixty-eight French Army divisions could not have overrun nine German divisions holding an incomplete 'West Wall' seemed totally implausible.[3]

Slessor and his colleagues on the Joint Planning Committee (JPC) begged to differ, stating in a policy paper that 'the Germans would be able to spare enough forces from an attack on Czechoslovakia to hold their fortifications in the West, and match any French offensive which – if it were to materialize – we thought would be a costly and ineffective operation'.[4]

With the overall *capabilities* of its 160 divisions, the French Army held a strong defensive position. However, when examining *intentions*, Slessor believed that, under its Commander-in-Chief General Gamelin, the French Army was useless, and its spirit was sapped during the late 1930s.[5] To make matters worse, their Air Force (*L'Armée de l'Air*) had been in decline since 1933 and though it had a first-line complement in late 1938 of 1,375 aircraft, most models were 'seriously obsolescent or downright obsolete'.[6]

The initial Anglo-French staff talks had taken place during March and April 1936, prompted by Germany's remilitarization of the Rhineland. The French hoped at that time that if British resources were added to their order of battle, it would strengthen their hand in any diplomatic moves.[7] Specifically they were looking to the British to provide a strong mechanized army field force, together with RAF fighter squadrons to be based in France. In particular, the French were acutely aware of their vulnerability in the air. Paris was well within range of German bombers based in the Rhineland. Consequently, throughout the late 1930s the French sought a greater contribution from the British to supplement their air defences. The air defence issue continued to cause strains between the French and the British, with the latter even refusing to discuss the issue.[8]

Even after Munich, the Chamberlain government withheld authority for closer military contacts or a stronger military commitment to the continent. In that time of indecision Slessor submitted a paper to Newall, Chief of the Air Staff (CAS), 'urging that we could no longer disinterest ourselves from the French strategic plans, which might vitally affect our own security'.[9] However, he recalled that in late 1938 'we were not in a position to influence the French plans, fully aware 'that Britain's contribution would amount to two weak [army] divisions and a few aeroplanes'.[10] The situation would eventually change considerably. By May 1940 Britain's contribution would amount to ten divisions of 390,000 troops, representing 10 per cent of the overall Allied defence forces in France. On the Air side the contribution would amount to twenty-nine squadrons comprising 464 bombers and fighters.[11]

Newall, as both CAS and chairman of the Chiefs of Staff (COS), now thought the time was right to launch proper Anglo-French staff conversations 'to ensure that Britain had a substantive input into joint plans, in order to counteract weaknesses and misconceptions in Gamelin's strategic thinking'.[12] The British worried that their army would become irrevocably committed to the French battle-line as had been the case in 1914.[13] Reticence and mistrust remained, along with doubts over the French Army's morale, the reliability of the French High Command, and the strength of its fortifications. Equally, on the French side there were continuing dark thoughts of *La Perfide Albion*: a suspicion that Britain sought to fight on land to the last Frenchman.[14] In this atmosphere of mutual mistrust Slessor accompanied Newall to the first high-level Anglo-French meeting held in London on 26 September. It was attended for the British by Thomas Inskip, Minister for the Coordination of Defence, Leslie Hore-Belisha, Secretary of State for War, and Lord John Gort, Chief of the Imperial General Staff (CIGS), and for the French by General Maurice Gamelin, Commander-in-Chief of French land forces, and General Pierre Lelong, the French military attaché. The French did not reveal their detailed plans at the meeting and Slessor suspected that the 'whole thing was a *projét*' rather than a detailed plan with firm tactical and administrative details. His suspicions were confirmed a week later when he received further indications that this was the case. Slessor then told Newall that he thought the French 'plans', such as they were, to be 'optimistic to the point of lunacy'.[15]

The Anglo-French staff conversations and the Phoney War

With preparations being made for war, it is remarkable that the formal Anglo-French staff conversations did not start until 29 March 1939, almost six months on from that initial London meeting. The series of staff conversations with the French over the next four months went well and, despite previous reservations, there was surprisingly good agreement on several points: that neither France nor Britain would come to the aid of Poland, if attacked; and that the Germans would most likely attack in the West through Holland and Belgium to attempt an invasion of France. And these predictions came to pass. But on the Air side of discussions there was a distinct suspicion of British intentions. Whereas the French felt that the RAF fighters and bombers should be deployed primarily in tactical support of the French Army, the British continued to propose a strategic response to any invasion that would entail the bombing of key targets in Germany that, through a programme of interdiction, would disrupt the flow of troops and matériel to their front lines. Slessor could never convince Gamelin or his colleagues, who were more concerned that such a move would invite retaliation against French cities and factories. They treated this whole concept with a suspicion that Slessor felt he was never able to dispel.[16] It was obvious that the French themselves were 'ill-equipped in the air, believing that all bomber forces should be used in direct support of the army'.[17]

During the month of May Slessor found that the staff talks were drifting towards discussions of establishing an Eastern European military alliance in the Balkans rather than addressing a military response to direct German aggression. In August Slessor and his staff colleagues were relieved of their duties by the Permanent Military Representatives to the Anglo-French Supreme War Council (SWC), and Air Vice-Marshal Douglas Evill took Slessor's place as the RAF representative in the continuing round of Anglo-French staff conversations.

On 1 September Slessor was promoted to the rank of air commodore. He continued to be deeply involved with French issues until their capitulation in June 1940. Newall valued Slessor's clear and incisive qualities and chose him as his staff officer to accompany him on the several high-level meetings that were held at the French Army's headquarters located at Château de Vincennes on the eastern outskirts of Paris.

Those meetings gave Slessor an even deeper insight into the thinking of the French High Command following the declaration of war and before the Battle of France, a period known in France as *La Drôle de Guerre* and in Britain and America as the 'Phoney War'. General Gamelin as commander in chief was well-respected by both his allies and his opponents. During the First World War he was credited with planning the successful counterattack during the First Battle of the Marne in 1914 and was subsequently promoted rapidly through the officer ranks. In 1931 he became Chief of the General Staff, and in 1935 he became Inspector General of the French Army and vice president of the Higher Council of War. He was naturally conservative in his planning, and his vision for France's defence was based upon a static defence perimeter along the Franco-German border that included the ill-fated Maginot Line. Slessor described how Gamelin lived a remote and cloistered existence at Vincennes surrounded by a coterie of his chosen army planners who were also out of touch with day-to-day developments. Surprisingly, there were no air staff representatives based at Vincennes.[18] Nonetheless, Slessor and Newall were introduced to General Joseph Vuilleman, commander in chief of the Air Force, who attended those meetings. Unfortunately, Vuilleman had poor leadership qualities. As John Terraine wrote, 'he was considered to be an elderly bomber pilot who was not over-endowed with dynamism, and who could put up no more than 250 fighters and 320 bombers, all of doubtful performance'.[19] In September 1938 Vuilleman had told his government that he hoped to be supported by 120 British bombers in the first week of hostilities and a further 120 over the course of the ensuing month. Slessor recalled Vuilleman insisting 'that the French were anxious to do nothing calculated to open up the war in the air and in general to keep this "an army cooperation war" if they could'.[20]

The French grand strategy involved settling in for a long war with all effort put into adopting a strong defence posture against the threat of German invasion, and instead to weaken Germany elsewhere through economic warfare in other areas, notably the Balkans and Scandinavia. Those two areas were highlighted because of their ability to supply strategic raw materials – crude oil and high-grade iron ore – that were vital to sustaining Germany's war industries. However, from the British military perspective Lord Ironside (CIGS) complained, 'everything was hopelessly defensive everywhere'.[21]

In early 1939 the Air Staff had decided that the best way to respond to a German invasion of France would be to put the 'Ruhr Plan' into immediate effect. Slessor pointed out that twenty squadrons of light and medium bombers would be located initially at airfields in the Rheims and Laon area of eastern France. Known as the Advanced Air Strike Force (AASF), it was in effect Bomber Command's French outpost, well within range of targets in western Germany: specifically oil refineries, depots and railway links located primarily in the Ruhr Valley. It would see the fulfilment of Western Air Plan WA5(C) that Slessor had originally proposed in 1937.

Throughout this period those who subscribed to the long war strategy on either the British or French side continued to promote the idea of diversionary moves in either the Balkans or Scandinavia. The Balkan plan never found favour with the British, nor with Gamelin.

The Norway Campaign

However, the Scandinavian plan came to be considered seriously after the Soviet Union invaded Finland in November 1939. At this stage in the Phoney War period British and French politicians favoured some action to aid the beleaguered Finns. However, the underlying appeal of Scandinavia was the fact that Germany was at that time importing 40 per cent of its iron ore from the Gällivare area of northern Sweden. The ore was of high grade and important in the production of steel needed for the manufacture of armaments. Shipments of ore were transported by rail to two ports for onward export by ship to Germany: either westwards to Narvik on the Norwegian coast, or south to Luleå on the Gulf of Bothnia. On paper this looked like an ideal way to wage economic war against Germany. One report by the British Ministry of Economic Warfare assured the War Cabinet that if deprived of the Swedish ore, Germany could not continue to wage war for more than a year.[22] However, the superficial appeal of a campaign to deny ore to the Germans and at the same time provide military aid to the Finns came up against several serious challenges. A joint Anglo-French military presence would almost certainly not be welcomed by either Norway or Sweden, both neutral countries at the time. The Germans would almost certainly retaliate, which would inevitably bring war to both countries. Furthermore, there was a high likelihood of the Soviet Union becoming involved as an unwelcome adversary against the Allies. To complicate matters further, the Soviet Union had entered into a non-aggression pact with Germany in August 1939.

Slessor, as the senior member of the JPC at the time, reviewed the situation and presented his conclusions and recommendations to the Chiefs of Staff in January 1940.[23] Slessor and his JPC colleagues now believed that the long war strategy was open to serious criticism. By 1940 the Germans could field 170 army divisions and, with seventy to eighty divisions considered ample to hold a defensive front in the West, it would still leave ninety to one hundred divisions available for campaigns elsewhere.[24] Despite all these concerns Churchill, then First Lord of the Admiralty, continued to be highly enthusiastic about intervention in both Norway and Sweden.

Slessor and the other members of the Joint Planning Committee agonized throughout January and February to manage expectations and not give the impression to Norway, Sweden or Finland that they could expect any substantial assistance in either troops or matériel. Both French and British politicians continued to propose bold plans, but without much regard for the longer-term consequences. Inevitably, mindful of the necessity of keeping focused on the main strategy of defending France, the JPC felt compelled to address the situation to the Chiefs of Staff as follows:

> Our only sound strategy must be to remain on the defensive and build up our strength, and we should on no account undertake added commitments if they can possibly be avoided, before we are in a position to meet them. The only thing that should make us depart from this policy would be if we could be quite certain of getting into the Gällivare fields.[25]

Churchill rejected this advice, and Slessor recalled that 'he invented a terrible sobriquet for the JPC as "that machinery of negation" ... long staff studies of various operations, as the result of which I was usually convinced that they were better left alone, or else that they could not be fitted in with the general conduct of the struggle'.[26]

But on this issue Slessor and the other JPC members were entirely correct. Inevitably, the Scandinavian campaign was doomed from the start. The British had two plans. Operation Wilfred would involve launching marine mines into Norway's nearshore coastal waters in an attempt to stop ore from being exported from Narvik. Plan R-4 would involve landing Allied troops at key ports on the Norwegian coast if there was a German military response. However, that response took place sooner than anyone envisioned. Germany invaded both Denmark and Norway on 9 April and this marked the point at which the Phoney War came to an end. Despite valiant Allied efforts, German forces eventually dominated everywhere: on land, at sea and in the air. The speed of the German operations led to hastily prepared military plans being continually revised or cancelled. As John Terraine commented, 'From the beginning to the end the Allied operations in Norway ... displayed an amateurishness and feebleness which to this day can make the reader alternately blush and shiver.'[27] Over the following six weeks the RAF lost fighters and bombers that they could ill afford to lose while they operated in difficult conditions against continuous German air superiority.

The Battle of France

It came as no surprise that the Germans had finally decided to invade in the West. On 10 May Slessor was woken by his official green telephone ringing early in the morning at his London Ebury Street flat in Victoria. The caller informed him that German paratroopers were dropping in Holland, and that the AASF squadrons' airfields in France were being bombed. After all the uncertainty during the Phoney War and the Scandinavian fiasco, he had a feeling of relief. 'At least one knew where we stood.'[28]

The Battle of France had opened with the simultaneous invasion of Holland, Belgium and Luxembourg. The British Expeditionary Force (BEF) that comprised ten divisions moved up through Belgium to the river Dijle southwest of Antwerp and to the defence line that was agreed in 1939. It was known as Gamelin's Plan 'D'. On paper, the two sides looked evenly matched, with the order of battle in May 1940 of 136 Allied divisions facing 135 German divisions. As the historian Martin Alexander wrote, 'No-one who mattered in the Franco-British leadership believed that they were running a real danger of an early, quick and complete defeat.'[29] In fact, that was also the view of the majority of the German High Command, namely that an attack in the West would almost certainly result in a stalemate, and a repeat of the position in the First World War. However, the numbers did not tell the whole story. The elements of surprise, speed and manoeuvrability would make the difference. In February 1940 the maverick Prussian general Erich von Manstein convinced Hitler that a manoeuvre through the Ardennes, though risky, would succeed in outflanking the Allies. The key differences lay in the German application of their military doctrine. In adopting their *Blitzkrieg* approach of speed and agility, the Germans were able to hold the initiative from the first day. The real surprise, however, was the speed of movement of Army Group A from an unexpected quarter, the supposedly impenetrable Ardennes forest, which caught the French Army off guard. This tactical masterstroke continued with the employment of *Schwerpunkt*: the concentration of German ground and air assets that struck key points of French resistance between Dinant and Sedan.[30]

The German forces were also coordinating all their operations in what twenty-first-century military tacticians would describe as C3I (command, control, communication and intelligence). This was far from the case for the defending Allied forces. The French High Command had extremely poor communications and a Byzantine organizational structure, and distrusted much of its intelligence.[31] The BEF often had difficulties during the first week of the battle at getting clear information and instructions from the French high command. In addition, its communication and coordination with the RAF air component was poor.

German Army Group A cut a westerly swathe through the French Ninth and First Armies. On 17 May, just seven days into the campaign, the Germans had already reached a line between St Quentin in France and Mons in Belgium. The situation had become increasingly desperate. The BEF withdrew to a defence line along the river Escaut (Scheldt), with the Belgian Army on its left flank retreating southwards; both the First and Ninth French Armies on its right flank were disintegrating. Fearing encirclement, Gort, Commander-in-Chief of the BEF, signalled that the outcome looked extremely uncertain.

On the same day the British War Cabinet met to discuss the grave situation. The crisis had led to immediate changes in France's key leadership. In the midst of panic, chaos and despondency at the centre of the French government, the Premier, Paul Reynaud, sacked Gamelin and appointed as his replacement General Maxime Weygand, who had been recalled from Beirut on 19 May.[32] This abrupt change at the top of the French High Command at this critical juncture did not help the situation.

On the evening of Sunday, 19 May Slessor became directly involved in the crisis when he was called to attend an emergency meeting at Admiralty House. The attendees included Newall and the other Chiefs of Staff, Ironside (CIGS), and the three service ministers. There was a sombre mood as the newly installed Prime Minister, Winston Churchill, chaired the meeting. Slessor recalled that 'the atmosphere in that long room was grave and tense, and during the discussion one's eyes could not but keep straying to the big map on the end wall with a strip of blue tape showing the terrible bulge spreading towards Arras and the coast'.[33] General Ironside was instructed to travel directly to Gort's headquarters in France to instruct him to move the BEF southwest and away from the Flanders pocket and towards Amiens, and there to take station on the left of the French Army.

Newall instructed Slessor to accompany Ironside to coordinate the urgent redeployment of all the RAF squadrons operating in France. Ironside and Slessor left immediately by a special government train from Charing Cross to Dover. From there they travelled by destroyer overnight. It was a hazardous journey. Even from Dover they could see the flashes of bombs bursting along the French coast between Dunkirk and Boulogne. In mid-Channel an aircraft flew over at low level and dropped either a bomb or magnetic mine that fortunately missed the destroyer.[34] The destroyer arrived off Boulogne in the early hours of Monday morning 20 May, having waited several hours for German air raids to cease.

At the port they were met by Gort's ADC and were taken by the GHQ Rolls-Royce to Gort's headquarters at a chateau near Wahagnies, south of Lille. They arrived around 8am and after settling in, Slessor found Gort pacing up and down on the front lawn. Gort was already discussing evacuation points on the French coast, including Ostend, Nieuport and Dunkirk. Ironside proceeded to show Gort the written Order 'A' issued by the War Cabinet to move south, despite, as Slessor wrote later, 'realizing that the order bore no relation to the situation as it existed'.[35] German units were rapidly advancing westwards, breaking through the French Armies' lines and consequently had created a gap in the Allied lines that had to be closed if disaster was to be averted.

Seeing the situation as critical, Ironside decided immediately to visit the French GHQ in Lens. He took Henry Pownall, Gort's Chief of the General Staff, with him. They arrived in Lens and met Billotte and Blanchard, Commander of the French First Army. Both generals gave Ironside the impression of being totally defeated without any idea of what to do next. Ironside was a formidable individual, standing at 6ft 4in, and known by his humorous nickname 'Tiny'. Towering over the two generals, Ironside lost his temper. He shook Billotte by the button on his tunic and insisted that they attack southwards toward Amiens. Both French generals were completely rattled by Ironside's behaviour and gave an unconvincing assurance that they would attack jointly with the BEF on 21 May. Ironside now understood the true situation. The scale of the defeat being inflicted on the French Army was much clearer in his mind.[36]

Back at the British GHQ Slessor realized the troops of the BEF were now cut off from further supplies of food and ammunition and for the first time believed there was every chance of them being rounded up and captured *en masse*, without a round of ammunition to enable them to continue fighting.[37] At 0900 hours Slessor contacted Air Vice-Marshal 'Sholto' Douglas, DCAS, requesting that Blenheims from 2 Group of Bomber Command be dispatched from England with fighter cover to attack the German tank spearheads and supporting infantry columns. The first attack was over the target area at 1130 hours and bombed a tightly packed infantry column moving west across the Bapaume road; the second attack, arriving shortly after, saw only a few enemy troops. In such quick-moving warfare both were, of course, too late for the original targets. Targets reported at 0830 hours were 'cold'

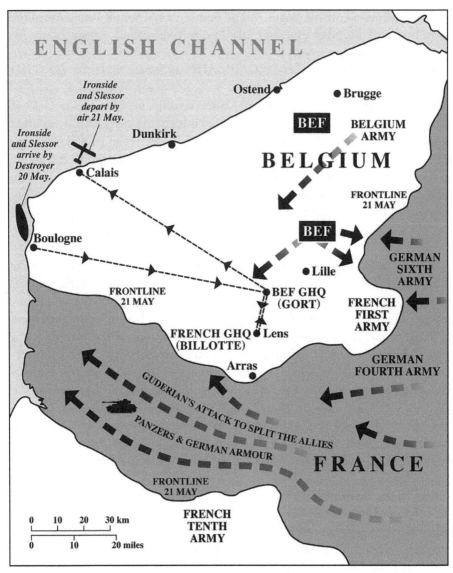

Ironside and Slessor's trip, 20–21 May 1940. Battle of France: the race for the coast to encircle the Allies in Flanders. (Adapted from maps by Major L.F. Ellis, *The War in France and Flanders, 1939–1940*, HMSO, 1954.)

three hours later. Long before 1130 hours the leading units of six German armoured divisions had advanced across the Canal du Nord. By noon the divisions were widely dispersed in the open country between Arras and the Somme.[38]

At the start of the Battle of France the RAF had twenty-nine squadrons based in France:

- the Air Component of the BEF comprising sixteen squadrons of Hurricanes, Blenheims and Lysanders, located at airfields between Abbeville in the west and Péronne to the east, tasked to provide air reconnaissance and air cover; and
- the AASF, located farther to the south, comprising thirteen squadrons of Battles, Blenheims and Hurricanes at airfields between Clermont to the west and Nancy in the east. These squadrons were originally tasked to attack targets in the Ruhr but would mainly be used in bombing the advancing German forces. They had not been trained for this role and their sorties were largely ineffective, suffering significant losses of both aircraft and aircrew.

Many of the airfields had now been subject to repeated air raids, with significant numbers of aircraft damaged beyond repair. Furthermore, the enemy's Army Group A advanced rapidly towards Arras, cutting all phone lines, thereby denying any communication with the AASF squadrons to the south. It was now imperative to withdraw all the remaining aircraft and their supporting ground echelons. During that morning Air Vice-Marshal Charles Blount, commander of the RAF's Air Component, arrived at the chateau. Blount and Slessor agreed a joint plan and Lord Gort agreed with their decision to get squadrons either out to England or right back to the Seine as quickly as possible. Three squadrons had already left for Kent airfields. 14 Group's fighters were ordered to operate during the rest of the day, and then to fly back to Kent that night. Ground echelons and their equipment had already been moved west to Beauvais, with some cleared out as far west as Cherbourg.

Slessor then went off in the Rolls to meet Ironside at the French GHQ in Lens, only to be slowed down to a crawl by two streams of refugees: one leaving Lille and travelling southwest and the other leaving Arras moving northwest. Chaos reigned. As Slessor noted:

Every road and lane was choc-a-block, with the pathetic flood – everything from motor cars to handcarts to wheelbarrows, perambulators, bicycles, and little trollies drawn by dogs, piled with mattresses, cooking pots and odds and ends of household property, and everywhere the heart-breaking streams of wretched, frightened people mingled with exhausted stragglers from Belgian or Dutch armies, thick as a crowd coming away from a cup final.[39]

After a difficult, slow journey Slessor arrived in Lens only to learn that Ironside had already left. He also found that the French Army HQ was already being packed up to move to Lillers. The remaining army personnel were in a sombre and defeatist mood. Slessor wandered down the corridors and looked into a room 'where there were a few utterly dejected-looking officers wandering listlessly about or sitting staring at the wall while an orderly rolled maps and packed up office gear ... I distinguished in *sotto voce*, half understood conversation – *rien à faire, fini,* and for the first time, that ghastly word "armistice"'.[40] The historian John Cairns was to write after the war that 'the spirit of 1914–18 had gone out of France, and her people were not what they had once been'.[41]

Slessor got back in the Rolls for what he thought would be another slow and difficult trip back to Gort's GHQ. Fortuitously, a Royal Military Police motorcyclist outside asked if he needed assistance. 'Certainly,' said Slessor, and the motorcyclist rode ahead, making a way for the Rolls and guiding it through streams of refugees 'like a hot knife through butter', arriving back at GHQ in a quarter of the time it had taken on the outward journey.[42] From there both Ironside and Slessor had another difficult, slow journey to their rendezvous point at St Inglevert airfield on the outskirts of Calais, where a Flamingo (a small passenger aircraft) and its Hurricane escort had been arranged for 6pm to take them back to England that evening.

Unfortunately, they arrived late only to find both planes had left. In the circumstances they decided to drive into a heavily bombed Calais and look for accommodation. They found rooms in a small hotel and settled down with what Slessor described as an 'excellent dinner and a bottle of Beaujolais that sticks in my memory'.[43] The fatigue of the preceding twenty-four hours caught up with him, but he was to wake up suddenly later that night with the bedroom floor covered with broken glass. During the early hours of that morning, 21 May, two sticks of bombs had exploded close to the hotel, one of which demolished the adjacent café. Ironside and Slessor left for England later that morning having cheated death twice during the previous thirty-six hours.

*   *   *

During that catastrophic week in late May Slessor returned to his role as RAF Director of Plans and as the senior member of the inter-service Joint Planning Committee. The situation in France was deteriorating by the hour. Late on the night of Friday, 24 May he wrote a covering letter to Newall that began with the words, 'This is unquestionably the most serious paper ever produced by the JPC and it is devoutly to be hoped that no future Director of Plans will ever again be called upon to participate in such an appreciation or write such a brief.'[44] That paper, largely authored by Slessor, formed the basis of a historic Chiefs of Staff memorandum. The document did not pull any punches. It set out a candid assessment of the chances of Britain holding out against further German aggression and possible invasion. Prophetically, it stated that 'the crux of the matter is air superiority, and Germany could not achieve this unless she could knock out our Air Force and aircraft industries'. It went on to state that Germany had a four to one superiority in aircraft and that she held most of the cards. The real test was whether 'the morale of our fighting personnel would counterbalance the numerical and material advantages which Germany enjoys. We believe it will.'[45]

Slessor wrote later, 'the best way of summing up our feelings at that horrible time is that we felt in our bones that we could not be defeated, but it was extremely difficult to see how we were going to win'.[46] Churchill himself commented that the report was written before the 'Dunkirk Deliverance'.[47] Much would depend on help from the Empire and the United States.

On Sunday, 26 May Operation Dynamo, the plan to evacuate the BEF, was put into effect. Over the next eight days over 338,000 British and French troops were eventually evacuated from Dunkirk's beaches and port. It marked the nadir of Anglo-French military relations, with each ally blaming the other for failing to cooperate and act swiftly.[48]

During the Battle of France the RAF lost nearly a thousand aircraft over a six-week period. During the first week 248 aircraft were lost from both the Air Component and the AASF. The fighting revealed inherent weaknesses. The Fairey Battle light bombers were obsolescent and fell easy prey to German fighters at high altitude and to the heavy concentration of flak from German army units at low level. On 14 May seventy-one Fairey Battles took part in a bombing raid in the Sedan area, with forty-four failing to return – a 62 per cent loss rate.[49] These loss rates were clearly unsustainable. Hugh Dowding, the Air Officer Commander-in-Chief of Home (Metropolitan) Fighter Command, wrote a historic memorandum to the Air Ministry on 16 May pointing out convincingly that if Britain was to avoid defeat 'not one fighter [will] be sent across the Channel however urgent and insistent the appeals for help may be', and concluding 'if the Home Defence Force is drained away in desperate attempts to remedy the situation in France, defeat in France will involve the final, complete and irremediable defeat of this country'.[50]

From this point onwards Newall, as CAS, gave his support and was 'the chief protagonist of what can be called the Fighter Command point of view'.[51] The following day he met the other Chiefs of Staff, stating, 'I do not believe that to throw in a few more squadrons, whose loss might vitally weaken the fighter line, alone would make the difference between victory and defeat in

France.'[52] Finally, on 19 May Churchill ruled that 'No more squadrons of fighters will leave the country whatever the need in France.'[53]

The Anglo-French relationship continued to deteriorate. The historian John Cairns wrote, 'To the British it seemed that the French, having sadly neglected their own air forces, were all too ready to direct the operations of the RAF. The French commanders were for ever asking for the RAF to tackle unsuitable targets. They had already suffered irreparable losses by attempting to answer such calls.'[54] Air Marshal Sir Arthur Barratt, who was overall commander of the RAF in France, bluntly told Vuilleman, his French opposite number, that 'if the French infantry doesn't hold, it is useless to send aeroplanes'.[55] The relationship had become even more acrimonious as Churchill became adamant that he would not release any more of the RAF's fighters for operations over France. Paul Reynaud, the French Premier, would repeat again and again that 'History will then doubtless record that the Battle of France was lost for want of aeroplanes.'[56]

Slessor felt the frustration of being unable to put the AASF into operation from the opening of hostilities, and ultimately doing so when it was too late to have any beneficial effect. It was only after the *Luftwaffe* bombed Rotterdam that the 'gloves came off'.[57] Attacks were then authorized on German and Dutch targets. Between 15 and 17 May a hundred RAF heavy bombers attacked oil targets on the Ruhr, marshalling yards in Cologne and the approaches to Maastricht to disrupt the German Army's movements through southern Holland into Belgium.[58]

By then it was a case of too little, too late. They would have not done much to delay the enemy's inevitable advance. At that stage of the war Bomber Command had no modern navigation aids, and even with a full moon they found it difficult to locate their targets.[59] Unfortunately, Bomber Command was then ordered to switch to tactical targets that included communications and the Meuse crossings. The lessons learned from the RAF's inadequacies during the Battle of France would eventually be remedied. They were to relearn the close air support and air land coordination skills they had originally used in 1918 in the closing stages of the First World War.[60] During the Battle of Normandy in July 1944 the RAF also had an air strength that had grown ten to twenty-fold with significant technological improvements. At that stage of the war, the highly effective use of aircraft in both close air support and interdiction roles – by both the RAF and the USAAF – often prevented German troops and matériel getting to the battlefield.

In early June it was becoming increasingly inevitable that France would fall. On 14 June Slessor recalled being at a JPC meeting in a neon-lit basement room below the Cabinet office when they were interrupted by the duty officer with a message from the British liaison officer with General Georges. It read 'Organised resistance is at an end.'[61] But this did not mean the end of Slessor's involvement with France. What would become of France's significant navy, its merchant navy, gold, negotiable securities, its secret equipment and documents?

Destruction of the French fleet at Mers-el-Kébir: a further example of the 'Machinery of Negation'

Slessor and his JPC colleagues submitted a policy document regarding the French Navy that concluded 'even the successful destruction of the French warships would not be justified if it carried with it the genuine danger of resulting in the active hostility of France and her colonial possessions'.[62] It was not what Churchill wanted to hear. He vehemently disagreed with the conclusion, countering that if the French naval fleet were commandeered by the German Navy, it would become a serious threat to Britain. Admiral François Darlan, Admiral of the Fleet, reassured Churchill that the Germans would never get the ships and that it 'would be contrary to our naval tradition and our honour'.[63] However, Darlan never issued any order, as Churchill had requested, for the ships to sail to British, American or French colonial ports. It became a major moral dilemma for the British War Cabinet. The French Navy was the fourth most powerful navy in the world and it became an imperative to prevent the ships becoming part of the German or Italian navies.

On 2 July Churchill ordered Admiral Somerville to sail with Task Force H from Gibraltar to Oran in Algeria and there to demand that the French warships moored in Mers-el-Kébir either surrender or face destruction. The French Admiral, Marcel-Bruno Gensoul, refused to surrender and 40 per cent of the entire French fleet was destroyed or damaged with the loss of 1,297 sailors. Somerville was never enthusiastic about the action, later saying that 'it was the biggest political blunder of modern times and will rouse the whole world against us ... we all feel thoroughly ashamed'.[64] As Martin Alexander wrote, 'after the Dunkirk evacuation the image of Britannia "fighting to the last Frenchman" ceased to be a cynical jibe between friends and allies. It became the twisted, treachery-tainted undercurrent to an ugly new bout of cross-Channel xenophobia, one with a ferocity – and with the bloody and tragic consequences at Mers el Kébir'.[65]

Churchill's criticism of the JPC

Churchill was adamant that the action at Mers-el-Kébir was the correct decision, and that despite the impression that Britain was now 'down and out, which strangers had supposed to be quivering on the brink of surrender ... it was made plain that the British War Cabinet feared nothing and would stop at nothing'.[66]

But Churchill felt that the JPC's view of considering an attack on the French navy as unwise was yet another example of the 'machinery of negation'. On 24 August he took what he called 'the only formal step which I ever found necessary to bring the JPC under his personal control'.[67] Newall was unruffled by the change, expecting 'an unorthodox genius to behave in an unorthodox manner'. Slessor wrote of Churchill in *Central Blue* that, 'like all men of very strong character he has his likes and dislikes, and it has not been my good fortune to be among the former', adding, 'I do not think Mr Churchill has ever quite forgiven [the JPC] for their too frequent inability to fall in with his strategic ideas.' He noted that even in 1949, when *Gathering Storm* was published, Churchill was still stigmatizing the JPC for its 'vain boggling hesitation, changes of policy, argumentation between good and worthy people unending'.[68]

But Slessor soon found that reporting directly to Churchill was nowhere near as bad as he might have predicted. He recalled that, 'after some initial waste of time the excellent machinery of the Chiefs of Staff and the joint planners soon got back on track and with the added inspiration and impetus of the PM'.[69] The new role also had its lighter moments, which included several weekend visits to Chequers, the PM's country retreat in Buckinghamshire, during the remaining months of 1940. On one occasion Churchill, Slessor and their colleagues were walking in the garden after dinner. London was being bombed and the eastern sky was red with the glare of great fires. The PM gazed at it sadly, shaking his head. Then he said unexpectedly that it was strange that this war, unlike the last, had produced no good songs – no *Tipperary* or *Keep the Home Fires Burning*. 'I must write to [Ivor] Novello and tell him to write a good war song', and then with a chuckle, 'but this time it will have to be *Stop the Home Fires Burning*.'[70]

The collapse of France left a clean slate for future strategic planning. Before the start of the Battle of Britain, Slessor wrote of his thoughts to Air Marshal Richard Pierse, VCAS, on 19 June:

Everything had to be thought through afresh in the lurid light of the new and intensely grim situation in which we now found ourselves alone – our only major ally overwhelmed, our enemy in possession of the whole coastline of Europe from North Cape to the Bay of Biscay, and possibilities of further calamity looming in the Near and Far East. With the Luftwaffe concentrating for the knockout blow and the invasion barges beginning to pile up in the Channel ports, the task of the planners was to free their minds from these immediate perils and turn them to long-term consideration of future strategy, of the probable future threats that we must be ready to counter, and of the means to which we must look for the ultimate defeat of Germany.[71]

Chapter 7

Secret Emissary

American Preparations, June–September 1940

During the summer of 1940 Air Commodore Slessor and his fellow joint planners reported directly to Churchill. They were at the centre of momentous events as Britain's future as an independent nation hung in the balance. Many international commentators considered that, after the fall of France, it was unlikely the nation would survive the German onslaught, and that invasion was inevitable. Joseph Kennedy, America's ambassador to London, was a well-known Anglophobe. His messages back to Washington consistently reported that Britain was now 'a lost cause'. President Roosevelt was not convinced. He considered that Britain would fight hard and, with its strong navy and air force, might well prevent an invasion. However, he was convinced that if Britain was overrun, then only what would be left of the Royal Navy lay between the American east coast and Hitler's rampaging armies in Western Europe.[1] Slessor knew that in the immediate term national survival would depend on the RAF's ability to retain air superiority over Britain. In the longer term Britain needed America's help to build up the forces that would eventually be capable of defeating Germany and Italy. Slessor's direct involvement in setting up Anglo-American military staff conversations in London, deploying his innate ability in building long-standing relationships with key American military and civilian representatives, marked the start of a vitally important alliance.

The proposed increase of American air attachés in London

In February 1940 President Roosevelt and General George C. Marshall, Chief of the Army Staff, attended an Air Corps flying display. After the event the President asked Marshall how many air attachés were accredited to their London embassy. On learning that there were only two specialist officers employed in that role he suggested doubling the figure.[2] The British embassy in Washington contacted the Air Ministry to pass on the Air Corps' request. Slessor gave his qualified support to the proposal, recognizing that it would give the Air Ministry the opportunity to open more discussions, and to address the urgent need for additional aircraft that the Americans could provide.

But Newall, the Chief of the Air Staff, was sceptical. He wrote a guarded and somewhat acerbic note to Sir Archibald Sinclair, the Secretary of State for Air, questioning security and American motives: 'What guarantees have we that this information will not find its way back to our enemies?', and adding, 'I am not prepared to be rushed by the Americans who, as always, wish to have the best of both worlds. They would like to be our allies, but without any obligations and they are not blind naturally to the pecuniary advantages of such a state of affairs.'[3] But he was not alone in his suspicious view of American motives. Many in government circles. including Prime Minister Neville Chamberlain, were equally sceptical. Chamberlain did not want an American entry into the war. Perhaps mindful of President Wilson's key role in setting the harsh terms of the Treaty of Versailles in 1919, he wrote to his sister in January, 'Heaven knows ... I don't want the Americans to fight for us – we should have to pay too dearly for that if they had a right to be in on the peace terms ...'.[4]

Lord Lothian's initiatives in Washington

Britain was truly fortunate to have Lord Lothian as its ambassador to Washington during 1940. Lothian liked and understood Americans and their political system better than any of the Foreign Office's career diplomats. He had many valuable connections in their government, the universities and the media, and he was also a highly effective orator. At a time when isolationist views were common in America, he did much to publicize the British situation through keynote lectures, interviews and newspaper articles. He also had numerous conversations with Roosevelt. During 1940 Lothian was involved in negotiations for the supply of fifty ageing American destroyers in return for rights to eight air and naval bases in Bermuda, Newfoundland, the Caribbean and British Guiana. Later in the year he was also instrumental in concluding the Anglo-American Lend-Lease Agreement before his untimely death in December.

During February Roosevelt raised the air attachés issue with Lothian. By early March Lothian was concerned that the lack of response was starting to create an unfavourable impression. Finally, Newall relented: 'Information made available to these air attachés should be treated with complete secrecy, and we should expect to obtain a reasonable amount of information in return for what we give.'[5] However, the Chiefs of Staff retained the full right to refuse the American attachés any access to operations rooms and their work-ings, or to tell them anything about stabilized bombsights and radar.[6]

The first pair of additional air attachés, known officially as 'Military Air Observers', arrived in April. Lieutenant Colonel Gardner and Major Carroll spent a month investigating bomber tactics and ways to increase their effec-tiveness, the role of escort fighters and the effectiveness of bombing. At the end of their stay they concluded that if America supplied B-17 bombers to the RAF, then experienced Air Corps officers should train RAF aircrew in Canada. This recommendation was received enthusiastically by Slessor, who responded: 'we welcome any reinforcement that the U.S. could make avail-able to our long-range bomber force operating against Germany. It is sug-gested that plans should be based on an initial contingent of four heavy bomber (B-17) squadrons, which could be flown across the Atlantic, to operate from bases in the U.K.'.[7]

During early May General Arnold, Chief of the Army Air Corps, decided to send Colonel Carl A. Spaatz to London. Spaatz had been Chief of Air Corps Plans since early 1939. Arnold recognized that he was the ideal choice for the most senior air attaché in Britain during the summer of 1940. The US Army Air Corps insisted that it needed to get a first-hand view of the current state of the air war in Europe. Spaatz came with considerable knowledge and experi-ence. He had a broad knowledge of Air Corps capabilities, training, procure-ment and war plans. Officially, he was in Britain to study RAF training and tactics. But unofficially, he was sent to discuss the RAF's air requirements in light of America's own military aircraft production plans and schedules.

Slessor, as Director of Plans at the Air Ministry, was the ideal Air Staff officer to have discussions with Spaatz. They met for lunch on 3 June in London during one of the darkest periods of the war, as the Dunkirk evac-uation was nearing completion. Slessor briefed Spaatz on the RAF's combat experiences with the Luftwaffe over France and Belgium. Spaatz's biographer, the aviation historian Richard G. Davis, noted that Spaatz was particularly impressed with Slessor's commitment to the primary importance of the bomber offensive. Spaatz 'learned that the RAF "apparently thinks as we do, but [has] been hindered by the higher-ups" with regard to the feasibility and desirability of the strategic bombing of the German economy'.[8]

As the scale of the calamity in France became apparent, the urgent require-ment for American assistance became ever more pressing. The six-month period between the Dunkirk evacuation and the successful outcome of the Battle of Britain was a tense and uncertain time, and particularly for Slessor. The defeat of the Allied Front in Western Europe meant that Britain now stood alone. In early June Churchill requested Slessor to prepare a strategy paper to address in the broadest terms British policy for the future conduct of the war and to outline the programme of military expansion required for national survival. It was entitled 'Future Strategy, 1940'.[9] It could be argued that with so much uncertainty, it would be impossible at that time to come up with any clear strategy. However, Slessor reflected after the war that 'we had to take things as we found them at the time, and the "Future Strategy Paper" was far from being a waste of effort. It did at least clear our minds, and it provided a broad basis of strategic policy which had an influence that endured long after many of the basic premises had profoundly altered and set a pattern for the future development of supply policy.'[10] Slessor believed that Britain could lose the war unless: (1) air superiority over Britain was maintained, and (2) that, ultimately, Britain must achieve a significant numerical increase in RAF aircraft and aircrew. Slessor was now convinced that Britain would only succeed in the longer term with American support. Specifically, that would require a proportion of America's military production of aircraft, ships, tanks and guns. Slessor's acknowledgement of America's importance was stated clearly in the Munitions Memorandum that he sent to Churchill in June:

> We have open to us the potentially enormous capacity of the U.S.A. But if we are to exploit this vast advantage it is absolutely essential that we should insist on the production in America of the very best and newest type of aircraft. It is impossible to exaggerate the importance of this; to accept American types of inferior fighting value actually in replacement of our own would be fatal ... the question is of such vital importance that we should dispatch to America a mission of the very highest calibre to bring home to the U.S. authorities and secure their assent to the production of our own superior types.[11]

Towards the end of June Slessor found he was once again needing to prompt Newall into responding to Lord Lothian's proposal to President Roosevelt regarding the desirability of joint senior military staff conversations with the Americans. The need for closer Anglo-American relations was self-evident. Looking back at the dark days of mid-1940, Slessor reflected that there was an urgent need for secret, informal conversations to counter the view in Washington:

> with what may now appear as unjustified optimism – that Germany might still be defeated by a combination of air attack, economic pressure, and revolt in the occupied territories. Here the crux of the matter was the full financial and material support of the United States and other American countries which would follow her lead. And we thought the best way

of securing that support (which we realised was far from certain) was to fight on against apparently hopeless odds.[12]

In mid-June Slessor became concerned that the British side was being too slow in responding to the American initiative for high-level military staff conversations and should strike while the iron was hot. Slessor and his colleagues on the Joint Planning Committee produced a memorandum to form the basis of high-level staff conversations, which was approved by the Chiefs of Staff.[13] One critical point related to divulging state secrets. One of those secrets that was jealously guarded was the use of radar. Slessor took a more pragmatic view when he wrote:

My own view is that we have now got everything to gain and very little at risk by being completely frank with them [the Americans]. In spite of the precautions we attempted, I feel that it is almost certain that the Germans will have got a great deal of information from the French. At the same time, I do not believe, in the present temper of the United States, that there is likely to be any very serious leakage to Germany ... and I feel therefore that it would pay to come clean.[14]

Slessor realized the immediate value of maintaining a good relationship with Spaatz and the other air attachés, and pointed out that if they wanted to spend a few days at operational stations, it would be difficult and embarrassing 'if we had to try to conceal from them RDF and the stabilized bombsight'.[15] The Air Ministry had now finally relented, and by early July the rules on divulging information were relaxed and reinforced with a written Air Ministry confirmation which read, 'in fact there is every reason why they should be told, so that they may report to their own country, and we may have valuable items which would make the exchange of technical information worthwhile from the American standpoint'.[16] Nonetheless, technical details and design information were withheld.[17]

July 1940: Pessimism in Washington, 'Wild Bill' Donovan and the start of the Battle of Britain

Many in America considered that, after the fall of France, Britain was in imminent danger of defeat. Some even believed that Britain's best hope lay in some kind of settlement with Hitler. Joseph Kennedy, America's ambassador in London, concluded that support for Britain was pointless and that any provision of aid would be flogging a dead horse. His view was shared by many in Washington. After America's involvement in the First World War there had been a surge of isolationism with a strongly held desire never again to become involved in another European war. That attitude was reinforced by the fact that France and Britain had both defaulted on American-financed war loans.

President Roosevelt was no isolationist but a committed internationalist, believing in free trade between democratic nations. His Secretary of the Navy, Frank Knox, had already decided to send an international lawyer, William J. Donovan, on a fact-finding mission to London to assess the legalities and arrangements to provide the Royal Navy with fifty ageing US Navy destroyers as a stop-gap measure. Ever the wily politician, Roosevelt saw real value in expanding Donovan's mission to assess Britain's chances of resisting invasion, and to determine the validity of Kennedy's assertion that the British had neither the will nor the means to beat back a German attack. Slessor summed up Donovan's visit: 'in a nutshell [he] was to see for himself and advise the President whether we in Britain had a sporting chance of pulling through what then seemed to most Americans an almost hopeless situation'.[18] Roosevelt had known Donovan since they were classmates at New York's Columbia University Law School before the First World War. Donovan was a Republican and, despite their differing political allegiances, they both shared a common view of internationalism and interventionism. Donovan was a genial Irish American and a very successful Wall Street lawyer. He had served with distinction during the First World War, receiving the Congressional Medal of Honor for the bravery he exhibited during the Second Battle of the Marne in July 1918. He was known to his friends and colleagues as 'Wild Bill' Donovan, a nickname that dated from his time as a battalion commander. His troops gave him the nickname out of admiration for his coolness and resourcefulness, but also for his insistence on hard physical drills for his troops prior to combat.

Donovan arrived in London on 16 July. On learning of his visit, Ambassador Kennedy retorted that 'Our staff, I think, is getting all the information that possibly can be gathered, and to send a new man here at this time was the height of nonsense and a blow to good organisation and his trip will simply result in causing confusion and misunderstanding on the part of the British.'[19] Lothian had cabled the Foreign Office to ensure key governmental personnel were aware of Donovan's arrival and to give him unprecedented access. Over the following two weeks Donovan met King George VI, Churchill and the Chiefs of Staff, and visited Bomber and Fighter Command airfields and naval facilities in Portsmouth. Churchill even assigned a seven-man team to ensure all Donovan's questions were fully addressed.

Newall detailed Slessor to escort Donovan on his visits to two Bomber Command airfields in East Anglia and to listen to aircrews returning from their sorties over Germany. He was given VIP treatment, travelling in the government's Flamingo small passenger airliner escorted by a Hurricane during the opening phase of the Battle of Britain. The timing was ideal for him to gain an assessment of Britain's chances of 'pulling through'.

Mid-July 1940 marked the first phase of the Battle of Britain with the bombing of ports on the south coast together with coastal shipping in the Channel. As a result, Spaatz decided to extend his stay in England; he would eventually spend fourteen weeks in England between June and September. He spent two weeks in July at Bomber Command airfields observing their tactics and methods, of which nine days were spent with a Wellington bomber group. He noted the small scale and ineffectiveness of their night sorties at that time. None of this detracted from the fact that he could see that aircrew morale was high. He realized that their true effectiveness still lay in the future with the eventual introduction of larger aircraft ('the heavies'), navigation aids and increased bombloads.

Spaatz's assessment of RAF Fighter Command's performance against the Luftwaffe led him to conclude that Britain could beat any invasion attempt, and on 31 July he informed General Arnold, head of the United States Army Air Corps, that if the Germans did not launch their invasion in August, they would have to postpone it indefinitely, 'unless the Germans have more up their sleeve than they have shown so far'.[20]

But back with the US attachés, Slessor was getting on well with Spaatz and was to see a lot more of him during those summer months. As he recalled, 'thus began another treasured friendship'.[21] Slessor appreciated Spaatz's dry sense of humour that, as he wrote, 'can reduce me to a state of schoolboy giggles quicker than anything I know'.[22] He also respected the fact that Spaatz was a 'man of action rather than speech, rather inarticulate but with an uncommon flair for the really important issue and a passionate faith in the mission of air power'.[23] Over one weekend he invited Spaatz to his home in Oxfordshire and remembers 'carting corn [after a harvest] and we lay on our backs in the stubble chewing straws and looking up at the summer sky where the Battle of Britain was then being fought away to the south-east'.[24] It is no exaggeration to state that Slessor was instrumental in forging important and long-standing personal relationships with senior American air commanders that would endure throughout the Second World War and through to his time as Chief of the Air Staff in the early 1950s. Spaatz was to rise to the rank of Commanding-General, and for the final eighteen months of the war, he was the overall commander of all the United States Army Air Forces in the European theatre of operations.

On 1 August Spaatz and his fellow air attachés joined Donovan for a breakfast meeting at Claridge's. Spaatz commented that the German chances of destroying the RAF were not particularly good, and he predicted that in air combat German losses in daylight raids 'will be huge'. Furthermore, he considered the accuracy of their night bombing was of a low order. He did not rule out the fact that an all-out attempt might lead to a win for the Germans but if not, it would be the beginning of the end for German air supremacy.[25] Donovan reported back to the President that the British would successfully resist invasion and were resolved to continue fighting. This was a highly positive view, particularly at a time when the chances of Britain succeeding were considered by the RAF's own Commander-in-Chief of Fighter Command, Hugh Dowding, as slim. Richard G. Davis, Spaatz's biographer, concluded that it was difficult to gauge the extent to which Spaatz's advice aided Donovan in reaching his positive conclusion. But, as an authoritative military observer, Spaatz's opinion must have helped to counter those in America who felt subdued by the 'great deal of hopelessness that had been coming over those in High Command'.[26] At the end of August Donovan wrote a letter to Newall stating, 'I still have confidence that my judgement as to your power of resistance to invasion and of your resolution is right.'[27] Slessor considered that Britain owed Donovan, 'a great deal ... for his unfailing confidence and support of our cause in a country [America] that, almost to a man, had written us off for lost'.[28] Slessor's diplomatic skills, his clubability and his natural warmth towards the Americans had played no small part in reshaping American sentiments.

Donovan returned to America on 3 August and briefed Roosevelt on his findings. Walter Lippman, the famous columnist and political commentator, wrote that he 'almost singlehandedly overcame the unmitigated defeatism that had paralysed Washington'. However, Roosevelt continued to worry how he might deal with a still strong isolationist mood in the country. He was justifiably concerned that a massive arms package for Britain could sink his re-election chances later in the year.[29]

The lead-up to joint staff conversations, May–August 1940

In his initial correspondence with Roosevelt after becoming Prime Minister in early May, Churchill had requested the immediate loan of between forty and fifty destroyers, and an urgent dispatch of anti-aircraft guns with ammunition. Roosevelt demurred on the 'destroyers proposal but promised to help as much as possible on the remaining requests. By late June, 500,000 rifles, 80,583 machine guns, 25,000 automatic rifles, 316 mortars and 895 75-mm anti-aircraft guns with 1 million rounds of ammunition were on their way to England'.[30]

On 11 June Lothian met Cordell Hull, the Secretary of State, to follow up Churchill's proposal to hold joint high-level naval staff conversations to discuss their respective fleet dispositions in the Atlantic and Pacific. He did not get a positive response. However, the following week Lothian met Roosevelt and asked whether he thought 'that the time had come for further secret staff talks as to how the British and American navies and, if necessary, air forces should deal with various situations which might arise in the near future. The President thought it was a good idea and should take place at once.'[31] Lothian immediately cabled London with Roosevelt's positive response to the proposal of Anglo-American staff talks.

Nearly two weeks later Slessor was incredulous that there was still no response forthcoming from the British side. He wrote a memorandum to Newall as follows: 'It is now over a fortnight since Lothian suggested it might be a good thing to have Naval and Air conversations and that the President thought they should take place at once', believing that Britain's best response:

> would have been immediately to follow this up by a signal asking them to nominate representatives, but, as far as I know, nothing whatsoever has been done and I am very much afraid that we might be missing a golden opportunity ... I am told, however, (but I cannot vouch for this) that the Prime Minister has decided that the moment would be premature to have conversations with the United States.[32]

Slessor was correct. Churchill was now far more hesitant about taking up Roosevelt's proposal for staff conversations. He preferred to wait and see some tangible evidence of American support. He also was suspicious of Roosevelt's motives, and he was aware that Roosevelt had repeatedly raised the issue of the future of the Royal Navy. Though never formally acknowledged, in the circumstances of a German defeat of Britain, what remained of the Royal Navy would be redeployed to America's eastern seaboard to avoid capture by the German Navy. But Churchill was also concerned about making any spontaneous offer of Britain's prized military secrets. He lamented, 'Are we going to throw all our secrets in the American lap, and see what they give us in exchange? If so, I am against it ... Generally speaking, I am not in a hurry to give away our secrets until the United States is much nearer war than now.'[33] Ultimately, Churchill relented and agreed to staff conversations but only after being pressured by Lord Halifax, Britain's Foreign Secretary.

While Roosevelt was keen to see Anglo-American military staff conversations taking place, he insisted that they be conducted in total secrecy and, because of the highly inquisitive press corps in Washington, that they should be held in London. To maintain total security and secrecy it was decided that the forthcoming 'Conversations' be given the anodyne title 'The Anglo-American Standardisation of Arms Committee'. In early August Slessor prepared a Joint Planning Committee memorandum for the War Cabinet Chiefs of Staff Committee in which he wrote:

> The Prime Minister has agreed that the Conversations should be conducted on a basis of complete frankness, and on the reciprocal understanding that the greatest secrecy be observed ... We propose to assure that they will be prepared to discuss the problem as active Allies ... that American representatives will be at pains to ascertain the true facts of the strategic situation, particularly in respect to our ability to withstand the full weight of a German attack on this country, and to bring the war to a successful conclusion.[34]

On 8 August Slessor wrote a Joint Planning Committee memorandum to the War Cabinet stating that:

> the American representatives to the forthcoming Conversations are understood to have sailed from America on 4 August. We have, as yet, no knowledge of the instructions which have been given to the American delegation ... it is essential that we should be ready with our own ideas on the subject matter for discussion and the general sequence in which the conversations should be conducted.' Slessor added that 'the Chiefs of Staff should meet the Americans and, shortly after their arrival, give them a very brief survey of the existing strategical situation and of our future strategy.[35]

He added that after the initial meeting the Americans would visit various key installations, defences and service establishments. On returning from their tours, the American representatives would then meet again with the British planning committee for detailed discussions. To ensure a firm basis for the next round of detailed talks, Slessor and the Joint Planning staff urged the Chiefs of Staff to sound out the Americans for the full extent of their authority.[36]

The American delegation arrived in England on 15 August. The three senior delegates included Rear Admiral Robert L. Ghormley for the Navy, Brigadier General George V. Strong for the Army and Major General Delos C. Emmons for the Air Corps. Prior to the opening meeting, Slessor ensured that copies were circulated of a report to the American delegation that contained a full statement of the British views on both the current military situation and the proposed strategy. Specifically, he included a relevant section entitled 'Lessons of the War: Air Operations' analysing the Battle of Britain and the bombing campaigns to date.[37]

The Anglo-American Standardisation of Arms Committee, 20–31 August 1940

The two sides met for the first time on 20 August. The British were represented by Vice Admiral Thomas Phillips for the Royal Navy, Air Marshal Sir Richard Pierse for the Royal Air Force, Lieutenant General Sir Robert Haining for the Army and Major General Hastings Ismay, Secretary of the War Cabinet. As the American military historian William Johnsen wrote, 'this was a very high-powered group, especially when compared to the composition of the American delegation'.[38] It demonstrated to the Americans just how seriously the British were taking the joint meetings.

For the Americans, Rear Admiral Ghormley opened the discussions to state their position. He remarked that neither he nor anyone else would exercise supervisory oversight within the US delegation. Furthermore, each member was an individual member of his Service, and consequently they could not, and would not, act as a corporate body. They had come to listen and analyse, but not to make any commitments on behalf of their government.[39] As Johnsen wrote, 'in the first few minutes Ghormley had swept away the underpinnings of the British hopes for a U.S. commitment to Britain's plans for the talks. He equally dashed the hopes for a U.S. commitment to Britain or any idea that the Americans were there to engage in formal staff talks'.[40] Ghormley's opening remarks must have unnerved the British team. The sombre mood probably did not improve when Brigadier General Strong noted that the greatest problem confronting Anglo-American cooperation was the conflicting requirements for the British and American proposed supply programmes. Consequently, he stated that the United States needed accurate information from the British side so that they could develop a coordinated plan.

Sir Richard Pierse for the British delegation took a conciliatory approach, noting that from the British perspective the priority was an agreed strategy from which they could derive production requirements. He added that the Americans would be in a better position to understand the problems of war after they had heard from the Chiefs of Staff reviews that would later form part of the meetings. The meeting was adjourned and during the following week the American delegates visited defence installations and Service establishments and met with key individuals within their respective Service ministries.

In their absence the Americans continued to probe for details of the overall British strategic concept for war. Colonel Raymond Lee, a military attaché from the American embassy in London, forwarded a detailed questionnaire to Slessor and the joint planners that had been compiled by the American delegates on a wide range of issues that included British ideas for offensive action in Western Europe; matériel requirements both short and longer term; plans for operations in the Mediterranean theatre; views on the short and longer-term role of Japan and Russia; and steps anticipated for the defence of British interests in the Western hemisphere.[41] This was a large shopping list of items and it was becoming increasingly obvious to Slessor and the other joint planners that the American delegates' precise functions had not been clearly defined. Consequently, the planners wrote, 'it may well be possible to lead them [the American delegates] into proper staff conversations which the President appeared to have in mind in the first place and which we expected the American delegation would be empowered to undertake'.[42] The British planners recommended that, despite the American delegates' statements about the limitations of their authority, the Chiefs of Staff should quickly sound them out again. The British should prepare for comprehensive and formal staff conversations.[43]

The second meeting of the Anglo-American Standardisation of Arms Committee (AASAC) was convened on 29 August. On that occasion the British team included Admiral of the Fleet Sir Dudley Pound for the Royal Navy, Air Chief Marshal Sir Cyril Newall for the Royal Air Force and Field Marshal Sir John Dill for the Army. Newall opened the session by delivering the British view of the current strategic situation under three broad categories: political, economic and potential enemy action. He summarized many of the key points contained in the current draft of the Chiefs of Staff 'Future Strategy' report.[44] He outlined the worsening British economic position and especially their dependence on overseas supply delivered by shipping, and the need for increased American economic and industrial cooperation. Newall posited that to win the war, Germany had to carry out a successful invasion of Britain or knock out Britain's industrial capacity by repeated air attack, or completely sever her overseas marine lines of communication.

Newall went on to emphasize the German vulnerability to economic blockade, and their dependence on external sources of crude oil supply, notably from Romania. This situation was expected to become critical during 1941. The Chiefs of Staff expected that future German war plans would continue to involve attacks on shipping in the North Atlantic, invasion in the Balkan area, attacks on Egypt from Libya, and a possible German advance through the Iberian Peninsula to attack Gibraltar with the objective of denying the Royal Navy any control in the Mediterranean and to cut off Britain's trade supply routes in that maritime theatre.

Newall then outlined the British domestic industrial production programme, particularly in terms of manpower and steel output. While Britain could manufacture ships, certain aircraft and armaments, he added that it was 'essential that we should get everything from America that could be supplied'.[45]

Turning to the Army's requirements, Newall, as British lead, stated they had planned for an Empire total of fifty-five divisions, of which thirty-four divisions would be committed to home defence. By spring 1942 between twenty and thirty divisions would be ready for offensive operations. The figures included five armoured divisions and ten independent armoured brigades.

The RAF expansion programme called for 6,295 aircraft of all types by mid-1942. This total would include a hundred squadrons of 1,600 heavy bombers, required for the strategic offensive against Germany and Italy.

Newall concluded his review by stating that the directors of plans (who included Slessor) would be available to clear up any specific questions and that they had full authority to discuss all matters.[46] He then opened the meeting for general discussion. Strong asked how they could obtain a definitive statement on Britain's aircraft requirements from the United States. Newall replied that Air Commodore Slessor could discuss both supply and production issues in some detail. The American delegation then asked how the strategy would be implemented, and ways of enforcing a blockade, and the RAF targeting policy and strategy in the air offensive against Germany.

Both sides met again two days later for further discussions. Newall again spoke for the British team and addressed the most urgent and pressing issue: the defence of the United Kingdom. He acknowledged that the situation was serious but maintained that 'we are confident of our ability to withstand any attacks on this country, and our whole policy is based on this assumption'.[47] He went on to take questions from the American delegation on other aspects of Britain's grand strategy, notably plans for the Mediterranean theatre of operations and Far East defence plans and policy.

On 31 August the joint meetings were concluded. As the historian William T. Johnsen commented, 'The Anglo-American Standardisation of Arms Committee talks represented a key transition point in Anglo-American collaboration ... Their final report reinforced Roosevelt's decision at a critical time: to continue *with all aid short of war*. This decision also opened the door for further and increased collaboration between the two countries' militaries.[48]

General Emmons of the US Army Air Corps remained in England to have further discussions with the Air Ministry. He met Slessor again on 2 September to discuss aspects of strategy, the RAF's command structure, and to get further details of aircraft requirements. During his time in England Emmons had been given the fullest opportunity to visit operational units and talk both formally and informally to RAF officers. The fact that all aspects had been covered in an atmosphere of utmost frankness must have influenced his optimistic assessment of Britain's chances of success in preventing a German invasion, and therefore its ability to pursue its longer-term strategy.[49]

On their return to Washington, Strong and Emmons briefed Stimson, Secretary of War, on the results of their visit. They compiled a lengthy report, and in their conclusions they considered that the home defence of Britain relied on air power and that the RAF would succeed in retaining air superiority, enabling the ability to repel any invasion. Both generals were greatly impressed by the British candour and methodology, and their willingness to share their experiences. They considered that unless the Germans invaded by 15 October the British strategic situation would improve considerably. As Johnsen commented: 'Perhaps the most important for Anglo-American collaboration was their final conclusion: "We both have the very definite feeling that sooner or later the United States will be drawn into this war."'[50]

However, the outcome of their briefings in Washington was not without a serious misunderstanding. Within a few days of the return of the American delegates to the United States, the Air Ministry received an indignant message from Henry Morgenthau, secretary to the Treasury, to the effect that, at a meeting of his 'Aid to Britain' committee, General Strong had reported that 'it was no good for the United States supplying Britain with aircraft if they could not produce the crews to fly them'.[51] This comment left Slessor totally mystified and with 'consternation not unmingled with resentment ... why he should ever have imagined that we should want to hoard aircraft that we could not use remains a mystery'.[52]

Slessor had already submitted a paper on 31 July to the Expansion and Re-equipment Policy Committee entitled *Expansion of the Air Forces of the Empire after June 1941*, better known as the ERP21 programme. As Slessor wrote later: 'The programme aimed to build a first-line force by 1942 of 6,600 aircraft of all classes, and included the provision of crew, training facilities, accommodation, fuel, bombs, ammunition, and all the innumerable items which go to make a modern air force.'[53] Slessor reflected that Strong himself could have resolved this erroneous deduction 'in five minutes with anyone who was in a position to know'.[54] In the event, Henry Self, one of Slessor's civilian colleagues in the Air Ministry, sent a signal to Morgenthau that quashed the issue. This misunderstanding only confirmed Slessor's conviction that 'there was however a good deal to be said for sending to America at that time a senior Air Staff officer who was thoroughly in the picture of the latest expansion policy and could discuss problems of our requirements from American industry'.[55]

On 2 October Slessor wrote a memorandum on the British supply programme, his views offer an illustration of his grasp of strategic considerations that sat outside a single-issue focus:

> The combined strength of America and the British Empire can certainly surpass and outlast that of Germany and her Allies ... It is essential that the programme of the United States and British requirements be as much as possible co-ordinated so as to prevent competition in the industrial field. To this end we must seek a common programme agreed and adjusted to the conflicting requirements of immediate and ultimate needs.[56]

But in Washington there was still a continuing suspicion that if Britain was not providing accurate figures on British aircraft production and aircrew, then they might well be allocated a disproportionate number of American aircraft relative to their direct needs. In early October Henry Morgenthau met Arthur Purvis, Head of the British Purchasing Commission in Washington, to address his concerns regarding the allocation of aircraft to Britain and reports from the US Army Air Corps that aircraft sent to Britain 'were sitting in their shipping crates because of the lack of trained pilots'.[57] Purvis recognized the gravity of the situation and contacted the Foreign Office promptly, writing that if Britain expected to continue to receive aircraft, it would need to provide accurate and updated information on British military aircraft production and the numbers of new aircrew, in addition to a nine-month projection for both categories. To assuage British concerns regarding disclosure of this highly confidential information, Morgenthau stressed that circulation would be restricted to President Roosevelt; himself; Henry Stimson, Secretary of War; and William Knox, Secretary of the Navy.[58] At the same time, in conversations with Sir Walton Layton, Director General of Programmes at the Ministry of Supply, President Roosevelt was expressing the same concern about ensuring reliable aircraft and aircrew figures.[59] Set against this American requirement, there was an underlying concern in London about disclosing such highly confidential figures to a neutral government.

The decision to send Slessor to America

By 6 October Morgenthau was still concerned. He still felt that Air Marshal Charles Portal, the newly appointed Chief of the Air Staff, or a similar high-ranking senior air commander should visit Washington in order to resolve this dilemma. Morgenthau stressed to Purvis that the Roosevelt Administration would attach great importance to such a visit, and that Portal, or an alternative high-ranking RAF commander, could familiarize the key American air commanders with a deeper insight into the RAF's current strategy, the status of the current air war, operational procedures, organization, training, equipment and tactics.[60] The Air Ministry responded to Lothian that Portal would be unable to leave England because of the ongoing air war over Britain but that 'an officer of the highest reputation and ability will, however, be sent as soon as possible'.[61] The officer selected was Air Commodore John Slessor, Director of Plans, who, as Johnsen wrote, 'despite his relatively junior rank – but not intellect or abilities as the U.S. staffs would soon find out – would prove to be a critical figure in building the evolving coalition'.[62]

Slessor must have been highly satisfied with the decision, but also relieved to have been chosen. He was the ideal candidate, given his background and experience. He had now been the RAF's Director of Plans for over three years, had a deep understanding of the RAF's strategy and the expansion plans, including his recent and direct involvement in the comprehensive ERP21 programme. Perhaps equally important – as we know – Slessor got on well with Americans. He understood their concerns but was also clear and persuasive in putting across the British case for the supply of American aircraft.

The Beaverbrook problem: refusal to agree to give aircraft and aircrew figures to the Americans

However, Slessor also recognized that his temporary posting to America posed significant challenges. In order to clarify his terms of reference in discussion with the American military staff, he asked Portal for his approval to talk openly, realizing he would only succeed *if he received accurate, up-to-date figures*: British aircraft production, aircrew figures, wastage, and losses in combat or air raids. He knew this would not be a straightforward process. Slessor had received a briefing from Lord Beaverbrook, then Minister of Aircraft Production, to the effect that the Americans could not be trusted and would be unable to maintain secrecy over any figures they might receive on British aircrew and aircraft. Slessor wrote a memorandum to Portal on 17 October underlining the importance of keeping the Americans on side:

> I am convinced that they [the Americans] are out to play, and that any risks we may run by adopting this very co-operative attitude will be more than outweighed by the advantages to be obtained. After all, we are largely in their hands over this matter, and if they don't play we are sunk;

and I am certain that the best way to get them to play is to treat them as one of us and be open and free with them.[63]

Perhaps even more problematic was that Beaverbrook did not like the Americans and considered that 'they would only help if they thought we were strong and going to win. If they thought we were going to lose they wouldn't lift a finger to help us out.'[64]

Beaverbrook was one of Churchill's closest friends and a member of his War Cabinet. It would now involve patience and tact to deal with this challenge. Slessor knew only too well that any withholding of reliable figures could easily frustrate his efforts to succeed in America. Slessor wrote to both Portal and Archibald Sinclair, Secretary of State for Air, that he could not agree to proceed with any negotiations with the Americans based on Beaverbrook's intransigence. He wrote that Beaverbrook 'had constantly made statements making out we were better off than we are and said he would only tell them [the Americans] what suited him and what he wanted them to think'.[65]

On 29 October the dilemma appeared to have been resolved. Churchill himself reported that Slessor had received a frank and detailed briefing on the expected British requirements for aircraft and aircrew through to June 1941. The statistics that he could share in meetings with the Americans included explicit figures on the distribution of aircraft and the pilot training programme.[66] On the night before he left for America, Slessor met both Churchill and Lord Lothian (who was on home leave) at Chequers. Lord Lothian 'expressed himself strongly in favour of frankness with the Americans and belittled the chances of our confidence being betrayed to the enemy'.[67]

Chapter 8

Clandestine Mission

Slessor in America, 8 November 1940–10 April 1941

Travelling to the United States from Britain in late 1940 was difficult. The North Atlantic sea lanes were under constant threat of attack not only from U-boats but also from German long-range aircraft based in western France and from their surface warship raiders such as *Scharnhorst* and *Gneisenau*. Furthermore, Germany now controlled the European coastline from northern Norway to the Spanish border. At that time the only way to cross the Atlantic by air involved catching Pan Am's flying boat service from Lisbon to New York. Their 'southern route' had been inaugurated in June 1939 and under normal conditions the flight took twenty-nine hours with technical stops in the Azores and Bermuda.[1] In November 1940 Pan Am was operating a weekly service on its southern route.

Since both Portugal and America were neutral countries, Slessor left England travelling in civilian clothes, carrying a 'doctored' passport to avoid recognition by Axis spies in either country.[2] He was accompanied by his young civilian Air Staff assistant, John Orme. They arrived in Lisbon on 1 November. Unfortunately, Pan Am's Boeing 314 flying boat had been delayed in the Azores because of poor weather and a heavy swell, and was delayed again by poor sea state conditions when the plane arrived in Lisbon. However, the upside of the unfortunate delay was a week's enforced holiday in Estoril, 15 miles west of Lisbon. Slessor certainly did not complain about the delay. As he recalled: 'after months of really strenuous and exacting work ... after weeks of blackout in the London Blitz, the luxurious ease of the Palacio hotel [and the] bright lights of Estoril were anything but unpleasant'.[3]

Jack's one reservation about the hotel, as he wrote home to Hermione on Palacio notepaper, is the 'taut nervousness about the place. It seems fairly taken for granted that Boche will walk in sooner or later'; such was the extraordinary milieu created by Portugal's neutrality and location. The same letter concludes, 'I don't know how long I shall be in the States – perhaps a fortnight, perhaps a month.'[4] Slessor's brief for his mission was clearly highly flexible and to some degree open-ended, offering a diplomatic and creative freedom he relished. It was to be five months before he returned to Britain.

A month later, on 4 December, Slessor expressed frustration in another letter home, this time from the salubrious surroundings and safety of Washington's University Club, sitting in stark contrast to the perils afflicting his countrymen 3,000 plus miles to the east. Impatient to make real progress, he met 'that God-damned yellow son of a bitch [Joe] Kennedy', briefly back from his ambassadorial role in London. Jack considered telephoning Roosevelt to rail about Kennedy's animus towards the British, threatening to throw the '——r [Slessor's self-censorship] into the Potomac'.[5] Presumably this was letting off steam and Roosevelt did not actually find himself on the end of such indelicacy. Whilst Jack could be ruthlessly forthright in private conversations, this was uncharacteristically pugnacious language for his private letters and certainly not for public exposure. Amusingly, it revealed a new appreciation for the direct, uncompromising vernacular of his hosts.

But back to the start of his mission. Slessor finally arrived in New York on 8 November. He was met at La Guardia airport by Colonel George McDonald, whom he already knew from his time as air attaché at the United States London embassy. It was Slessor's first wartime visit to the United States. It would not be his last. During his five months there, he achieved much. He forged new and lasting relationships with his opposite numbers which significantly enhanced the evolving Anglo-American alliance. His visit involved numerous informal and formal meetings with members of the Army Air Corps, visits to military aircraft factories, and discussions with key individuals in Roosevelt's administration, including a meeting with the President himself. Slessor was promoted to the rank of Air Vice-Marshal (Temporary) on 10 January 1941.[6]

On 5 November 1940 Roosevelt had been re-elected for an unprecedented third term of office, and with a convincing landslide majority. Shortly thereafter he announced that, in future, Britain would receive 50 per cent of America's military aircraft production.[7] This news was highly encouraging for the British. In his radio broadcast to the nation on 29 December he pledged that America must become the 'Arsenal of Democracy'.[8] It was an endorsement of Roosevelt's continuing support for Britain through arms shipments and the forthcoming Lend-Lease financial arrangements. It also signalled the green light to commence formal military discussions between the Americans and the British. In early December Portal instructed Slessor to remain in America and to be his representative at the forthcoming talks. Over two months between 29 January and 29 March Slessor was the RAF's representative in the Anglo-American ABC staff conversations in Washington.[9]

In early December Slessor wrote to Hermione, describing his initial impressions of his first few weeks in America:

> We must rely on U.S. collaboration to win this war … This is a grand country, and they are, on the whole, a grand people. I am astonished at the almost complete pro-British feeling here … and there is genuine and universal admiration for the British, and the way they are taking it. The RAF stocks are as high as they could be … Bill Donovan has been inexpressively kind to me, and through him I have met a mass of people that otherwise I never should have met. He is the sort of unofficial emissary of Roosevelt and Knox – a sort of person behind the throne in this country, knows everything and everyone. I think he is certain to be in government soon – either that or as Ambassador to London in succession to that swine Kennedy, who is actively working against us in this country.[10]

William Donovan was never offered a senior position in Roosevelt's administration nor was he appointed as the ambassador in London. However, in July 1941 the President appointed him as the Coordinator of Information, which included intelligence and propaganda, and he was instrumental in laying the groundwork for a centralized intelligence programme. In 1942 Donovan was appointed as the commander of the newly formed Office of Strategic Services (OSS), the forerunner of the Central Intelligence Agency (CIA).

Beaverbrook and the continuing problem of the lack of full disclosure of British aircraft and aircrew figures

Shortly after his arrival in America, Slessor had hoped to meet Henry Morgenthau, US Secretary to the Treasury, in order to clarify the British position on the overall air strategy, and the future aircraft and aircrew expansion plans, in addition to current information on military aircraft production and aircrew. To Slessor's surprise, Morgenthau was away on vacation in Puerto Rico until late November, but he had left instructions with Philip Young, the Treasury under-secretary, to deal with the issues. On 21 November, and unbeknown to Slessor, Churchill and the War Cabinet had decided that future details of aircraft and aircrew figures 'should be steadily damped down, and its circulation restricted as far as possible'.[11]

Slessor finally met Morgenthau on 3 December. Their meeting was cordial and positive. Slessor did his best to allay any lingering suspicions on the veracity of the aircraft and aircrew figures that had been provided previously. But, as Slessor recalled, Morgenthau 'did not fail, however, to rub in the essential need to keep him and his colleagues fully informed if we were to get the help we wanted. "The way to help us to help you is not to try and scare us with a string of bad news but to give us the facts;" and he asked again for a regular monthly statement of our position in respect of aircraft and crews coming off production.'[12] It was clear that Morgenthau was not getting all the information that had been requested. This left Slessor in a difficult position, and he concluded that Beaverbrook and his Ministry of Aircraft Production (MAP) were not complying with the Prime Minister's assurances that had previously been given to him at the end of November. Slessor immediately contacted the Air Ministry to get the planned and actual domestic aircraft production for October and November, the projected deliveries of aircraft from America, and anticipated and actual pilot losses. However, the Air Ministry itself had difficulty in getting the requested information from the MAP.[13] Furthermore, American officers noted a marked discrepancy between actual and published aircraft figures, sometimes by as much as 200 aircraft per month.[14] During this period Slessor would be asked repeatedly to provide the more complete figures that had been requested and was to find himself constantly embarrassed by the lack of accurate and up to date information on British aircraft and aircrew.[15]

Slessor was frustrated and felt compelled to contact Portal regarding his inability to provide complete sets of figures, as requested by the Americans. In his letter to Portal he wrote: 'I do not mind being made to look a fool, though the Americans cannot be expected to understand and I cannot explain to them why the Director of Plans who had been sent to America to discuss this sort of thing with them is kept in ignorance of so vital a factor as British production ... we must take them into our confidence and tell them the facts even if unpalatable.'[16]

However, despite the War Cabinet's mercurial behaviour regarding the level and detail of full disclosure to the Americans, Churchill sent a long, candid and incredibly detailed letter to Roosevelt on 8 December. In relation to aircraft production, he wrote:

> We look to the industrial energy of the Republic for reinforcement of our domestic capacity to manufacture combat aircraft. Without that reinforcement reaching us in substantial measure we shall not achieve the massive preponderance in the air on which we rely to loosen and disintegrate the German grip on Europe. We are at present engaged on a programme designed to increase our strength to seven thousand first-line aircraft by the spring of 1942 ...
>
> May I invite you Mr. President, to give earnest consideration to an immediate order on joint account for a further two thousand combat

aircraft a month? Of these aircraft I would submit, the highest proportion should be heavy bombers, the weapon on which, above all others, we depend to shatter the foundations of German military power.[17]

The letter made a deep impression on Roosevelt, who read and reread the contents of Churchill's long letter over several days while he was relaxing on USS *Tuscaloosa*, the presidential flagship at that time.

Slessor made the point to Portal that 'if we really attached importance to the Americans making the necessary efforts to organise additional production on the lines of the Prime Minister's letter to the President of December 8, we should have to take them into our confidence'.[18] Unfortunately, the full disclosure issue continued to rumble on into the new year and beyond.

On 10 January Portal again reminded Churchill that Morgenthau had repeatedly stated that he would only agree to approve the export of the military aircraft that Britain had requested when he received complete, accurate and timely figures on British aircraft production and aircrew, with forecasts. Portal went on to tell Churchill that he had 'consulted Lord Beaverbrook about this and he is of the opinion that we should confine ourselves to supplying information on current stocks and future programmes'.[19] The problem had been resolved a few days earlier. Beaverbrook had already relented, having contacted Purvis of the Purchasing Commission in Washington and authorized the release of all the required information to Slessor. Despite the assurances, however, the issue was not resolved.

During November Slessor visited the Bell Aircraft Corporation near Buffalo in upstate New York. He was accompanied on that trip by Colonel Carl Spaatz, whom he had got to know well during his visit to England between June and September. He saw flight trials of the prototype P-39 Airacobra fighter. However, Slessor commented that at the time there were no American fighters to compare in quality or firepower with the British fighters.[20] That situation was to change dramatically from 1942 as the Americans started to produce air superiority fighters such as the P-47 Thunderbolt and the superlative P-51 Mustang (especially once fitted with the Rolls Royce V-12, 27-litre, Merlin engine).

The 50/50 Plan for Future Aircraft Production

Roosevelt's announcement on 8 December allocating 50 per cent of all future aircraft production to Britain ought to have made Slessor's job easier. Instead, it created both resistance and resentment in America's Armed Services. In reality, this policy gave Britain preference over their own military requirements and had the effect of delaying their expansion plans. General Marshall, the Army Chief of Staff, told Slessor that in November only six new aircraft were delivered to the Army Air Corps while some 300 were allocated to the British.[21] As William Johnsen wrote, 'Colonel Orlando Ward, assistant secretary of the War Department, noted in his diary, "the 50-50 deal is working with 33 planes for the U.S. and 409 for the foreigners. A 50-50 deal like one horse for them, one rabbit for us ... We are like a pointer pup. If someone with a red moustache, a swagger stick, and a British accent speaks to us, we lie down on the ground and wiggle."'[22]

The request for more heavy bombers

It was an article of faith that the RAF's prime objective in the war was to defeat Germany with a sustained bomber offensive. To that end, the top-secret 'Future Strategy Plan' of September 1940 envisaged a hundred squadrons of 1,600 first-line heavy bombers, with reserves, during 1942.[23] The key target sets in Germany had already been selected and categorized into sixteen 'Western Air Plans' that had been chosen by Slessor and the Air Staff in the late 1930s. Priority was given to destroying Germany's industrial centres, including iron and steel works, aircraft factories, munitions works, shipyards, and oil storage and refining sites.

Churchill had already made direct reference in his letter to Roosevelt of the need for additional heavy bombers 'to shatter the foundations of German military power'.[24] Slessor was already in discussions with senior American air staff regarding the RAF's requirements, and the Air Ministry wanted a breakdown by category of the forthcoming production programme of aircraft destined for Britain by 1942.

On 20 December Portal felt it was important to remind Slessor to ensure that he kept his focus on the supply of heavy bombers. In his letter he wrote: 'we impressed upon Purvis [Head of the British Purchasing Commission] of the vital importance of an almost unlimited supply of heavy bombers as the key to ultimate victory and the danger of ourselves or America going too much for numbers and collecting hordes of superfluous fighters'.[25]

The challenges of meeting aircraft production targets in America

During December Slessor visited more aircraft factories and quickly realized that the production targets that had been set for mid-1942 would not be met without drastic changes in work practices. America was still operating as a peacetime economy in late 1940 without the sense of urgency brought on by wartime conditions. Slessor recalled that at that time the US aircraft industry was 'a huge uncoordinated mass with no-one to settle priorities or exercise control'.[26] More out of concern and frustration Slessor wrote to Portal as follows:

> I am sure the vital thing to get across to these people, who are genuinely out there to help, whereas their declared policy is to do everything short of war, on present form they are doing about twenty-five percent of what they do short of war ... they must really take their coats off and we must have the end, for instance, to this absurd condition in which owing to the five-day week twenty-eight percent of their precious machine tool capacity is unused. In fact, if they want to keep out of the military war they must mobilise themselves for industrial war, and do it *now*.[27]

In late 1940 the forecast of aggregated production for Britain and the Empire amounted to 26,000 aircraft of all types by June 1942: 14,000 on existing orders, and a further 12,000 to be achieved by expansion of the manufacturing facilities.[28] Slessor considered that the issue needed to be resolved as soon as possible. He wrote to Morgenthau:

> It seems impossible to sit back and accept a situation in which the British and U.S. air forces are backed by so inadequate a production ... Our aim therefore, should be first to create immediately capacity for at least an additional 250 [aircraft] a month of an improved type of heavy bomber – a class which are [*sic*] of vital importance to the defeat of Germany and in which there is a serious deficiency in present programmes.[29]

But serious consideration was already being given to the planning of a massive expansion of aircraft production. During December the Secretaries of War and the Navy, Henry Stimson and Frank Knox, joined William Knudsen, Chairman of General Motors, to form a task force to address the challenges of ramping up aircraft production. As in Britain, they decided to turn to the large American automotive manufacturers and utilize their skills and experience in mass production. Knudsen was appointed as Chairman of the Office of Production Management and member of the National Defense Advisory Commission.

Despite early teething problems – keeping up with continual improvements and modifications, assuring consistent production quality, and recruiting and training skilled workers – the Americans performed marvels. After the war Slessor recalled that it was 'almost incredible to look back on the subsequently gigantic achievements ... to which the Royal Air Force owed so much as the war progressed and the great programme swung into its stride'.[30] By 1944 American aircraft production was over four times that of Britain, and five times greater than German output.[31] By June 1945 the United States had produced 324,810 aircraft of all types.[32] At its peak 1.3 million employees were directly involved in aircraft production. When asked following the war about the contribution of aircraft production to the war effort, Bill Knudsen responded, 'we won because we smothered them in an avalanche of production, the likes of which he [the enemy] had neither seen, nor dreamed possible'.[33]

Slessor in Hollywood, southern California, late December 1940

It was not all work for Slessor. He spent the Christmas period in Los Angeles, and he received VIP treatment. He wrote to Hermione on 28 December to report that he had been taken to a restaurant where Dorothy Lamour, Spencer Tracy and James Cagney were dining at an adjacent table. The starstruck Slessor talked to all three. On another occasion he had drinks with Vivien Leigh and her husband Laurence Olivier. Vivien Leigh had recently won an Oscar for her role as Scarlett O'Hara in the movie version of *Gone with the Wind*. Laurence Olivier told Slessor that he was returning to Britain to join the RAF. However, to Slessor's disappointment, he subsequently joined the Royal Navy's Fleet Air Arm, where he met up with his friend and actor Ralph 'Pranger' Richardson. Olivier rapidly achieved the distinction of exceeding Richardson's reputation for crashing aeroplanes. Slessor also went to a boxing match, a fundraiser in aid of British War Relief, where various film stars were invited to take a bow, including 'a distinguished RAF officer'. Slessor wrote that he received the loudest round of applause of his whole life. He visited Hollywood and spent time with Cecil B. DeMille, the producer and director, and watched another director, King Vidor, at work on set.[34]

The aircraft ferry issue, December 1940–July 1942

With a marked increase in American aircraft production, Slessor and many of his Air Staff colleagues could see a looming logistical crisis in North Atlantic ferrying[35] operations. Since May 1940 ferrying arrangements for American aircraft had come under the control and responsibility of Lord Beaverbrook and the Ministry of Aircraft Production. Beaverbrook had appointed Morris Wilson, the president of the Royal Bank of Canada, to organize a plan to ferry American aircraft to Europe. He established the Atlantic Ferry Organisation (ATFERO), a Canadian civilian agency that was under contract to the British government to fly American-built bombers across the Atlantic from Newfoundland to Scotland, a distance of 2,100 miles.[36] This was not only the shortest route, being a geodesic line on the Earth's globe, but also kept unarmed aircraft far away from German interference. However, a key issue was the lack of numbers and qualifications of the pilots who would be required to ferry the ever-increasing quantity of aircraft. The question was one of scale. In early December, recognizing this emerging problem, Slessor wrote to Portal as follows:

> The present system whereby we bribe a few American pilots to fly machines over will not touch the fringe of the problem when we begin to get delivery in really large numbers. Ultimately, we shall see something in the order of 1,000 pilots on this job, and that, as far as I know, is a commitment which we have never faced up to in our calculations. No doubt, we shall be able to raise many of them in the U.S.A. but nothing like all, and there isn't the least doubt that the RAF will be called upon to find crews in very large numbers for this ferrying job. I know that this is a matter for MAP, but it has many direct implications for the RAF and I think you will want to satisfy that the problem is being tackled on sufficiently broad and imaginative lines.[37]

Slessor sent a further message to the Air Ministry on 22 January 1941 stating that by June 1941, 200 aircraft per month would need to be ferried across the North Atlantic and that number was forecast to double to 400 aircraft per month by year's end. He concluded by recommending that the entire ferry operation should be taken over by the Air Ministry as the Atlantic Ferry Service. It became yet another source of confrontation between Beaverbrook and the MAP against Slessor and the Air Ministry.

But there was also little support for the continuation of ATFERO's ferrying operations from the American side, who cited an absence of leadership, control and representation to coordinate the transfers of aircraft. It was also increasingly obvious that ATFERO could not provide a sufficient number of qualified pilots to handle the ever-increasing aircraft inventory. The situation came to a head when President Roosevelt intervened. On 29 May he wrote to Churchill of his concern regarding the rising number of aircraft awaiting shipment from North America as follows:

> In spite of best efforts of the organisation now handling the flight delivery of combat aircraft from this country to England I am advised that substantial numbers of these planes are accumulating in this country and this condition is apt to grow worse as production reaches an accelerated level over the next few months. In our common interest and in order to relieve the situation as soon as possible, I am prepared to direct the Army and Navy to assume full responsibility from factory to the point of

ultimate take-off and to supply maintenance and surviving facilities along the way to the ultimate staging field ...

I am advised that the close co-operation necessary to carry through successfully this continuous operation can best be obtained if responsibility for the Atlantic flight could be undertaken by their sister service under the Air Ministry using of course the present civilian pilots and such additional ones as may become available.[38]

Slessor's concern about the future ferry operations was totally vindicated by the text of Roosevelt's telegram. On 21 July ATFERO operations were transferred to the newly formed RAF Ferry Command under the leadership of Air Chief Marshal Sir Frederick Bowhill, based in Montreal. Roosevelt had insisted that aircraft be transferred to a military command rather than a civilian agency. Henceforth, American service personnel flew all the new aircraft from their factories to transfer points in Canada. Thereafter the British would be responsible for the transatlantic ferry operation. As the historian Jeffrey Davis wrote: 'Within three years the ferry scheme transferred from a daredevil operation run by "the strangest collection of pilots ever gathered together in the history of flying" into a highly organised section of the RAF which ensured that a steady stream of aircraft flew from Newfoundland to Northern Ireland or Scotland. Eventually, 10,000 aircraft were ferried on this route.'[39]

Preparations for the American-British Staff Conversations (ABC), November 1940–January 1941

Following Roosevelt's resounding election result in early November 1940, Lord Lothian considered that the time was now ripe for more comprehensive bilateral military staff conversations. Lothian was unaware that Admiral Stark had already submitted a memorandum to the President on 12 November on the 'National Defence Policy'. Stark had authored a war plan known as 'Plan Dog', which envisaged full military cooperation with the British against Germany and Italy if the United States were drawn into war, but with the proviso of making every effort to keep on the defensive in the Pacific and, to the extent possible, to avoid war with Japan. Furthermore, Stark recommended that the President should authorize secret, formal staff conversations with the British. On 29 November Lothian learnt that Roosevelt had agreed to the proposal, but with the proviso that the talks be held in conditions of top secrecy.[40] Roosevelt was always acutely aware of the prevalent public mood. Most American citizens had considerable sympathy for the British cause, but they also had a strong desire to stay out of the conflict. Consequently,

Roosevelt had two concerns regarding the forthcoming joint talks. First, the disclosure of the talks would compromise America's neutrality and signal to the Axis powers that plans were already under way to form a military alliance with Britain; and second, it would provide evidence to the still significant number of isolationists in America that serious war plans were being discussed with the British, which they believed would inevitably lead to a wholly regrettable repetition of American involvement in a European war.

The talks, which came to be known as the American-British Staff Conversations (ABC), were originally scheduled to commence in mid-December, but sadly Lord Lothian's untimely and sudden death, following a kidney infection, on 12 December led to a delay.[41]

In a demonstration to the Americans of Britain's still significant naval power, Churchill had authorized the battleship *King George V* to cross the Atlantic carrying important passengers including Lord Halifax, who was sent to replace Lord Lothian as the British Ambassador in Washington, and four new members of the British delegation to the forthcoming ABC talks. The British delegation comprised Rear Admiral Roger Bellairs as chairman, Rear Admiral Victor Danckwerts and Captain Arthur Clarke for the Royal Navy, Major General Edwin Morris for the Army, Air Vice-Marshal John Slessor for the RAF, and Colonel A.T. Cornwall-Jones of the War Cabinet Secretariat.

Brigadier General Raymond E. Lee, formerly an Army attaché at the American embassy in London, who had also travelled from Britain on *King George V*, noted in his diary, 'it is a strong team, Slessor, who is now in Washington, were all together on the Joint Planning Committee two or three years ago, and should know what they are about'.[42] Before leaving London, Lee met General Hastings 'Pug' Ismay, Churchill's personal military assistant, for a farewell luncheon. Over lunch, Ismay remarked that, in his estimation, Slessor was the best of the whole delegation.[43]

During their time in Washington the delegates dressed in civilian clothes and, as a cover, took on the role of civilian advisers on technical matters for the British Purchasing Commission. Slessor commented that 'the only criticism of the selectors of the team was that it would have been difficult for the least suspicious enemy agent in Washington to take us for anything but British officers: Ted Morris and 'Dancks' in particular were caricatures of what a British general and admiral ought to look like'.[44] He might well have added that he himself would appear to be everyone's idea of what a senior RAF commander should look like. They kept a low profile during the talks, and they managed to maintain their disguises successfully over the two-month period. During that time they were accommodated on the top floor of the British embassy with office space and bedrooms.

Slessor had previously worked with all his fellow delegates. He had met Bellairs during the late 1920s when both were involved in planning within their respective Services. Danckwerts was on the Joint Planning Committee (JPC) with Slessor during the period of Anglo-French staff conversations between 1939 and 1940. Cornwall-Jones was the secretary of the JPC in that period. Slessor had worked with Morris during their time at the Army Staff College at Camberley during the early 1930s. Finally, Slessor had been working with Captain Clarke of the Royal Navy at the British embassy since the previous November.

ABC talks, Washington DC, 29 January–27 March 1941

The members of the Planning Committee who were responsible for selecting the US representatives and staging the ABC were highly suspicious of British motives and were careful to ensure that their delegates maintained their guard throughout the meetings.[45] It was a strong team, comprising senior experienced officers drawn from the Army, the Navy and their respective air services.

Lieutenant General Stanley Embick was chosen to be their chairman. He was a seasoned Army veteran who had been recalled from retirement, having served during his long service career in many parts of the world. However, he was no admirer of British military strategy and had been distinctly unimpressed since his time as the American representative on the Allied War Council during the First World War.

The Navy was represented by five officers: Rear Admiral R.L. Ghormley, who had spent several months in England in 1940 and who was their key representative on the obliquely named Anglo-American Standardisation of Arms Committee; Rear Admiral R. Kelly Turner, head of Plans, who was to become known after the ABC talks as 'Terrible Turner' and who, as the American military historian James Leutze wrote, 'seemed to see himself as the sole guardian of American national interest';[46] Captain Alan Kirk, who had recently served as the naval attaché in the US embassy in London; Captain Dewitt Ramsay of the Naval Aviation Section; and Lieutenant Colonel Omar T. Pfeffer of the war plans section of the US Marine Corps.

The Army was represented by Brigadier Generals Sherman Miles of Intelligence and O.T. Gerow, Director of the War Plans Division; and Colonel Joseph T. McNarney of the Army Air Corps. In addition, they were accompanied by several technical experts. The American attendees at the first plenary session outnumbered the six members of the British team by a considerable margin. Colonel Cornwall-Jones, the secretary for the British delegation, commented that when the full American team filed into the meeting room the British side was stunned.[47]

The first plenary session of the ABC talks took place at the Navy Building in Constitution Avenue, Washington DC, where General Marshall welcomed the delegates and dwelt on the need for secrecy, warning that public knowledge of the mere fact that conversations were in progress might have an unfavourable effect on the passage of the draft Lend-Lease Act that was passing through Congress.

The British delegation opened the discussions with their three propositions on general strategy:

(1) the European theatre is the vital theatre where a direction must be sought;

(2) the general policy should therefore be to defeat Germany and Italy first, and then to deal with Japan; and

(3) the security of the Far Eastern position, including Australia and New Zealand, is essential to the cohesion of the British Commonwealth and the maintenance of the war effort. Singapore is the key to the defence of those interests and its retention must be assured.

The American delegation accepted the first two propositions, but not the third. This had been a bone of contention since the late 1930s and had led to the failure of earlier talks. The British had wanted the Americans to establish a naval presence in Singapore which they felt would have a deterrent effect on Japanese intentions for the Malay peninsula and the Dutch East Indies (present-day Indonesia).

During their second meeting on 31 January General Embick set the tone with his full and frank dialogue. He asked bluntly what plans the British had in the event of the British Isles being overrun. The British responded that there were no contingency plans and, since Slessor had been Director Plans, and given his privileged involvement in recent events and negotiations, he was in a unique position to address the point. It was never something they had formally considered, and, in any event, Churchill had forbidden any planning for such a contingency.[48] Churchill had requested Slessor, as Director of Plans, to prepare two papers on Britain's future strategy and options. Written in the dark days of June 1940 and after the Dunkirk evacuation, neither paper made any mention of contingency plans in the case of Britain being overrun.[49] In fact, Churchill had secretly created Auxiliary Units or Operational Patrols, nicknamed 'Scallywags'. These individuals were constituted from the best of the Home Guard and others with country skills and weapons (game-keepers, landowners, and the like). They prepared and trained in small guerrilla groups of four to ten men, an adumbration of IRA active service units that were so effective during the Irish 'Troubles', 1969–1998. The Scallywags' existence was, anyway, highly secret and inappropriate for talks at this strategic level.

Those discussions were followed up with the British delegation's turn to ask awkward questions. Noting that the Japanese had already invaded Hainan Island and French Indo-China (now Vietnam), and there were strong rumours of Japanese intentions to invade Malaya, they asked how the United States would react if Japan continued its southwards advance into Malaya, then further into the Dutch East Indies (now Indonesia). Surely, they asked, this would be a *casus belli*? The Americans would not be drawn on the point, only offering economic coercion and diplomatic pressure as their likely response.

The discussion, therefore, exposed the considerable differences between Britain and America in their Far East strategies. The British continued to push back by restating their belief that Singapore, with a strong naval presence, was pivotal to their Far East strategy, not only for Malaya and the Dutch East Indies but also for Australia and New Zealand. In all this the British delegation were considering the cohesion and stability of the Commonwealth and insisting that 'Singapore is the key to the defence of these interests and its retention must be assured.'[50] This view contrasted sharply with American remarks during the talks. Brigadier General Sherman Miles stated that the 'concerted British pressure on us to commit ourselves in the Far East would be a strategic error of incalculable magnitude'.[51] The American delegates were united in this view. Slessor summed up his thoughts on the American view succinctly as 'the traditional dislike of "colonialism" and to a feeling that it was not up to them to protect British trading interests in Malaya with American arms'.[52] This was certainly a view held firmly but quietly by Roosevelt – less quietly as Allied victory became more certain as 1944 turned into 1945. But the Far East issue, despite its importance, was the only serious and irreconcilable difference that the delegates confronted during their two months of talks.

The main body of the ABC-1 report focused on areas of strategic principle, and how the forces would be deployed in the event of America entering the war. Notably, the Americans put down an early marker that their military commanders could neither subdivide their forces nor attach them to units of another power. In areas where the two nations operated together, the senior officer in that area would assume overall command.[53] After the mistakes and misunderstandings during the First World War, the Americans were not going to sacrifice the control and autonomy of their forces. The Americans in 1940 were determined that the history of 1917–1918 should not be repeated.[54]

There were significant differences in style and approach between the American and British delegations. Whereas the British were careful to co-ordinate their small inter-Service team to develop agreed positions prior to the plenary sessions, the Americans, operating on a single-Service basis, often only came together at the joint meetings. The Navy and Army delegates would sometimes argue openly during the plenary sessions, and the British would very quickly take note of the lack of harmony and try to take advantage of the situation. The British delegates had considerable experience of Cabinet government, recognizing that inter-Service cooperation and agreement was a cardinal rule. They were also well acquainted with formal minute taking. The joint minutes taken during the talks were drawn up on the British model and were primarily the product of Cornwall-Jones.[55]

The exchange of military missions

One of the more positive outcomes of the ABC talks was the unanimous agreement to exchange military missions to be established in Washington and London. Slessor had always been an active proponent of the idea and con-sidered that it was key to building up and improving the Alliance relationship. He noted years later that the British Joint Services Mission (BJSM) became the nucleus of the British side of the Combined Chiefs of Staff by whom, under the Prime Minister and the President, the higher direction of the com-bined war effort was conducted in an intimate and integrated manner, one without precedent in the history of alliances.[56]

Aircraft allocations: more confrontation with Beaverbrook

On 1 February Slessor was yet again confronted with the accusation that the British were hoarding unduly large reserves of American aircraft which could not be matched with British aircrew numbers, and the American side bluntly stated they had not been treated with frankness. The American Air Service delegates, Colonel Joe McNarney of the Army Air Corps and Captain Dewitt Ramsay of the Naval Aviation Section, were aggrieved that all this was occur-ring at the expense of aircraft being denied for their own expansion plans. Slessor was again finding it exceedingly difficult to dispel the lingering suspi-cion. He was now clearly concerned that any withholding of the requested information might permanently damage the air power relationship. He cabled Portal promptly: 'Our production position both of aircraft and crews is essentially pertinent to this question of American air assistance ... the RAF should not accumulate more than we really need while the United States Air

Corps, which at present has virtually no modern combat planes, continues to be starved of aircraft.'[57] Portal was now alarmed and realized that this continuing problem would endanger the outcome of the talks. He wrote to Churchill: 'Slessor reports that the point has come up again, in the course of the second meeting of the British – United States technical conversations … I quite appreciate Lord Beaverbrook's reluctance to release this information but now that the matter has been raised directly by the US Staff I feel most strongly that failure will imperil the success of the technical conversations.'[58]

Churchill left it for Beaverbrook to respond. In a further demonstration of Beaverbrook's unregenerate 'silo mentality', his curt response to Portal on 14 February revealed his dislike of Slessor and an obvious lack of any concern in maintaining good relationships during the ABC talks:

> It seems to me that the Air Commodore [sic] Slessor is impinging on the duties and responsibilities of the Aircraft Ministry … communication should pass through this Ministry [of Aircraft Production] and should be handled entirely by us. I hope you tell Air Commodore [sic] Slessor to take this course as you will see at once we cannot both handle the American programme. The authority must be left with us.[59]

This episode characterized Beaverbrook's persistently unhelpful and combative attitude towards many of the senior RAF commanders and the Air Ministry on a range of key issues. He often referred to them as 'the bloody Air Marshals'.[60] Portal's short reply to Beaverbrook emphasized the importance of Slessor's role in the ABC talks: 'The nature of Slessor's work in America is such that I am afraid it will be impossible for him to avoid points of this character being put to him by the US delegation.'[61] The problem dragged on and Beaverbrook chose not to respond immediately. Over a month had passed before one of his assistants sent a message to the Air Ministry. It read: 'Lord Beaverbrook has seen your note to me of 19 March on the subject of Slessor and has asked me to answer it to the effect that he has not very much faith in this officer and does not propose to become involved in any negotiations about him.'[62]

The ABC air discussions and negotiations

This problem could have derailed any Anglo-American agreement on future aircraft allocations. Fortunately, Slessor's diplomatic approach and his friendly outgoing manner ensured that he could continue to develop a fruitful working relationship with his American opposite numbers. Together they represented the Air subcommittee and they negotiated and produced a final report in late March that dealt with plans for the expansion of, and aircraft allocation to, both the British and American air forces. Much would depend on the future course of events. The American Army Air Corps plans centred on an expansion target of fifty-four air combat groups by mid-1942 (the First Aviation Objective), on the assumption that the United States had not entered the war. However, in the case that Britain were to be successfully invaded in 1941 and knocked out of the war, the expansion target would be raised to 100 air combat groups, the minimum required by the Air Corps for its proportionate effort in achieving its air security of the United States and its Western hemisphere interests (the Second Aviation Objective).[63]

In their discussions Slessor continued to emphasize the importance of heavy bombers to implement the strategic air offensive against Germany. He requested that within the first three months of America entering the war, the Army Air Forces should provide four squadrons at a minimum of ninety-six heavy bombers to be deployed in England. This would only be the start of a build-up of bombers and fighters. The bombers would continue the air offensive, with the fighters being used for the air defence of Britain and as escorts for the bombers.[64]

ABC-2 'the Slessor Agreement': future British and American aircraft allocations

A specific agreement was reached between the three members of the Air subcommittee; it was known as the ABC-2 agreement, and later more commonly as 'the Slessor Agreement'. On the assumption that Britain would continue as an active belligerent in 1942 and beyond, and that America had not entered the war, the agreed aircraft allocations to Britain would be as follows:

(1) all UK British and Commonwealth aircraft indigenously produced;
(2) 26,357 aircraft already ordered from future American production up to mid-1942; and
(3) 100% of *new* aircraft production from mid-1942 onwards, emphasizing the assumption that the US had not become a belligerent.

The Americans would receive the balance of remaining production *less* allocations already committed to other countries. However, following America's entry into the war, the arrangement would revert to the existing allocations as already agreed, and with all new production split 50/50 between America and Britain.

This was an extremely good deal for Britain and was a mark of Slessor's negotiating skills. However, as Slessor himself reflected, 'there was amongst some Americans a view that the British had taken the pants off Hap Arnold', but adding 'that some Americans are curiously liable to suspect that they are going to be "outsmarted" by the subtle British ... they cannot take them at face value but suspect them of some dark design'.[65] He praised Joe McNarney, his opposite number, as a tough negotiator.[66]

As a postscript to the agreement, the key element of 100 per cent of new aircraft production for the British was never put into effect. Only nine months later America entered the war after the Japanese attack on Pearl Harbor on 7 December 1941, compounded by Hitler's declaration of war on the USA just four days later on 11 December.

Whereas Slessor got on well with his colleagues on the Air subcommittee, it was certainly not the case with Rear Admiral R.K. Turner of the US Navy. Slessor described 'Kelly' Turner as 'an able and forcible officer whose influence in the Navy department was perhaps more powerful than his position warranted ... he could best be what one of his colleagues called "as ornery as hell" and was rather liable to start from the assumption that he was right and everyone else were either fools or knaves'.[67] When it came to the final scrutiny of the draft ABC agreement, Kelly Turner proved to be obdurate, and for the British, Rear Admiral Roger Bellairs commented 'every paragraph had to be fought'.[68]

On 27 March, during the closing session of the talks, Colonel McNarney suddenly announced that the Air subcommittee would include their report on aircraft allocations – the ABC-2 *Report on Air Collaboration* agreement – as an annex to the main body of the ABC-1 agreement. This was an unfortunate case of poor timing and, rather than surprise his fellow delegates, perhaps McNarney should have given more notice of the report's inclusion. In any event, as Leutze noted, 'Kelly Turner, who did not reserve his acerbity for the British, went through the roof.'[69] 'Why', Turner wanted to know, 'should the needs of the air forces be given special consideration?' This was followed by a full-blown row between Slessor and Turner. Slessor now realized that if the ABC-2 Air agreement, 'which had been hammered out with such blood, sweat, toil, and tears did not have the full standing and authority of the ABC-1 document, its validity would surely be dangerously weakened, and he felt he could not sign any of the documents and the matter must be referred to the British Chiefs of Staff'.[70] The 'final' session then closed without the ABC agreements being signed. Back at their accommodation on the top floor of the embassy that evening, even Slessor's colleagues were embarrassed by his outburst, and were even starting to doubt the wisdom of his attitude.

The following day Slessor and Turner continued to argue. Fortunately, Turner's Navy colleagues, Ghormley and Stark, finally convinced him to drop his strongly held objections. Slessor's stand on the matter had been vindicated.

The British and American delegations met for the last time on 29 March. Exactly two months had passed since the start of the talks, and much had been achieved. The ABC-1 agreement with the ABC-2 annex was signed by all delegates and passed on to their respective chiefs of staff for their approval.

The ABC talks, held only nine months prior to America entering the war, provided the emerging Anglo-American alliance with a template for their future joint policies and strategies and would guide them through the next four years. Lowenthal commented that 'ABC was an important step forward, a means of fleshing out grand strategic agreement.'[71] Churchill was advised that Americans regarded and quoted the ABC agreement 'as the bible of our collaboration'.[72] But the talks also threw up some sharp differences in British and American policy and strategy. The issue of joint defence in the southwest Pacific was never resolved. The Americans almost universally disliked Britain's colonial policies. The US Navy refused to consider a joint base in Singapore and there continued to be moments when there was an underlying distrust of Britain's motives. Leutze commented perceptively that 'it is unduly simplistic to label it as a time of Anglo-American cooperation ... collaboration is perhaps the best word to describe it, for that word implies a relationship based on calculation and convenience'.[73]

Slessor meets President Roosevelt, 8 April 1941

In early April, and two days before he departed back to Britain, President Roosevelt asked to see Slessor, who was clearly honoured to be invited to the White House. He commented that the President had an 'extraordinary knack of making one feel that he was really pleased to meet one, as well as an infectious enthusiasm about anything he was at all interested in'.[74] Slessor was left in no doubt about his wholehearted enthusiasm and determination to see Britain win the war.

Slessor travelled back to Europe by the same southern route as his outbound trip five months earlier. He departed from La Guardia's marine air terminal on 10 May by Pan-Am Clipper to Portugal. During his time in America he had gained a much greater understanding of the American political and military systems with their strengths and shortcomings. His experiences would later give him a major advantage in steering the policy direction in 1942 of coalition air warfare with the Combined Bomber Offensive against Germany, and in his operational experience as the Deputy Commander of the Anglo-American Mediterranean Allied Air Forces in 1944.

Chapter 9

Bomber Command

Air Officer Commanding 5 Group,
Bomber Command, April 1941–March 1942

On 12 April 1941 Air Vice-Marshal Slessor took up his new operational posting as Air Officer Commanding (AOC) of Bomber Command's 5 Group. For the ensuing eleven months he was based at 5 Group's headquarters at St Vincent's Hall near Grantham in Lincolnshire. 5 Group had overall responsibility for eleven squadrons of approximately 160 Handley Page Hampdens and 60 Avro Manchesters that were based at six airfields located primarily in central Lincolnshire.[1]

1941: a low point in 5 Group's history

In 1939, and prior to the outbreak of war, the previous Commander-in-Chief of Bomber Command, Air Chief Marshal Sir Edgar Ludlow-Hewitt, lamented that he 'still had to face the fact that over forty percent of a force of his bombers were unable to find a target in a friendly city in broad daylight'.[2] Training, particularly of navigators, was at the centre of the problem. For too long during the late 1930s the 'air observers', forerunners of navigators, were regarded as part-time aircrew and, as the aviation historian Malcolm Smith wrote, this was perhaps the 'epitome of the amateur aircrew at that time'. Despite Ludlow-Hewitt's assiduous drive to get comprehensive training for all his bomber aircrews, the attitude persisted throughout the early war years. In 1938 he did finally get the Air Ministry to agree to air observers receiving ten weeks of intensive training in navigation.[3] Hence in early 1941 the bombers were regularly sent at night-time over Germany and the occupied territories, often with extensive cloud cover over the primary targets. Even when the navigators were well trained, they lacked the navigation and bombing electronic aids, *Gee*, *Oboe* and *H2S*, that only made a significant appearance from 1943 onwards. It was little wonder that targets were regularly missed. All this was a far cry from the confident pre-war rhetoric about the primacy of the bomber that had been espoused by senior air commanders since Trenchard's time.

Since 1929 the RAF had adopted a doctrine in which the strategic bomber offensive would be the key determinant of victory in any future major conflict. Portal, Harris and Slessor were all strong believers in the bomber doctrine and Slessor was now experiencing first-hand the result of delays, political prevarication and budget constraints that occurred in the pre-war period. In Slessor's own words, 1941 and early 1942 was a time that was 'a bleak and sometimes depressing period of trial and error ... in the early stages of the first bomber offensive in history ... we were still on the strategic defensive and likely to be for some time to come; and we had nothing like enough of anything to go round – even for a defensive strategy'.[4]

The aircraft: Hampdens and Manchesters

5 Group was operating with squadrons of medium bombers (Hampdens) and underpowered heavy bombers (Manchesters).

The Hampden medium bomber had originally been designed around roles as a fighter-bomber, tactical ground support, maritime patrols and air reconnaissance aircraft. They were now being pressed into service to attack strategic targets such as aircraft factories, shipyards and armaments factories in the Ruhr with their limited bombload of 6,000lb. The reason for the extensive use of medium bombers by 5 Group could be traced back to the pre-war defence budget constraints in 1937. Thomas Inskip, the Minister for the Coordination of Defence, adopted a deliberate policy to limit and delay the manufacture of heavy bombers.[5] Slessor had originally proposed an expansion of heavy bomber numbers in his Scheme 'J' that was submitted in October 1937. Inskip cancelled that proposed expansion and insisted the focus was given instead to the increased manufacture of medium bombers: the Battles, Blenheims and Hampdens. By early 1941 that policy had fed through to Bomber Command, and particularly 5 Group, in the form of too many relatively ineffective medium bombers and a shortage of the much-needed heavy bombers. In addition, Slessor knew that overall he was operating with an insufficient number of aircraft. The number of aircraft in Bomber Command had been reduced by nearly 24 per cent. Nearly 200 aircraft had either been sent to Coastal Command or to Egypt. Slessor wrote to Air Vice Marshal John Baker, the Director of Bombing Operations at the Air Ministry, complaining about the reductions. Baker admitted that aircraft numbers were not going to improve during 1941 and explained that this was partly due to the decision taken by Beaverbrook and the Ministry of Aircraft Production in late 1940 to focus on fighter production.[6]

Arthur Harris, who had previously commanded 5 Group, considered that the Hampden was highly vulnerable to fighter attacks in daylight raids and considered it was 'a most feebly armed aircraft with a single gun on top and a single one underneath manned by a gunner in a cramped position'.[7] The aircraft was certainly not designed around comfort, and many aircrews nicknamed it 'the flying suitcase' on account of its claustrophobic conditions.

The Avro Manchester was the twin-engined forerunner of the successful four-engined Lancaster. The Manchester had been rushed into service in 1940 initially with 207 Squadron, based at Waddington. The aircraft suffered from a range of engine problems. The underpowered Rolls-Royce Vulture engines were prone to overheating, premature engine wear and lubrication problems. Over two extended periods during 1941 all the Manchesters were grounded for remedial work and consequently their crews were transferred to flying the increasingly obsolescent Hampdens. Although the Manchester could accommodate a 10,000lb bombload, its service ceiling altitude was only 18,000ft. Slessor saw the aircraft as a stopgap measure until the Lancasters started to roll off the production lines. The one glimmer of light in the gloomiest of years for 5 Group was the appearance of the first Lancasters that were delivered to 44 Squadron at Waddington on Christmas Eve 1941.

5 Group flight operations, March–November 1941

In the first two months of 1941 the Battle of the Atlantic had resulted in sixty-two merchant ships being sunk by U-boat attack. Churchill was becoming increasingly alarmed by the losses and the immediate threat that it posed to critical food and matériel supplies from America. In early March Churchill ordered that all Bomber Command's aircraft were to give the highest priority to stemming the catastrophic assault on merchant shipping. To that end a directive was issued on 9 March for a four-month campaign against U-boat shipyards and port facilities, the Focke-Wulf 'Condor' manufacturing plant, and diesel engine manufacturing sites. The target list included German coastal sites in Kiel, Bremen, Hamburg, Vegesack and inland engine manufacturing sites in Augsburg, Mannheim and Dessau. A number of U-boat facilities and airfields in western France, including Lorient, St Nazaire and Bordeaux, were on the target list.[8] However, throughout the year the raids were largely ineffective. The campaign was extended with daylight raids over targets in western France. Eleven of ninety-one bombers were shot down by fighters and flak on one particular raid on port facilities in Brest on 24 July. A further two crashed on their return journey.[9] With loss rates of more than 10 per cent per raid, Slessor queried the wisdom of further daylight raids over France. He wrote to Peirse, Commander-in-Chief of Bomber Command, stating that it was 'uneconomic' continuing with the daylight raids.[10]

When time permitted, Slessor went out to his airfields to see the aircraft depart for their targets and again when they returned. He listened to aircrew debriefings with the intelligence officers and recalled the 'early morning smell of stale cigarette smoke, the taste of strong, bitter tea out of heavy NAAFI cups, and also the sinking feeling in the pit of the tummy as the orderly chalked up the time landed against one after another of the names on the board, and the clock ticked round towards the ominous moments when the "time landed" column would mean there would be no return for C-Charlie or P-Peter'.[11]

As the year progressed, the focus shifted towards inland targets in Germany. On 9 July a directive from the Air Ministry to Bomber Command stated that 'the weakest points in his [The German] armour lie in the morale of the civilian population and his inland transportation system. The wide extension of his military activities is placing an ever-increasing strain on the German transportation system, and there are many signs that our recent attacks on industrial towns are having great effect on the morale of the civilian population.'[12] This change of targeting policy was almost certainly influenced by Lord Trenchard. On 2 June he had met Portal and suggested that serious consideration be given to bombing city areas in his strong belief that the morale of the German people 'stood up very badly to the strain of repeated bombing', adding that 'no town of any size should consider itself safe'.[13] Trenchard considered the morale of the German people to be a weak point, and less stalwart than the British.[14] The focus was shifting further down the path of unconstrained city area bombing. Irrespective of the Air Ministry's selection of targets, the bomber crews were failing to find and attack them. On the night of 12/13 June 5 Group sent ninety-one Hampdens to attack railway yards at Soest, a small town 20 miles east of Dortmund. The attack failed on account of poor visibility, although forty-two crews claimed to have bombed the primary target.[15] Slessor knew that many of his crews were 'really just loosing off [bombs] blind into the overcast or unloading over concentrations of flak or searchlights or at fires which as often as not were dummies lit for the very purpose of attracting bombs away from their proper targets'.[16] Slessor wrote to Peirse after the Soest raid making an early plea for accurate target marking by special aircraft going in ahead of the main force and lighting up the target with heavy loads of incendiaries. In the case of Soest, he wrote, 'a wing-commander at 3,000 feet watched bomb after bomb tumbling into a burning wood' but in defence of his aircrews admitted that 'the chaps are getting more cunning at spotting dummies'.[17] Slessor was not the first, or the only, senior air commander to request specialized crews to mark targets ahead of the main force. Air Commodore Sidney Bufton, who later became Deputy Director of Bombing Operations at the Air Ministry, had been an early and strong advocate of the idea. The practice was formalized in August 1942 when the Pathfinder Force (the PFF) was formed as 8 Group Bomber Command under the direction of Air Vice-Marshal Donald Bennett.[18]

On 30 August a further directive outlined an attack on twenty-one small towns along railway routes with the intention of causing 'a serious, even though temporary, breakdown in communications'.[19] The directive went on to state that the targeting policy would have a considerable effect on civilian morale. During this time Slessor continued to be consulted on policy by the Air Ministry. He relayed important policy issues to his old mentor, Trenchard, who used the information in the House of Lords.[20] However, it is not known what views Slessor himself held at the time on city area bombing with the intention of affecting the morale of the German civilian population. He had previously discussed the ethical dilemma of bombing industrial targets in city areas but had not supported a deliberate policy of morale bombing. As Director of Plans in September 1939 Slessor was quite clear when he wrote 'indiscriminate attacks on civilian populations as such will never form part of our policy'.[21] But equally it was a grey area. The line between genuine military and civilian targets had become blurred. Slessor posed the moral and ethical dilemma in *Central Blue*. Why would a tank depot outside Dusseldorf be an acceptable target when a tank factory surrounded by workers housing was not? However, irrespective of Slessor's views it is important to note that at this stage of the war 'the gloves had come off' after the Luftwaffe's air raids on British cities during 1940 and 1941.[22]

The Butt Report, August 1941

Irrespective of the ethical and moral issues surrounding area bombing, Bomber Command was still failing to find and destroy targets on a regular basis. The continuing disappointing results of bombing raids led Lord Cherwell, the chief scientific adviser to the War Cabinet, to appoint one of his assistants, David Bensusan-Butt, to carry out a survey of bombing results over a two-month period in June and July 1941. The survey involved the examination of 650 photographs taken by aircraft that were involved in a hundred raids over twenty-eight targets on forty-eight nights. Butt and his team, which included the Photographic Interpretation Section, concluded that only one-third of aircraft claiming to reach the target area actually got within 5 miles of the target. Butt's report was released on 8 August. Slessor would not have been surprised by the report's findings, knowing that his crews were 'failing to find and hit any but the most obvious on the clearest moonlight nights ... but for the most part our bombs were going lamentably wide of the mark'.[23] Churchill's faith in the efficacy of the bomber offensive was shaken, but it did not signal a change of heart in the bomber offensive representing the primary method of attacking the enemy at that stage in the war. Navigation skills and the need for sophisticated electronic navigation and bombing aids were now of paramount importance.

This was an exceedingly difficult moment for Bomber Command. Churchill had backed the bomber offensive throughout the early wartime period and had given it his fullest support, but as he wrote, '[Heavy bomber] Production has been planned to conform with this strategic conception and we are deeply committed to it. If it is now to be accepted that the best heavy bombers can do would be to cause a heavy and increasing annoyance, then, as I see it, the strategic concept to which we have been working must dissolve'.[24] Portal was under extreme pressure to justify the fundamental role of Bomber Command. He responded with a coherent defence: 'given the necessary production, the Royal Air Force is capable by itself of carrying the disruption of Germany to a very advanced stage. If that assumption is no longer tenable; we must produce a new plan. The worst plan of all would be to continue our preparations after we had ceased to believe in the efficacy of the bomber as a war winning weapon.'[25] Despite Churchill having reservations, he accepted the point, responding, 'one has to do the best one can, but he is an unwise man who thinks there is any *certain* method of winning this war, or indeed any other war between equals in strength. The only plan is to persevere.'[26]

But 5 Group's problems did not abate. Poor weather continued throughout the last quarter of 1941. Slessor always had a healthy respect for his meteorologists. At 5 Group he recalled 'we had an exceptionally good Senior Meteorological Officer ... Mr Matthews – the 'Gremlin' as he was affectionately known by group staff and squadrons alike ... and he never hesitated to give an opinion on the suitability of the weather for the operation ordered for the night'.[27]

On the night of 7 November the extremely worried meteorologist was quite insistent that the Group aircraft would be undertaking 'a quite unjustifiable risk in sending Hampdens to Berlin in the icing conditions to be expected'.[28] Slessor immediately contacted Peirse at Bomber Command Headquarters and requested an alternative target. He managed to convince Peirse, although it was rare for a group commander to query the Commander-in-Chief's directive. Slessor and his senior meteorologist were vindicated when 5 Group lost only two of seventy-five Hampdens dispatched. However, for the other Groups the night of 7/8 November was remembered for the considerable loss of thirty-eight aircraft, a 9 per cent loss for the night's operations.

The night of 7/8 November became a major source of concern not only for the air commanders, but also for Churchill and the War Cabinet. Loss rates of 9 per cent could not be sustained. Churchill immediately ordered the Air Ministry to issue a directive that ensured the conservation of both bomber and fighter aircraft 'in order to build a strong force to be available by the spring of next year [1942]'.[29]

Peirse was never a convincing Commander-in-Chief for Bomber Command. The Air Staff investigated the Berlin raid and concluded that he had been negligent in dispatching the aircraft with the knowledge that the crews would encounter high winds, storms and icing. Portal had also become aware of Slessor's request for permission to attack an alternative target (Cologne) because of the forecast unfavourable meteorological conditions.

The official history summed up the period during which Peirse had been Commander-in-Chief of Bomber Command as 'one of progressive disillusionment as the limitations which beset the night bomber were gradually and ruthlessly revealed ... In the view of some observers, the morale of the force and the confidence of its commanders in the success of their attacks was beginning to decline.'[30]

In early January 1942 Peirse was relieved of his command and Air Vice Marshal Baldwin took over as the interim commander. Despite the directive to conserve the bomber force, 5 Group continued raids on the port facilities in Brest with failed attempts to attack the German warships *Scharnhorst*, *Gneisenau* and *Prinz Eugen*. The Group was also involved in raids on port facilities in Hamburg, Wilhelmshaven, Emden and Bremen, again with negligible to poor results.

'The Channel Dash', 11–13 February 1942

On the night of 11 February *Scharnhorst*, *Gneisenau* and *Prinz Eugen* left Brest in atrocious weather conditions, together with six destroyers and fourteen torpedo boats. They were shielded in the air by a Luftwaffe force of thirty-two bombers and more than 250 fighters. The breakout had been anticipated by the British and preparations had been made to attack the German ships in Operation Fuller. An unforgivable breakdown in communications prevented the implementation of the operation until it was too late. The group of German warships was only detected at 1030 hours when they were already 20 miles off Boulogne. In the severe weather the Fleet Air Arm's Swordfish aircraft failed to hit the ships with their torpedoes. No fewer than 242 sorties were launched by Bomber Command in extremely poor weather conditions throughout the course of the daylight hours on 12 February. 5 Group lost eleven aircraft to enemy fighters, flak and collisions in the murky weather. Only minor damage was sustained by *Scharnhorst* and *Gneisenau* by mines that had recently been laid by 5 Group's aircraft. The German ships arrived at their home port on 13 February. It was a propaganda success for the Germans, and a period of acute embarrassment both for the Royal Navy and the Royal Air Force.

In early March Slessor was instructed to take up his new posting as Air Officer Commanding of 11 Group, Fighter Command, based at their head-quarters at Hillingdon House in Uxbridge. It was strange that he was being transferred after less than one year, and just at the point at which 5 Group was improving with the phasing-out of Hampdens and the introduction and build-up of Lancasters within the squadrons. It was a turning point for 5 Group's fortunes.

On his arrival at 11 Group Slessor and his predecessor agreed that drawn-out hand-over/take-overs were a bore so with no further delay they signed the required papers effecting the transfer of command. Even as he was being introduced to his new staff at Uxbridge and had settled down at his new desk to read his various briefs, Slessor received a phone call from Air Vice-Marshal Wilfrid Freeman, Deputy Chief of the Air Staff at the Air Ministry. Freeman told him not to take over the Group as plans had changed – but it was too late. He apologized for disappointing Slessor, but 'it had been decided that the burden of work on the policy side of the Air Staff had now become so great – especially with the entry of America into the war – that it was necessary to create a new appointment, Assistant Chief of the Air Staff (Policy)'.[31] Slessor was the first incumbent. His tenure as AOC 11 Group had lasted five hours.

Following the attack on Pearl Harbor in December 1941, America was now in the war. Following the Anglo-American Arcadia Conference held in Washington during January, the United States Army Air Forces (USAAF) were making plans to deploy their B-17 squadrons to air bases in eastern England. There was no better senior air commander than Slessor to coordinate the Anglo-American strategy in the forthcoming Combined Bomber Offensive (CBO). Wiser heads prevailed.

Chapter 10

Allied Strategic Priorities

Anglo-American Talks and Casablanca, March 1942–January 1943

In late March 1942 Air Vice-Marshal Slessor returned to the Air Ministry. He was now based in King Charles Street, close to the War Office. He was to spend most of the next ten months deeply involved in discussions with his American opposite numbers. Despite the broad agreements reached during the ABC staff talks, both America and the Soviet Union were now in the war, there was a considerable divergence of view between the British and American High Commands on the next steps, and how, when and where to deal with the Axis powers. There were unexpected reductions in the originally agreed allocation to Britain of American aircraft, particularly of heavy bombers. Anglo-American discussions during the year were often difficult and some-times fraught. Furthermore, 1942 was not a good year for the Allies, who were still on the defensive. Fortunately, towards the end of the year the tide was finally starting to turn. Slessor made two trips to Washington at that time. Then, in January 1943 he accompanied Portal to the Casablanca Conference where he made an important, perhaps vital, contribution to the success of those proceedings.

The Arcadia Conference, 24 December 1941–17 January 1942

Following the Pearl Harbor attack on Sunday, 7 December, Churchill wrote to Roosevelt proposing a meeting at the earliest opportunity but was advised that any meeting would not be possible for at least another month.[1] However, during the remainder of that momentous week other key events unfolded: Japanese troops had simultaneously invaded Siam (Thailand) and the Dutch East Indies (Indonesia) on 7 December, and the Philippines on 8 December; two British warships, *Prince of Wales* and *Repulse*, were sunk by Japanese planes on 10 December off the Malayan coast; and Hitler declared war on the United States on 11 December, making the United States a belligerent in

Europe. The war now took on a truly global dimension, and this was a key turning point for Roosevelt. He now agreed to meet Churchill with their military staffs at the earliest opportunity.

In short order Churchill arranged for the Chiefs of Staff to accompany him on the battleship *Duke of York* for the transatlantic crossing. Churchill's entourage included Sir Dudley Pound, the First Sea Lord; Field Marshal Sir John Dill, Chief of the Imperial General Staff; Air Chief Marshal Sir Charles Portal, Chief of the Air Staff; Lord Beaverbrook, Minister of Supply; Averell Harriman, Roosevelt's special envoy; Lord Moran, Churchill's personal physician; and the secretariat that included Brigadier Leslie Hollis and Colonel Ian Jacob.

Duke of York left Greenock on 13 December. It was a rough crossing, and to avoid even worse weather the battleship, accompanied by an escort of three destroyers, took a southern route that for some time put them in danger of U-boat attacks. The trip took ten days, during which time Churchill wrote four memoranda setting forth his views on the best way to defeat the Axis, proposing a strategy that the Western Allies were to follow in the next phase of the war.[2] *Duke of York* finally arrived in Chesapeake Bay in Virginia on 22 December, docking at Norfolk naval shipyard. The group travelled immediately to Washington DC and were met by President Roosevelt personally.

During the next three weeks over Christmas and the New Year Churchill, Roosevelt and their respective military staffs were in frequent discussions in the conference that was later better known by its codename Arcadia. The talks enabled both sides to reconfirm the grand strategy of the ABC negotiations that had been mapped out nine months previously and in which Slessor had played a key role. In their discussions both sides reaffirmed that dealing with Germany remained the number one priority. Churchill and the Chiefs of Staff were reassured by the 'Germany First' commitment, particularly in view of the attack on Pearl Harbor and the invasion of the Philippines. Churchill had become concerned that significant volumes of munitions and other war matériel might well be diverted to the Pacific and away from Britain and its North African campaign.[3] However, the 'Germany First' priority would not go unchallenged within large sections of the American public and senior military leaders, notably by the US Navy, and on multiple occasions during 1942 and early 1943.

On 24 December Admiral Stark announced that in the future American heavy bombers sent to England would be manned by American crews. Portal was surprised by this announcement and pointed out that this was not in accordance with the ABC-2 'Slessor Agreement' that had been finalized eight months previously. However, General Arnold, Commanding General of the

Army Air Forces (AAF), reassured Portal that the new proposal would not prejudice existing agreements in terms of numbers. To endorse those original arrangements, the Arnold-Portal Agreement was signed on 13 January 1942. The agreement called for the provision of 9,530 aircraft of all types during 1942, listed by categories and delivery dates.[4] In Slessor's view this rearrangement was not so very different from the original 'Slessor Agreement' and importantly 'included nearly 600 heavy bombers – among which were those we wanted so badly for the long-range anti-submarine work in the Atlantic'.[5]

The US Army Air Force comes to England

On 12 February 1942 General Arnold announced that the USAAF would be sending sixteen heavy-bombardment groups that would consist of a total of 512 B-17s during the year. In addition, he would also complement this force with three fighter groups (225 aircraft), and eight photoreconnaissance squadrons (96 aircraft). Carl Spaatz was named as the commanding general of the newly established Eighth Air Force in England.

Later that month Brigadier Ira Eaker arrived in England and established the Eighth Air Force's Bomber Command headquarters at Wycombe Abbey in Buckinghamshire. The site was a requisitioned independent girls' school located in 250 acres of parkland and conveniently close to the RAF's Bomber Command headquarters in High Wycombe. Throughout the war it was known through its codename 'Pinetree'. The ABC-1 talks held in early 1941 had clarified the organization and control issues of American units in any future war and the Eighth Air Force in England was to be a fully autonomous body answerable only to the American High Command. However, the Eighth Air Force was to work closely with the British and would eventually co-ordinate its operations with the RAF during the Combined Bomber Offensive (CBO) that lasted from mid-1943 until the end of the war.

On 10 May General Spaatz met General Arnold at Bolling Air Force Base in Washington DC to discuss the overall deployment of aircraft and logistic support being sent to Britain. Spaatz made it clear that the build-up would proceed slowly and carefully at first, and that it would develop in a phased manner. He hoped that the bomber force would not be stampeded into any premature action by political pressures.[6] Spaatz was a realist. He knew that defeating the Luftwaffe would be an immense task; he was acutely alive to the impending months of a constant bleeding away of experienced pilots and loss of first-line machines if the Allies were to draw the sting of the Luftwaffe and make a cross-Channel invasion possible.[7] On 14 May Spaatz met General Marshall to address the tactical role the USAAF would play in such an invasion. Spaatz stressed the importance of timely air reconnaissance to identify

German armoured formations and columns. He also ensured that Marshall was aware of the significant difference between air superiority and air supremacy. Air superiority meant that the stronger force could operate confident of overwhelming dominance, but it could not guarantee that the opposing force would be unable to inflict damage. Air supremacy would indicate complete, unhindered control of the skies over the battlefield, shutting down the enemy's ability to hinder Allied operations. He wrote later, 'No such effort [a cross-Channel invasion] should be attempted until the Allies gain complete SUPREMACY [sic] in the air.'[8]

The first phase of the American bombing offensive would involve raids on short-range targets in France and protected by British fighter cover. The second phase would entail deeper penetration sorties using the cover of the longer-range American fighters. The final phase would involve large numbers of B-17s flying deep into Germany as a self-defending unit.

The B-17s would fly in a close formation that would be known as the combat box. In theory, the B-17s would be able to cover the airspace around the box with their impressive array of .50 calibre machine guns, thereby protecting the entire bomber force itself as a unit.[9] Spaatz and his officers had great faith in what they saw as a relatively invulnerable bombing force that would be capable of achieving the precision bombing of key strategic targets from high altitude. Slessor considered Spaatz's careful introduction of his combat units was the correct course of action in that it involved breaking in his new units by degrees, profiting from the RAF's combat experience, and not throwing green units straight into action.[10]

But Churchill was genuinely concerned about the ability of the USAAF to carry out its daylight bombing raids without suffering punishing losses over Germany. He asked Slessor and the Air Staff to examine an alternative use either in the Battle of the Atlantic, or in joining the RAF in the night bombing offensive. Those suggestions were at total variance with the function for which the USAAF crews had been trained: to fly at high altitude, in daylight, and to carry out precision bombing utilizing their Norden bombsights. The USAAF remained confident that with increased aircraft numbers during late 1942 they would succeed.

Criticism in the British press did not help. Newspaper articles outlined the differing American and British approaches to bombing. On 16 August 1942 *The Sunday Times* ran an article by Peter Masefield, a respected aviation expert, that concluded, 'unless the Fortress or the Liberator can be adapted for employment at night they are unlikely to achieve more than intermittent harassing operations in daylight in a European theatre and in the face of modern air defences'. The following day, 17 August, Spaatz held a joint USAAF/RAF press conference to demonstrate the cooperation between the two air forces. He also launched the USAAF's first bombing mission in Europe against the Rouen-Sotteville marshalling yards in northern France. The force of B-17 bombers was escorted by RAF Spitfires. The raid was a minor success and bomb damage assessment indicated that 50 per cent of the bombs fell within the target area. Spaatz told Arnold: 'it is my opinion and conviction that the B-17 is suitable as to speed, armament, armour, and bomb load. I would not exchange it for any British bomber in production.' Arnold followed up by forwarding Spaatz's message to the President, adding 'the above more than vindicates our faith in the Flying Fortress and precision bombing'.[11]

Cognizant of how essential it was for Anglo-American unity not to be damaged by British faint hearts and, most particularly, condescension, on 26 September Slessor wrote a detailed memorandum to both Portal and the Secretary of State for Air, Sinclair, arguing that the Americans should be given a chance to implement their tactics without the British pooh-poohing their efforts:

A bit cock-a-hoop as a result of their limited experience to date. They are setting about it in a realistic and business-like way, paying special attention to gunnery training, distribution of ammunition, cutting of the bomb load and increasing the ammunition of wing aircraft, and so on. And making allowances for their natural optimism I have a feeling that they will do it ... They have hung their hats on the day bomber policy and are convinced they can do it ... To cast doubts on it just at present would cause irritation and make them very obstinate. It is yet to be proved whether it is possible to carry the war deep into Germany by day. But they believe they will and I am inclined to agree with them *once they really get adequate numbers.* Their early operations [over France] lend support to their belief – the B-17 (i.e. Fortress) has shown that it can defend itself and take an enormous amount of punishment.[12]

Over the following two months the USAAF raids increased in both frequency and the number of heavy bombers involved. By late September 178 heavy bombers were stationed at seven airfields in eastern England.[13]

On 9 October a force of B-17s and Liberators bombed targets near Lille in north-eastern France. Exuberant claims were made of high numbers of German planes shot down and destroyed. Encouraging articles appeared in the American press. The *New York Mirror* wrote that 'the Lille raid established the American Flying Fortress and Liberator bombers are veritable battleships of the air, self-sufficient in both offence and defence ... the pursuit ship [the escort fighter] is becoming obsolescent and will be replaced. The bomber is no longer a clay pigeon to the fighter. The American strategy of high-level precision daylight bombing by crews coordinated as teams is justified.'[14]

The debate over daylight bombing continued throughout the remainder of 1942 and all of 1943. Portal had been frustrated at being denied the 512 American bombers that had originally been agreed in the Arnold-Portal Agreement during the Arcadia Conference earlier in the year. At the end of October Portal wrote to Sinclair, 'Far from dropping bombs on Germany, the American daylight bombers have not ventured beyond Lille ... the American public is led to believe a serious contribution is being made by the American Air Force. It is not for us to undeceive [sic] them. But there can be no doubt they will find out for themselves before very long.'[15]

Slessor was becoming increasingly optimistic over the daylight bombing issue. Together with other members of the Air Staff he wrote:

The view of the Air Staff is that the Americans and the RAF will be able to bomb Germany in daylight. Given sufficient strength to saturate their defences, they think it quite possible that our losses on the aggregate will be no heavier than by night and that the results combined with night attack should be doubly effective. No-one can say for certain until it has been tried – and tried repeatedly. It can, however, be said with confidence that it would be a mistake to try it prematurely, with insufficient numbers and with crews inadequately trained.[16]

Slessor was to admit later that he was unduly optimistic about the potential of unescorted daylight bombers. The heavy losses and failures of the Schweinfurt and Regensburg raids in October 1943 were to provide ample evidence of the daylight bombers' vulnerability to both flak and fighter attacks. In addition, however, no one in senior positions – including Spaatz, Portal and Slessor himself – could have predicted during 1942 and 1943 the vital role that the long-range, high-performance fighter would come to play in turning the tide. As addressed previously (see Chapter 4), during Operation Argument ('Big Week') in February 1944 and beyond, long-range USAAF fighters destroyed significant numbers of the Luftwaffe's fighter defence force. The official air war historians Charles Webster and Noble Frankland noted:

The peculiar irony of the situation was, however, that Sir Charles Portal, who had no confidence in the future of a long-range fighter, was pressing for the development of the [Rolls-Royce Merlin-powered] Mustang, which the Americans did not regard with favour. A further and perhaps even greater irony was introduced by the fact that Air Vice-Marshal Slessor, whose judgement of the prospects of the self-defending formation was almost as wrong as that of the Americans themselves, had by his advice rendered a service to the bombing offensive, which was of outstanding and perhaps even of decisive value.[17]

Despite all his misgivings, Churchill himself was early in recognizing the importance of the high-performance fighter. In a letter to Roosevelt on 16 September he remarked 'for keeping up and intensifying the pressure on Germany, the Fortress and the long-range fighter are indispensable'.[18]

Sinclair, too, had come to recognize the risks of an open debate with the Americans over daylight bombing. He understood that such a move would play into the hands of Admiral King and the US Navy, who might tempt the USAAF to focus on the Pacific theatre. Slessor's remarks had their effect and Sinclair made an important intervention, writing to Churchill as follows:

> Americans are much like other people – they prefer to learn from their own experience. In spite of some admitted defects – including the lack of expertise – their leadership is of a high order, and the quality of their aircrews is magnificent. If their policy of day bombing proves to their own satisfaction to be unsuccessful or prohibitively expensive they will abandon it and turn to night action ... they will not be convinced except by their own experience. With 4,000 to 6,000 bombers operating from this country we can pulverise German war industry and transport and bring the harvest of victory within the compass of such land forces as we shall have available in 1944.[19]

The differing Anglo-American views on grand strategy

On 9 March Brigadier General Dwight D. Eisenhower, head of the Operational Plans Division (OPD) of the United States Army, delivered a new plan that emphasized the need for a massive frontal assault from England to France either in September 1942 or April 1943.

This overly ambitious plan called for forty-eight army divisions, thirty American and eighteen British, supported by a combined force of 5,800 aircraft, of which 3,250 were to be American and 2,550 British. The plan, code-named Roundup, would be preceded by a military build-up phase in England known as Bolero. Many on the American side considered that there needed to be an early assault on Occupied Europe, rather than what they saw as wasteful and diversionary operations in North Africa and the Mediterranean. At an early stage of the Arcadia Conference in December 1941, General Arnold had his say on how the war should be won:

> I think the way to win the war is to hit Germany where it hurts most, where she is strongest – right across the Channel from England, using the shortest and most direct road to Berlin. We will have the air power to destroy her factories, communications, facilities, concentration of supplies, and to defeat her air force. We can then isolate, by bombing, any part of the coastline in the area we desire to use for landing troops. We will be able to secure command of the air and remove that threat from the troops making the landings.[20]

This view did not have support on the British side, primarily because of the timing. They were mindful of the high risks of failure. They had seen the mistakes made during the 1915 Gallipoli campaign and the inability to overcome the enemies' defences, and the consequent failure followed by evacuation. Both Slessor and Portal preferred an initial campaign in North Africa and the Mediterranean. Even before America's entry into the war Slessor wrote to Lord Trenchard in autumn 1941:

> Whether the Germans gain a military decision against Russia or whether (as now seems more probable) the Eastern Front settles down to a stalemate, it appears that the enemy must turn on us on the Mediterranean front. His last hope of defeating the British Empire is to turn us out of Egypt, seize West Africa, and the Atlantic bases of Casablanca and Dakar and turn the Mediterranean into an Axis lake, with the probable result that Japan will come into the war against us.[21]

Despite British reservations, the Americans continued to consider that an early and direct assault on 'Fortress Europe' represented the best strategy. Marshall and Stimson, the Secretary for War, presented the Bolero/Roundup plan to President Roosevelt, who approved it, making his support of the plan clear to the British. He sent General Marshall and Harry Hopkins, his chief aide, to London. They arrived on 8 April and presented their plan to the Chiefs of Staff. The British were polite, but they were also non-committal. Nonetheless, Slessor became involved in examining the plans.

One additional scenario envisioned a cross-channel raid known as Operation Sledgehammer to establish a bridgehead in an area between Boulogne and Le Havre. If successful, it would enable follow-up forces to achieve a breakout into western Europe should conditions prove favourable. Little consideration was given to military intelligence and the fact that the experienced and well-supplied German 15th Army, with strong air support, would be waiting for such a move. They would be in a dominant position to prevent any successful Allied operation during 1942 or 1943. As Slessor wrote, 'the War Office were extremely cagey about the whole idea'.[22] At that point in the war three key factors still needed to be fully addressed: first, the challenge of logistics and the transportation of American troops and matériel to Britain at a time of extreme U-boat danger during the Battle of the Atlantic; second, the training of sufficient troops to be ready for combat in less than a year; and third, the necessity to ensure Allied air supremacy over the battle space. But none of these pressing concerns dissuaded the Americans from promoting what became known as the 'Marshall Memorandum'.[23] Stalin was an additional factor. He agitated for a second front in western Europe to take the pressure off his beleaguered troops on the Eastern Front. The strategic disadvantage of delaying the opening of a Western Front centred on the possibility of Soviet defeat, for if the Soviets were knocked out of the war in 1942, Hitler could avoid fighting on two fronts. With memories of a similar situation occurring in 1917 during the First World War, both Churchill and Roosevelt were, therefore, eager to provide every assistance to ensure the Soviet Union was kept in the fight. In early June Roosevelt assured the Soviet Foreign Minister, Vyacheslav Molotov, who was on a visit to Washington, that he was committed to opening a second front in 1942.[24] Nothing came of these scenarios and, as Slessor later commented, 'the Russian situation improved, the idea of any kind of half-cock operation became less popular after the Dieppe raid, and by the end of the year I was minuting CAS that "I don't believe we need worry unduly about Stalin patching up a peace – unless we sit and do nothing for the next nine months preparing for a Roundup that shall anyway not be strong enough to launch [in 1943]'.[25]

Inevitably, by July no Anglo-American agreement had been reached on Sledgehammer. The British had listened politely and agreed to consider the operation *in principle*. Feeling that the British had reneged on previously agreed strategic decisions, General Marshall and Admiral Ernest J. King, the new Chief of Naval Operations, proposed that either London should reach an agreement on Sledgehammer or the United States should turn its main attention to the Pacific.[26] The proposal was, in effect, an ultimatum to its closest ally. Roosevelt recognized the political repercussions and in a terse memorandum he rejected their proposal, signing it simply 'Roosevelt, Commander-in-Chief'.[27] For a second time he sent Hopkins, Marshall and King back to London to reach agreement on either Sledgehammer or Operation Gymnast, the invasion of North Africa, that had originally been proposed in the opening sessions of the Arcadia Conference in December 1941.[28] However, Roosevelt also instructed them not to preclude the European Roundup option during 1943. Gymnast was renamed Torch, but there were continuing disagreements as to what the operation would entail, and when and where the landings in North Africa would occur. The Anglo-American Combined Chiefs of Staff continued to disagree about the future strategy. The American Joint Chiefs of Staff continued to demur over Torch, which would preclude Roundup.[29] The British Chiefs of Staff did not rule out Roundup, but they were more concerned about the time needed to prepare for a successful cross-Channel invasion (as described above). In the event Torch was agreed by the Combined Chiefs and was put into operation in early November. The chiefs were still at variance over their forward plans and matters were only resolved at the Casablanca Conference in January 1943.

The sudden change of American aircraft allocations to the RAF, April 1942

'In April', Slessor wrote, 'a horrid rumour circulated that it was the future President's policy that American aircraft would only be manned by American crews.'[30] The new policy would therefore affect the allocations to Britain of aircraft, and particularly the supply of heavy bombers that were part of the Arnold-Portal Agreement signed only three months earlier. Slessor had concluded correctly that this change had resulted from General Marshall's plans for Roundup and the requirement for the USAAF to have around 3,500 first-line aircraft to be based in England in early 1943, and ready for a cross-Channel invasion. It also meant that the RAF's plans for the build-up of its heavy bombers in 1942 would be directly affected.

In early May Air Marshal Douglas Evill, the RAF representative on the Combined Chiefs of Staff, discussed the planned reductions with General Arnold, who suggested that the RAF should only receive enough aircraft to maintain the numbers in squadrons already equipped with American aircraft. Two days later it was further proposed that all American heavy bomber production would be allocated to its own air forces after July 1942. Portal, Slessor and his Air Staff colleagues were shocked by this latest news and the direct effect it would now have on the RAF's bomber offensive strategy. It was now obvious to Slessor that there would be no change of attitude on the American side. As he wrote, 'Even Harry Hopkins [President Roosevelt's assistant] made no bones about the fact that both the Slessor and Arnold-Portal agreements must now be regarded as obsolete.'[31]

However, these changes had to be viewed in the context of the momentous changes that had occurred since the original Slessor Agreement of March 1941. First, the German invasion of the Soviet Union in June had changed the fundamental dimension of the war. Roosevelt had agreed with Stalin that

America would now provide war matériel including aircraft to the Soviet Air Force. Second, in December America had entered the war that would now involve them on two fronts: the Pacific and the European theatre of operations. This placed unexpected demands on the both the USAAF and US Naval Aviation. Slessor appreciated that now America was an active participant in the war, they would no longer be willing to subordinate the needs of their air forces to the extent that they had done before Pearl Harbor.

There was an additional problem. During early 1942 the massive ramping-up of American aircraft production was also running up against several organizational problems with consequent delays in reaching the planned production targets. The British were not now going to receive the numbers of heavy bombers considered critical to the RAF's bomber offensive against Germany. Instead, they were receiving fighters and light bombers which were, as Slessor wrote, 'a type that the RAF was least interested in'.[32]

On 24 May General Arnold and Admiral John Towers of the Bureau of US Naval Aviation arrived at Prestwick in Scotland. Slessor gauged Arnold's frame of mind at the time when he wrote, 'on seeing British B-24 Liberators parked up on their stands Arnold noted, "from my point of view too many planes were standing there when they were badly needed elsewhere"'.[33] Slessor commented that Arnold obviously considered these planes were not being used by the RAF, but he failed to appreciate that they were in the process of being modified with the installation of anti-submarine radar that would be critical in the Battle of the Atlantic.

United Nations Air Forces Conference and the Arnold-Towers-Portal Agreement, 26–31 May 1942

The first meeting of what was described as the 'United Nations Air Forces Conference' was convened in London on 26 May. Slessor was keen to push back on Arnold's revised proposal and to demonstrate the negative effect it would have on RAF strategy. Slessor wrote the opening remarks that were delivered by Churchill, who opened the proceedings by noting that America had a production capacity of 60,000 aircraft during the year, and he had difficulty understanding why an outstanding order for 5,000 aircraft for Britain should really prejudice the build-up of the USAAF. Arnold replied that the American public expected action from the USAAF in Europe now and consequently he could not continue with the Arnold-Portal Agreement. Furthermore, he told Churchill that existing production volumes could not yet meet the present allocation of aircraft not only to the USAAF, but also for the defence of the west coast of the United States, the US Navy, the Russians and the Chinese.

Over the next few days the British and American teams had further meetings to iron out the specifics on aircraft types and future aircraft allocations for the British during the second half of 1942. The RAF had to forgo its requirements for American heavy bombers apart from the Liberators that were earmarked for anti-submarine duties with Coastal Command. Portal met Arnold to agree a draft agreement that would be signed in Washington as the finalized agreement on 26 June.

The Arnold-Portal Agreement had scheduled the delivery to the British of 9,530 aircraft of all types during 1942. The RAF considered that the 589 heavy bombers were the most important part of the consignment. The Arnold-Towers-Portal (ATP) Agreement now revised those figures downwards. The RAF would receive 3,048 aircraft of all types during the second half of 1942, of which only fifty were heavy bombers (B-24 Liberators).

Slessor initially saw this as a serious setback for the strategic offensive. But as Webster and Frankland wrote in their official history of the bomber offensive against Germany:

> From the point of view of the strategic air offensive the question of who flew that aircraft was not important. What mattered was how many long-range bombers the Americans would produce and to what purpose they would apply them ... After 1942 it is no longer possible to follow the history of the British air offensive without repeated reference to the policy, operations and achievements of the United States Air Forces.[34]

In late May Portal sent Slessor to Washington as his representative to finalize the details of the ATP Agreement to conform with the established principles. He travelled with Arnold in his special USAAF Stratoliner, together with Averill Harriman, Major General Mark Clark, Vice Admiral Lord Louis Mountbatten and Brigadier Vivian Dykes. Travelling in the state-of-the-art luxury airliner was uneventful until they encountered extremely poor weather with almost zero visibility in the Washington DC area. Even Slessor, as a seasoned flier, found this a hair-raising experience. He wrote that 'it was as thick as pea soup right down to ground level'. He praised the very experienced pilot but commented that he gave at least one of his passengers a miserable five minutes. 'At one moment the dome of the Capitol appeared on the starboard side for a second out of the fog; at the next, one caught a glimpse of the top of the Washington Monument whizzing past our port wing tip ... I have seldom been more thankful to feel the wheels touch ground.'[35] Slessor was to spend three weeks finalizing the aircraft allocation arrangements for the second half of 1942. The ATP Agreement was finally signed off on 21 June.

The year 1942 proved to be a very uncertain one for the Allies. Transatlantic shipping was central to all logistical planning. Throughout the year a significant number of American cargo vessels in the Gulf of Mexico and on the eastern seaboard were sunk by U-boats in what their crews referred to as 'the happy time'. Between September and November U-boats were sinking Allied shipping in the Atlantic as fast as it was being produced. The Battle of the Atlantic continued to be finely poised. Earlier, in June, the British Eighth Army had received a serious setback in the western desert when Tobruk fell to Rommel's Afrika Corps. By mid-year the Germans had advanced deep into Soviet territory and the Allied leaders and military planners became concerned as to whether the Soviet Union would survive at all, or alternatively that there might be a military stalemate on that front. Either scenario would see large elements of the Luftwaffe being redeployed to the west during the winter of 1942/1943.

Consequently, in August President Roosevelt demanded an updated and revised plan to consider the requirements to defeat the Axis powers. The plan was known as Air War Plans Division/42 (AWPD/42) and argued for simultaneous air offensives against both Germany and Japan. However, the plan recognized that, with the resources available, priority would be given to the offensive against Germany. The USAAF would concentrate on the 'systematic destruction of the German military and industrial machine through precision bombing in daylight. AWPD's baseline assumption relied on 139,000 aircraft being produced in 1943.'[36]

Towards the end of the year the tide was turning in favour of the Allies. In western Egypt the British finally won a decisive victory on 8 November in the Second Battle of El Alamein. They had now eliminated the threat of the Axis powers gaining control of Egypt and beyond into the Middle East. On the same day Operation Torch saw the Allied invasion of Vichy-held areas of North Africa with landing points in Vichy-controlled French Morocco and Algeria. Later that month the Red Army launched Operation Uranus, which led to the encirclement and eventual defeat of the German 6th Army at Stalingrad. In the southwest Pacific Allied forces, predominantly US Marines, were succeeding in retaking the Solomon Islands and Guadalcanal.[37]

The lead-up to the Casablanca Conference, September 1942–January 1943

In late September Portal produced and submitted a note which Slessor wrote 'is one of the best I can remember'.[38] Portal now considered that the time had come when the Anglo-American allies had to choose a clearly defined plan, and not to be deflected by something unexpected cropping up. There were sharp differences between the British and Americans on what, why and how to prosecute the war against the Axis powers. There was a strong body of opinion amongst politicians, military commanders (such as General MacArthur and Admiral King) and the public for far greater efforts to be deployed in the Pacific. The respective air forces debated whether to bomb Germany at night or in daylight. Politicians and military commanders continued to argue as to whether to mount an early frontal assault on Fortress Europe in 1943, as defined by Bolero and/or Sledgehammer, or initially to adopt a more peripheral plan that would see amphibious landings in the Mediterranean as a precursor to attacking what Churchill and others had described as the 'soft underbelly of Europe', with advances into Italy or through the Balkans. It was in this period of multiple strategic choices that Roosevelt and Churchill, with their respective Chiefs of Staff and senior military commanders, would meet at Casablanca to agree and decide the future course of the war.

Portal considered three separate policies:

Course A – the build-up of forces (as in Bolero) to get a decision by invasion *before* German industry and economic power had been broken;
Course B – to shatter resistance by air and then put in the Army (i.e. the Anglo-American Combined Bomber Offensive (CBO) followed by invasion (Overlord);[39] and
Course C – a compromise under which the Allies would build up strong land and air forces but, on a scale, unrelated to any particular task, without any clear intention of attaining a definite objective by a definite time.

Both Slessor and Portal, and ultimately the British Chiefs of Staff, favoured Course B. Portal considered that a bombing offensive would require a combined Anglo-American force of between 4,000 and 6,000 heavy bombers. But he was also concerned that divergent views in the upcoming Casablanca talks might well lead to Course C, with compromises having to be made and with inevitable delays to achieving victory. Portal's Course B proposal was to form the basis of the highly significant Casablanca Directive on the Bomber Offensive.[40]

Slessor had been Assistant Chief of the Air Staff (Policy) for only six months when he was informed that he was going to take over as Commander-in-Chief of Coastal Command from Air Marshal Sir Philip Joubert. However, before that move Portal wanted Slessor to travel to Washington to take part in the next phase of Lend-Lease negotiations and agreeing the allocation of aircraft for Britain during 1943. Slessor wrote, 'we had the usual tough bargaining, but the Americans met us with their customary friendliness'.[41] At the end of November Slessor was back in Britain.

For a second time Portal delayed Slessor's move to Coastal Command. He now wanted Slessor to accompany him to a major Anglo-American high-level meeting. Portal clearly valued Slessor's proven negotiating and diplomatic skills with his opposite numbers within the USAAF and he was 'so to speak, an American interpreter'.[42] Slessor commented that the truth of 'two great peoples divided by a common language' was certainly not a flippant remark. Slessor knew Americans well and was attuned to interpreting their manner-isms, plus the subtle differences and nuances of language, for his British colleagues, many of whom were unacquainted with American ways. Richard Overy, the British military air historian, considered that Portal picked Slessor because of his extensive planning experience and that 'he was a sociable air force diplomat'.[43] It was significant that Portal left Air Marshal Arthur Harris, Commander-in-Chief of Bomber Command, out of the forthcoming pro-ceedings, noting 'his bluntness would have been out of place in the delicate discussions to follow'.[44]

The Casablanca Conference, 14–24 January 1943

Slessor left RAF Lyneham in Wiltshire on an overnight flight on 11/12 Jan-uary. The destination was not disclosed before he arrived to board the flight and a friend in London had lent him her hot water bottle, because it would be cold in Iceland at that time of year! Slessor found he would be travelling in a converted B-24 Liberator bomber. It was a sharp contrast after the luxury of travelling in Stratoliners. Slessor complained that it was 'not a very comfort-able conveyance for very senior officers'.[45] Slessor's fellow passengers included Sir Dudley Pound, Sir Alan Brooke, and Lord Louis 'Dickie' Mountbatten. On arrival in Casablanca Slessor commented that the weather was warm and sunny – 'a pleasant change from blacked-out London in January'.[46]

The Conference was held at the Anfa hotel complex in a Casablanca suburb. Prior to the talks, the American military had secured an area that contained the large hotel and several large villas, two of which would be occupied by the President and the Prime Minister. The secured area was referred as the Anfa Camp. Slessor was accommodated in the hotel, which he considered ugly, but with the redeeming features that it at least contained a large meeting room with windows down one side, and gardens.

The British and American Chiefs of Staff arrived at Casablanca with con-siderable issues remaining on how to pursue an agreed grand strategy. First, there was a considerable difference of opinion regarding the concentration of effort to be applied in Europe versus the Pacific. The British Chiefs of Staff were unanimous in putting maximum effort and priority into the defeat of Germany. American military leaders such as Admiral Ernest King were strong advocates for an earlier effort being applied in the Pacific and against Japan. Second, whether to attack Germany at the earliest opportunity with an early frontal assault in a cross-Channel invasion (Roundup) as advocated by General Marshall, or whether to apply a more oblique or peripheral approach. This indirect strategy was favoured by the British Chiefs of Staff and would involve clearing the Axis from the Mediterranean, to be followed up by amphibious landings in Italy or the Balkans. Third, whether the USAAF should bomb Germany in daylight raids or alternatively join the British in their night bombing offensive.

With these considerable differences between them, the British and American Chiefs of Staff and their supporting staffs met between 14 and 18 January to seek out a common position on the future grand strategy. At times the meetings were fraught, with Admiral King stating that the war against Japan was absorbing only about 15 per cent of the Allied effort, and later objecting that any action in the Pacific was being construed as interfering with the defeat of Germany. For the British, General Alan Brooke, Chairman and Chief of the Imperial General Staff, continued to emphasize the need to defeat Germany first, but the British were certainly not opposed to action in the Pacific. At the end of the discussions on 17 January Brooke wrote in his diary 'What a desperate day! We are further away from obtaining an agreement than ever we were.'[47]

On the morning of 18 January the Combined Chiefs of Staff continued to be divided on the key issue: the amount of effort to be applied in the Pacific and European theatres of operation. General Marshall continued to press for 'vigorous action in the Pacific'. He went on to state that in his opinion 'the British Chiefs of Staff wished to be certain that we keep the enemy engaged in the Mediterranean and at the same time maintain a sufficient force in the United Kingdom to take advantage of a crack in the German strength either from withdrawal of their forces from France or because of lowered morale'. He implied that 'the British Chiefs of Staff would maintain such a force in the United Kingdom dormant and awaiting an opportunity rather than have it utilized in a sustained attack elsewhere. The United States Chiefs of Staff considered that they can use these forces offensively in the Pacific Theatre.'[48] General Brooke continued to emphasize the importance of defeating Germany first, but said that it should not preclude action now in the Pacific and Southeast Asia. Admiral King asserted it could be construed that any action in the Pacific would be represented as interfering with the defeat of Germany. After three days of discussions the Combined Chiefs were as far apart as ever. Worse still, they were scheduled to meet the President and Prime Minister at 5pm that day with the intention of presenting a unified strategic plan. Just prior to the lunch break Field Marshal Sir John Dill asked Slessor what he thought the chances were of agreement being concluded. Slessor felt the outlook for agreement was 'pretty bleak'.[49] But Dill knew the American Chiefs of Staff well, from his time as Chief of the British Joint Staff Mission in Washington from the end of 1941. He considered that the real positions were not so far apart, and that the underlying problem came down to mutual suspicion.[50] The Americans believed that the British did not care about Japan and were solely interested in the defeat of Germany, whereas the British felt the Americans were starting to waver on the agreed principle of 'Germany First'. But the suspicions were unfounded. The British saw that dealing with the threat posed by Japan was critical to stability in the Pacific and Southeast Asia – and, it should be added, to the British Empire. Over the past year the British had lost Malaya, Hong Kong and Singapore. General Marshall had already restated the American commitment to the 'Germany First' priority in his opening remarks on 14 January. In his words the allocation of effort was 70 per cent to the European theatre and 30 per cent to the Pacific theatre.[51]

After lunch Slessor went up to the hotel's roof terrace, where he started scribbling the draft of a memorandum in his small notebook which he thought might 'bridge the gaps' between the opposing points of view (cf. p. 5). As he wrote, 'the Pacific hurdle was jumped by the words':

> Operations in the Pacific and Far East shall continue with the forces allocated (by the Combined Chiefs of Staff) with the object of maintaining pressure on Japan, retaining the initiative and attaining a position of readiness for the full-scale offensive against Japan by the United Nations as soon as Germany is defeated. These operations must be kept within such limits as will not, in the opinion of the Combined Chiefs of Staff, prejudice the capacity of the United Nations to take any favourable opportunity that may present itself for the decisive defeat of Germany in 1943.[52]

Slessor's incisive analysis of the issues and finding the form of words in a truly short period of time to 'bridge the gaps' was a measure of his intellectual capabilities, his understanding of the strategic sensibilities and imperatives of both sides, and his ability to couch mutual needs in words that would be nigh impossible to gainsay. It was the point at which the strategy logjam that had built up between the Combined Chiefs was finally eliminated. Later he wrote modestly and unconvincingly that 'anyone with the necessary training and experience could have done it'. The memorandum went on to address specific planned operations in the Far East and the Southwest Pacific, in addition to addressing the issues in the European theatre of operations.

Slessor showed his handwritten notes to Portal, who altered a few words and considered it 'might do the trick'. Four copies of the draft memorandum were hurriedly typed up by Portal's personal staff officer, Squadron Leader George Wiles. These copies were circulated to the Combined Chiefs of Staff. A few amendments were made with paragraphs that addressed the priority of defeating the U-boat menace which remained the first charge on resources, and insisted that the supply of war matériel to Russia must continue. General Marshall said the US Chiefs were prepared to accept it. The Chiefs of Staff used the memorandum in their discussions with Roosevelt and Churchill at their evening meeting that day.

The remaining Combined Chiefs of Staff meetings during the following days of the Conference proceeded smoothly, with discussions on clearing North Africa of Axis forces over the ensuing months. Agreement was reached to launch Anglo-American amphibious landings in Sicily during July, known through the codename Operation Husky. The deployment of forces for Husky would now lead to a deferment of the cross-Channel invasion of Europe until 1944.

Having achieved agreement on the broad issues of strategy, the Combined Chiefs of Staff moved on to address the strategic bombing offensive in Europe. Sharp differences remained on the advisability of the Americans embarking on a daylight bombing offensive over Germany in 1943. Both Churchill and Portal had the deepest reservations, thinking it probable that the campaign would end in failure. Slessor, however, continued to consider that daylight bombing might well succeed once the Americans had enough aircraft.

General Arnold was not deterred by British negativity. He was convinced that the USAAF's counterforce strategy against Germany's vital war industries would succeed. The target sets were detailed in their recently completed plan, AWPD/42. Portal informed Arnold that he had read the plan 'with interest'.[53] Arnold was probably irritated by what he considered to be a patronizing comment. He complained to his fellow American commanders that in his view the British seemed incapable of thinking in global strategic terms, but 'simply chased the next operation'.[54] This was never the case. However, Arnold insisted that the Combined Chiefs of Staff should draft a priority bombing programme for review and agreement. In the meantime Arnold was committed to 'selling' the daylight campaign to Churchill. They had lunch together on 19 January 1943, and on the following day a further short presentation was given to Churchill by Ira Eaker, the commanding general of the Eighth Air Force's Bomber Command. Churchill listened with interest and finally said that he was willing for them to 'give it a trial'. Years later Arnold wrote 'that it was a great relief to me and my command. We had won a major victory, for we could bomb in accordance with American principles, using methods for which the planes were designed.'[55] At a meeting later that evening President Roosevelt and General Marshall gave their approval for the daylight campaign.

Slessor was then instructed to draft a directive that finally set out the objectives of the bombing offensive and agreed the position of bombing by both day and night. This was to become known as the 'Casablanca Directive'. The most important part of the directive is contained in the first paragraph:

> Your primary object will be the progressive destruction and dislocation of the German military, industrial and economic system, and the undermining of the morale of the German people to a point where armed resistance is fatally weakened.[56]

The directive then continued to describe the priority targets, and under paragraph 5 it stated: 'You should take every opportunity to attack Germany by day, to destroy objectives that are unsuitable for night attack' (see Appendix D for the full text of the Directive).

Slessor was to write later that 'it was in fact a policy, not an operational directive'. At the Thunderbolt Conference held at the RAF School of Air Support at Old Sarum in Wiltshire during August 1947 to examine the Bomber Offensive, Slessor pointed out that 'the much criticised directive was the first to define an agreed combined offensive that was signed off by both the British and American Chiefs of Staff and to establish a set of priorities', adding rather poetically that 'the milk was in the coconut' when describing the importance of the first few lines that stated the primary objective. 'All the other stuff that went in at the bottom had to be put in so that Allied agreement could be achieved on something important.'[57] As the official history stated, the directive did not seek to reconcile the different perspectives, but simply accepted them all. It was too broad in scope, but at least it resolved conflicts between services, let alone the national objectives.[58] Slessor's drafting of the 'directive' demonstrated his ability to write a diplomatic policy document that satisfied the various national and service positions, but also ensured that Germany remained the number one priority; that the Americans could proceed with their daylight campaign; and that the RAF and USAAF could proceed with varying bombing policies.

Slessor also wrote after the war that there had been no little misunderstanding about the object underlying the Casablanca Directive. Some have tried to make out that its intention was to bring about the defeat of Germany by bombing alone. Both Slessor and Portal expressly disclaimed any such idea at the time of the Casablanca Conference.[59] That said, Slessor did not believe 'that there was the slightest hope of establishing great armies ashore, over-running Germany, and defeating the Wehrmacht on land, until German resistance had been softened up from the air,' adding, 'As far as I am aware, no one on the Air Staff then imagined that Germany could be forced to surrender by air power alone.'[60]

Chapter 11

Victory over the Atlantic

Commander-in-Chief, Coastal Command,
February 1943–January 1944

In the first days of the Casablanca Conference the Combined Chiefs of Staff received reports of the sinking of seven of the nine tankers that were en route from Trinidad to Gibraltar as Convoy TM1, sailing with much-needed fuel supplies for the American forces in North Africa.[1] The convoy did not have sufficient escort protection, but its loss came as a shock to the Chiefs. The critical loss of fuel underlined the widespread threat of the U-boat menace in the Atlantic and the urgent need for a solution. The Chiefs presented their report at the first plenary session on 23 January; its first sentence read: 'the defeat of the U-boat must remain as the first charge of the resources of the United Nations'.[2]

Within two weeks of attending the Conference, Slessor had been promoted to the rank of air marshal (acting) and had taken up his post as Commander-in-Chief of Coastal Command,[3] headquartered at Northwood, 15 miles north-west of central London. Slessor was acutely aware of the top agenda item resulting from the conference, and he was now keen to ensure that this priority objective was met. He himself wrote years later that 'it was my great good fortune to hold this interesting command throughout the peak year of the Battle of the Atlantic',[4] in which 219 U-boats in total were destroyed by Allied action, in contrast to 81 in 1942 and 178 in 1944. This was to be his second wartime command and a notable contrast to his first as commander of 5 Group, Bomber Command. Whereas his time at 5 Group involved the frustration of operating with obsolescent or underpowered aircraft, at Coastal Command Slessor was now in charge of sixty squadrons of 850 aircraft of varying types.

The maritime roles ranged from anti-submarine operations through to fighter and torpedo strike, reconnaissance, air-sea rescue and meteorological operations. Inevitably, the primary role of Coastal Command during 1943 was anti-submarine warfare. Thirty-four squadrons, comprising 430 aircraft, were dedicated to anti-submarine operations through either convoy escort duty or their solo hunter-killer role in seeking and destroying U-boats in the North Atlantic. In writing about Slessor's role at Coastal Command, the British aviation historian John Terraine remarked that:

> in his eleven-month period he brought new energy and drive, a fierce aggressiveness which communicated itself to his crews and may be summed up in the definable, but always recognizable quality, leadership. This Slessor undoubtedly possessed to a degree that the more intellectual Joubert [his immediate predecessor] did not, and it was felt not only in the Command, but by his naval colleagues, by the Air Ministry, and by the U-boats.[5]

But Slessor was the first to respect the fact that he had inherited a 'definitely going concern' from his wartime predecessors at the Command: Frederick Bowhill and Philip Joubert de la Ferté.

Coastal Command, 1939–1942

At the start of the war Coastal Command had no strategy to deal with U-boats, and its principal aircraft was the Avro Anson, a short-range aircraft incapable of patrolling the vast North Atlantic sea-lanes. In addition, it had neither a dedicated detection system nor any effective ordnance to attack German submarines. The Royal Navy confidently believed that it alone could handle the U-boat menace with convoy protection, ASDIC (sonar) and depth charges. But so far the Navy had failed to stop the U-boat menace; however, over the next thirty-six months the situation was to change rapidly as Coastal Command concentrated on the development of technological aids, effective ordnance, operational research, training, and larger and longer-range aircraft. Even so, Coastal continued to be the RAF's 'Cinderella' Command throughout much of that period. Both Bowhill and later Joubert argued valiantly for more resources against strong resistance at the Air Ministry. In December 1940, after grievous shipping losses to U-boat attacks, Lord Beaverbrook, no friend of the Air Ministry, commented that 'the conditions of Coastal Command are a grave reflection on the Air Ministry which starves it of equipment and has not given it the right type of aircraft'. A proposal to transfer Coastal Command *en bloc* to the Royal Navy was made.[6] This idea had been proposed by Beaverbrook, Mr A.V. Alexander, the First Sea Lord, and Admiral Sir Roger Keyes but Churchill was unimpressed and at a War Cabinet meeting stated clearly that such a move 'would be disastrous to tear a large fragment out of the RAF. This is not a time for service rivalry.'[7] The aviation historian John Buckley wrote that 'Jack Slessor squarely blamed the whole fracas on

Beaverbrook's crass ignorance of air or sea warfare which was only excelled by the unsoundness of his judgement on anything connected with the conduct of war.'[8] But Churchill continued to be highly concerned during this early period of the war, writing later that 'the only thing that ever really frightened me during the war was the U-boat peril'. He pondered, 'How much would the U-boat warfare reduce our imports and shipping? ... Either the food supplies, and arms from the New World and from the British Empire arrived across the oceans, or they failed.'[9]

Coastal Command's evolving anti-submarine strategy, 1940–1942

Coastal Command's anti-submarine doctrine evolved through developments in technology, the application of operational research and the combat experience gained in the three years from the beginning of 1940 to the end of 1942. During that time considerable advances had been made in three key areas: armaments, the use of searchlights in night-time operations, and radar surveillance.

The RAF had worked on the development of an anti-submarine bomb during the 1930s. However, when attacks were made, they were found to be completely useless.[10] Fortunately, close collaboration between the Admiralty and the Air Ministry in December 1939 led to the use of air-launched depth charges. Initially, 450lb modified charges were used, but the results were disappointing. The Navy's operational research unit section then became involved. They analysed the results of over 300 attacks and concluded that the use of a smaller 250lb charge was more effective, particularly if they were released in an array with a stick spacing of 100ft. This configuration was found to be the optimum method of either achieving an outright kill, or at least inflicting serious damage on the submarine. The more powerful Torpex explosive was introduced in 1942, and from that time onwards air-launched depth charges were responsible for the destruction of many U-boats in the latter years of the war.[11]

During the first U-boat campaign between 1940 and mid-1941, it became obvious that U-boat packs tended to attack on the surface and under the cover of darkness. At that time Coastal Command did not have the means of detecting U-boats other than by eyesight in daylight hours. Several options were considered that centred on the use of either searchlights or star shells. One of Bowhill's squadron leaders, Humphrey de Verd Leigh, had developed a powerful searchlight that could be mounted on the underside of an aircraft's wing. It became known as the Leigh Light. During 1940 and 1941 other searchlight options were under consideration and were undergoing evaluation. When Joubert became Commander-in-Chief of Coastal Command in June 1941, he was distinctly unimpressed by Leigh's searchlight and told him to stop any further work on its development. However, it proved to be superior to other searchlights and so was eventually reconsidered by Joubert as a viable option. He changed his mind and became a strong supporter of the installation of Leigh Lights on the Command's aircraft. The Leigh Light came into operational service in 1942 and the first night-time U-boat kill was made by a Wellington bomber in July of that year.[12]

Joubert had been appointed with the specific objective of building up the technological side of the Command. Having been Assistant Chief of the Air Staff (Radio) at the Air Ministry, he was familiar with radar developments and their application to maritime surveillance. The innovative system relied on cavity magnetron diode technology and was then developed as an airborne radar aid for both navigation and bombing. The land-based surveillance version was known as H2S. The maritime equivalent was known as air-to-surface vessel radar (ASV). Initially, Joubert found that the aircrews were using ASV strictly as a navigation aid, so he formed an operational research team at Coastal Command to investigate how ASV could be enhanced as a U-boat detection tool. Aircrews were then trained to rely solely on their ASV radar sets for the detection of U-boats.[13]

The British had one key additional advantage. ULTRA was the codename given to British Military Intelligence at the Government Cipher School located at Bletchley Park in Buckinghamshire. With the help of captured German naval codebooks, the cryptologists had broken the German naval cipher earlier in the war and could follow the details of U-boat activities until early 1942. Unfortunately, at that point the German Navy added a fourth rotor to their Enigma encoding/decoding machines. During a period of ten months from February to early December of that year the Bletchley Park team were unable to decipher and read U-boat signals traffic. Fortunately, on 30 October 1942 a patrol aircraft from 47 Squadron spotted a U-boat 70 miles north of the Nile Delta and attacked with depth charges, signalling its position back to the Royal Navy, which diverted a destroyer group to continue the hunt. After bringing the U-boat to the surface, personnel from HMS *Petard* captured highly valuable material from U-boat *U-559* shortly before it sank. The material included codebooks and lists of the Enigma key settings for all U-boats in use at that time. This material helped to enable Bletchley's cipher team finally to break the supposedly unbreakable German naval cipher. Over the first few months of 1943 ULTRA could now provide an increased volume of decrypted signals traffic that revealed the disposition and activities of the U-boats in the North Atlantic. As John Terraine wrote, 'the significance of this victory was very great – indeed so great that some historians have seen in it virtually the whole explanation of the victory over the U-boats'.[14] Although this claim is probably an overstatement, this breakthrough provided 'operational intelligence about the departure and return of U-boats to their Biscay ports; the numbers and types of U-boats at sea; and the movement and disposition of their patrols'.[15] Importantly, it also eventually revealed evidence of the declining state of morale amongst the U-boat crews in the North Atlantic.

Disagreements on aircraft priorities: the North Atlantic air gap, 1942

One of the main killing zones for U-boats in the central North Atlantic was known as 'The Gap', an area several hundred miles wide that extended south from the southern point of Greenland and was beyond the range of the existing fleet of aircraft operated by Coastal Command and the US Navy. During 1942 and the early part of 1943 most of the shipping losses in the convoys occurred in the Gap. It therefore became crucial to mount longer-range air patrols in order to close the Gap at the earliest opportunity. One of the key aircraft capable of fulfilling that task was the very long-range (VLR) B-24 Liberator maritime variant, designed by the Consolidated Aircraft Corporation, which Slessor described as the *Prima Donna* of Coastal Command.[16] While the American B-24 Liberator was originally designed as a heavy bomber, Consolidated modified it for a long-range anti-submarine role by eliminating some heavy components such as armour plating, the ventral gun turret and its self-sealing fuel tanks. This modification gave the aircraft an operating range of 2,400 miles, and thus the ability to patrol, or loiter, over the Gap for three hours.

During 1942 it became increasingly obvious that the VLR Liberator aircraft were urgently needed to escort convoys in remote areas of the North Atlantic. In May, however, Coastal Command was informed that it would have to operate with its existing aircraft until 1943. Both the Admiralty and Coastal Command were dismayed. Most of the shipping was being sunk in the Gap, and the U-boats understood that this remained the safest area for them to carry out their attacks.

Both Portal and Air Marshal Harris had always been strong advocates for the Bomber Offensive against Germany. They had considerable influence on Churchill and the War Cabinet in giving the Bomber Offensive the top priority. In June 1942 Harris was certainly no supporter of Coastal Command and he complained to Churchill that Bomber Command was being drained

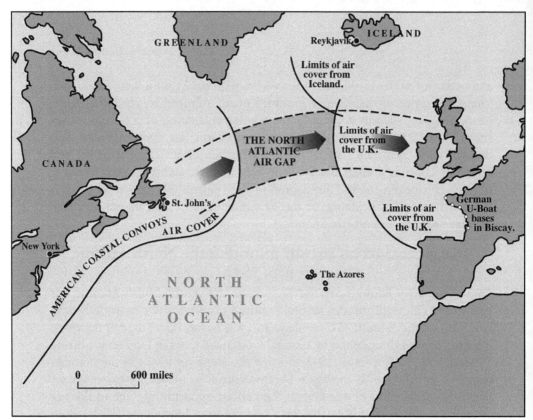

Air cover for North Atlantic convoy routes, August 1942. (Adapted from S.W. Roskill, *War at Sea*, HMSO, 1956, p. 204.)

'in order to bolster the already over swollen establishment of the purely defensive command'.[17] Despite Churchill's constant fear of losing the Battle of the Atlantic, he regularly sought ways of deferring the allocation of Liberators to Coastal Command. These views persisted throughout most of 1942, even after the publication of the Singleton Report in May.[18] That report concluded that unless the U-boat threat was addressed, Britain would collapse from marine trade strangulation long before the Bomber Offensive stood any chance of strategic success.[19]

During mid-June the British Chiefs of Staff requested that Rear Admiral Brind and Air Vice-Marshal Slessor ACAS (Policy) address the issue and recommend a solution. In their report they concluded that fifty-four long-range aircraft were required for operations in the Western Approaches and the Bay of Biscay, in addition to providing support for the Home Fleet; a further seventy-two long-range reconnaissance aircraft and two squadrons of thirty-six Lancaster bombers should be seconded from Bomber Command to Coastal Command on a temporary basis. These recommendations were promptly rejected by Portal.[20]

Reputed to be one of the greatest portrait photographers of the twentieth century, Yousef Karsh took this picture of Jack Slessor on 24 July 1954, nineteen months after he had retired from the RAF.

(*Above left*) Jack aged 3 months with his mother Adelaide, Ranikhet, India, 1897.

(*Right*) Jack with his father Arthur and younger brother Rodney, England, 1903; the youngest brother, Anthony, was born in the following year.

(*Above right*) John Cotesworth Slessor at Haileybury, aged 14, summer term, 1911.

lessor received his Fédération Aéronautique Internationale (FAI) aviator's certificate in 1915 after flying solo for only ninety minutes.

Jack flying at 4,000 feet, Heliopolis, Egypt, January 1916. This photograph was taken by Jack's observer, Cuthbert 'Turps' Orde.

BE2C with camera fitted.

'Lieut. J. C. Slessor, R.F.C., Wounded', excerpt from *The Draconian*, the journal of the Dragon School, Oxford, 1916. Photograph taken, prior to his service with 23, 17 and 4 Squadrons, wearing a RFC tunic showing his 2nd lieutenant's rank.

The flight commanders of 5 Squadron at Acq, near Arras, Western Front, 1917. Left to right: Captain Smart, Slessor, Captain Illingworth.

(*Left*) Slessor's self-portrait, France, 1917. Soigné and debonair, Jack Slessor's élan attracted many but could provoke jealousy. (*Right*) Doodles from flying logbook, Western Front.

Hermione Carter (née Guinness), in her widow's weeds, 1920. Hermione and Jack married in 1923, on his return from India.

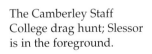

The Camberley Staff College drag hunt; Slessor is in the foreground.

A Wapiti IIA in 1937 over Shaktu, Waziristan, 150 miles northeast of the RAF air base at Quetta.

A Forward Operating Base of Wapitis at Gilgit desert strip, Kashmir.

A Forward Air Control
(FAC) party, Waziristan.
Slessor is standing on the
right.

Slessor was appointed Air
ADC (aide-de-camp) to
King George VI on
1 March 1939.

Air Officer Commanding 5 Group, Bomber Command, 1941.

A Handley Page Hampden of 5 Group. The Hampden, although still in service in 1941, was obsolescent.

Air Officer Commander-in-Chief, Coastal Command, 1943.

Battle of the Atlantic: Slessor with Captain D.V. Peyton-Ward RN at Northwood HQ, 1943.

onsolidated B-24 VLR Liberators at Aldergrove, Northern Ireland, 1943. (RAF Museum, Hendon)

A press photograph of Slessor with US General Ira Eaker, Mediterranean Allied Air Forces, 1944

Close air support. French troops are passing the wreck of a German column spotted by Allied airmen and destroyed by combined air/artillery on the Esperia defile as part of Operation Diadem, late May/early June 1944. (Andrew Brookes, *Air War over Italy*, p. 107)

ir interdiction. The result of an Allied air attack near Florence in July 1944. (Andrew Brookes, *r War over Italy*, p. 110).

Balkan Air Force Spitfire, based in Southern Italy, 1944. (© IWM, GOV CNA 3096)

Air Marshal Sir John Slessor with his family in 1945: his wife Hermione, their son John, and their daughter Juliet during her engagement to Lieutenant Colonel Jack Price DSO, MC, commanding officer of the 9th Lancers.

Slessor with Trenchard, 17 September 1950.

The V Force bombers. Bottom left to top right: Vulcan, Valiant, Victor. (© IWM, GOV CNA 9361).

...essor with his son, John, at the Queen's presentation of a new standard to 83 Squadron ...ulcans), Scampton, 1963.

Slessor's annotation on the back of the photograph: 'God knows when or where.'

In late October the War Cabinet, chaired by Churchill, met to discuss the dilemma. The conclusion was the same: 'in spite of the U-boat losses [sic] the bomber offensive should have first place'.[21] During the following month eighty-three ships (508,780 tons) were sunk, mostly in the Atlantic Gap. It was the critical wake-up call. Both Churchill and Portal finally relented and affirmed that priority should now be given to the protection of the convoys. At the newly convened Anti-U-boat Committee, Joubert pointed out that forty VLR Liberators would be sufficient to close the Gap and that, deployed earlier, they would have prevented, or at least reduced, shipping losses.[22] As the naval historian Marc Milner wrote, 'the Air Gap was the problem, and its elimination would have put an end to the wolf pack attack with or without ULTRA'.[23] However, it still would be a further six months before that objective was met.

Slessor's strategy for Coastal Command

When Slessor arrived at Coastal Command in February, he was confronted by the fact that the Germans had deployed over a hundred U-boats in the North Atlantic. But in considering the Atlantic as one battlefield, Slessor emphasized the point that the Allies had more than enough long-range anti-submarine aircraft but they had to be deployed 'in sufficient numbers, in the right place'.[24] Slessor also recognized that the only way to ensure the safe and timely arrival of shipping was to destroy the U-boats while they were at sea.

In the first months of his time at Coastal Command Slessor focused on two critical areas: the Air Gap where VLR Liberators could now be deployed and an area of the Bay of Biscay through which U-boats transited to and from their home ports. This area became known simply as 'the Bay'.

There was no shortcut to success by bombing the enemy's bases or build-ing yards, and, as Slessor wrote, 'you had to kill him at sea, or he would kill you'.[25] To underline his point, the early strategy of bombing the U-boat ports had not succeeded in stopping the U-boat menace. On the opening day of the Casablanca Conference in January 1943, Air Marshal Arthur Harris, Commander-in-Chief of Bomber Command, received a directive from the Air Ministry that specified raids on the U-boat home ports in western France: Lorient, St Nazaire, Brest and La Pallice. Over the following three months 3,056 bomber sorties were carried out and 4,178 high-explosive bombs were dropped. The roofs of the U-boat pens were constructed with 16ft of rein-forced concrete and exploding bombs made only slight indentations on their surfaces.[26] Photographic evidence of post-raid assessments revealed that the bombing destroyed most of the towns, with a significant loss of French civilian lives. Seventy-one Allied aircraft were lost, and further raids were called off altogether in April.

Only the appalling weather in the North Atlantic during January and February 1943 had protected the escorted convoys from U-boat attacks. March was a bad month. Seventeen convoys were attacked, with the loss of eighty-two ships and cargoes amounting to 500,000 tons.[27] However, despite the gloomy statistics, the Battle of the Atlantic was already starting to move in the Allies' favour. At Coastal Command Slessor had three distinct advantages: first, the introduction of longer-range centimetric radar, known as LRASVIII, which could detect convoys at 40 miles.[28] More critically, it could detect surfaced U-boats at 12 miles.[29] Whereas earlier versions of airborne radar could also be detected by the U-boats, for nearly eight months of 1943 the U-boats had no way of detecting its use by Coastal Command's aircraft. The element of surprise was key to the destruction of surfaced U-boats. Second, the increased use of high-frequency direction-finding (HF/DF), known to radio operators as 'Huff-Duff', was being used increasingly on the escort warships to detect the presence and location of U-boats in the vicinity of convoys. And finally, the third advantage was the increase in the number of VLR Liberators used for escorting convoys. Effectively, these factors together closed 'the Gap' in May of that year.

Offensive action in the Bay, April–August 1943

Plans to attack U-boats transiting the Bay had originally been suggested by Joubert. However, during his time in the Command, he had neither available aircraft nor LRASVIII radar. After Slessor took over the Command, he benefited from an increased number of aircraft, effective armaments, more effective search radar and more of the night-time Leigh Lights. In April he wrote to the Combined Chiefs of Staff:

> the Bay is the trunk of the Atlantic U-boat menace, the roots being the Biscay ports and the branches spreading far and wide, to the North Atlantic convoys, to the Caribbean, to the eastern seaboard of North America, and to the sea lanes where the faster merchant ships sail without escort.[30]

It was in this area of the Bay of Biscay that 120 U-boats were transiting each month to and from their Biscay ports and out into the North Atlantic. The U-boat transit area of focus in the Bay covered an area of 36,000 square miles, to which were allocated 150 aircraft actively engaged in what became known as the Bay Offensive. Over the period of those five months Coastal Command destroyed twenty-five U-boats in the Bay.

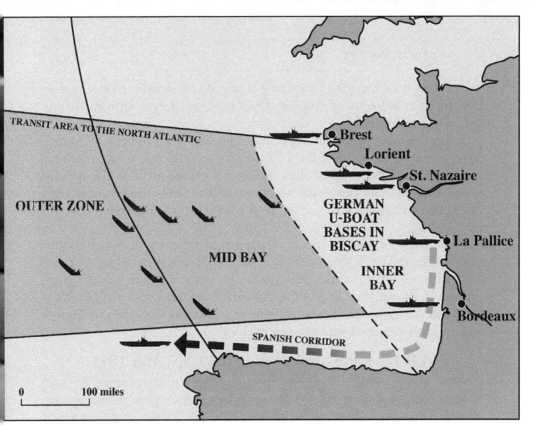

Slessor's initial Bay Offensive, May 1943. Eight U-boats were sunk between February and May 1943, but by early August, a total of twenty-five U-boats had been sunk by Coastal Command in the Bay. Patrol aircraft deployed: (Mid Bay) Whitleys, Wellingtons and Hudsons; (Outer Zone) Sunderlands, Catalinas and B24 Liberators. (Modified from S.W. Roskill, *The War at Sea*, HMSO, 1956, p. 368.)

Slessor described the Bay Offensive as having four phases. In the first phase between February and April only one U-boat was destroyed but the increased appearance of Coastal Command's aircraft produced the 'scarecrow' effect, compelling the U-boats that had been spotted to crash dive. Time was wasted as the U-boats remained submerged, travelling at less than 8 knots per hour, which meant that they could spend less operational time in the Atlantic.

Tactics changed in the second phase between April and June. U-boats that were spotted were now under orders to remain on the surface and fight it out with Coastal's aircraft using their anti-aircraft cannon and heavy machine guns. Some of Coastal Command's aircraft were lost to this action, but the U-boats were now finding themselves in an increasingly vulnerable situation. More than half of the U-boats spotted were also attacked with depth charges. During May seven were destroyed.

In the third phase between June and late July the U-boats transiting through the Bay stayed on the surface and travelled together in groups of five in what were known as group transits. This tactic proved to be a costly experience and it failed comprehensively. Over June and July a further thirteen U-boats were destroyed.

During the fourth phase between early August and November the U-boats chose to transit through the Bay of Biscay by staying close to the northern Spanish coast. This reduced their freedom to manoeuvre in the narrow coastal channels, and they came under surveillance and attack from aircraft based in Gibraltar and Morocco. In the first two days of August four U-boats were destroyed.

The killing rate over the period clearly affected the morale of the U-boat crews and forced them into a defensive posture. Slessor summed up the campaign when he wrote that the crucial factor lay not so much in having a large number of aircraft, 'but having the right sort of aircraft with the necessary range and the right sort of radar equipment – above all the long and longer-range aircraft equipped with ten-centimetre ASV'.[31]

VLR Liberators and 'closing the Gap', May 1943

Even as early as April 1943 it was becoming increasingly obvious that the U-boats could no longer employ their established 'wolf pack' tactics against the Allied convoys.[32] Admiral Dönitz started to suspect that there was a significant decline in the morale of his U-boat crews. Between 9 and 14 May thirty-six U-boats attacked two convoys, HX237 and SC129, but sank only five ships for the loss of five of their number.[33] In the following week two encounters with the U-boats were to prove decisive, and have been described as the last great Atlantic battles of the whole war. Thirty-three U-boats attacked convoy SC130. Six U-boats were sunk with no shipping losses. Two of the U-boat kills were made by escorting destroyers and the other four by Coastal Command: two sunk by Hudsons of 269 Squadron and two by VLR Liberators of 120 Squadron, based in Iceland. The effect on the surviving U-boat crews' morale would have been devastating. An ULTRA intercept of U-Boat Command signals traffic on 21 May revealed the underlying problem:

> If there is anyone who thinks that combating convoys is no longer possible, he is a weakling and no true U-boat captain. The Battle of the Atlantic is getting harder, but it is the determining element in the waging of war.[34]

This intercept was highly revealing. It pointed to the collapse of morale at the heart of the U-boat fleet. Much could be blamed on inexperienced U-boat captains who were replacing the now increasing losses of the more battle-hardened crews. A week later, on 24 May, Dönitz called off the convoy battle and admitted, 'the decision of the Battle of the Atlantic has gone to the enemy'.[35] Between March and May a total of seventy-one U-boats out of an operational fleet of two hundred had been destroyed in all areas by Allied aircraft or warships.[36] Slessor commented later that 'Dönitz must have regretted his boast that aircraft can no more eliminate a U-boat than a crow can fight a mole.'[37]

At the end of May Portal sent a message of congratulation to Slessor for his role at Coastal Command. Slessor chose to have it included in the next edition of *Coastal Command Review*, as follows:

> I wish to express to you and all under your command my admiration and warmest thanks for your achievements in the anti-U-boat war during the month just ended. The brilliant success achieved in this vital field is the well-deserved result of tireless perseverance and devotion to duty and is, I am sure, a welcome reward for the aircrews and others who have spared no effort during the long months of arduous operations and training. Now that you have obtained this remarkable advantage over the U-boats I know you will press it home with ever-increasing vigour and determination until, in conjunction with the Royal Navy, you have finally broken the enemy's morale.[38]

The U-boat war was far from over. But from this point forward Britain would not starve; British industry would continue to manufacture aircraft, warships, tanks and other armaments; the Combined Bomber Offensive against Germany would continue; and Bolero, the build-up of troops and matériel in Britain, would continue during the remainder of 1943 and into early 1944, leading to operation Overlord, the Allied invasion of Normandy in June of that year. Slessor wrote in the same edition of *Coastal Command Review*: 'What will happen when the Nazis at last hoist in the fact their last hope of avoiding decisive defeat has disappeared largely through the efforts of Coastal Command?'[39]

Slessor was to stay a further seven months at Coastal Command and spent much of that time coping with the challenges of coalition warfare and particularly his difficulties in dealing with Admiral Ernest King, Commander-in-Chief of the US Navy.

Slessor's challenges with coalition warfare

The North Atlantic trade routes from North America were critical to the Allied war effort and within one month of America's entry into the war, Dönitz had already deployed his U-boat wolf packs to attack American shipping. In early 1942 the US Navy was not operating a convoy system and aerial surveillance was limited. Worse still, the coastal ports were operating under peacetime conditions with no mandatory blackouts. The US Navy was ill-prepared for the considerable losses of both cargo ships and fuel tankers. For a period of over four months between January and April 1942 the U-boats undertook two operations: Drumbeat off the North American seaboard and Neuland in the Gulf coast and the Caribbean. In that period ships of all types were sunk in an area that stretched from the Panama Canal to Nova Scotia. The U-boat crews referred to the period as their 'second happy time'.[40] Admiral Ernest King, who was both the Commander-in-Chief of the US Navy and Chief of Naval Operations, took no responsibility for the lack of a convoy system with escorts, and the absence of a specific anti-submarine strategy. Rather, when he met Roosevelt, he blamed the entire catastrophic episode on the RAF's failure to destroy the U-boat pens in the Biscay ports during their construction in 1941.[41] Whilst technically King was correct, it was hardly a plausible excuse for his poor judgement and *laissez-faire* leadership. To boot, he had had plenty of opportunity to address the fact that the US Navy had made no specific preparations for trade defence following the ABC staff talks earlier that year. Slessor considered that 'for the first year of their war, the American Navy was manifestly unequal to the task of protecting American shipping'.[42] The situation only improved after the US Navy and their Air Forces started to implement anti-submarine strategies.

The disunity in the Allied command structure clearly frustrated Slessor, who wrote later that 'the violence of the inter-Service rivalry in the United States in those days had to be seen to be believed and was an appreciable handicap to the war effort'. Slessor considered that Admiral King was the real obstacle to progress and was frustrated that King consistently maintained that the Pacific theatre 'was the one that mattered'. Slessor added 'I'm afraid there was no disguising the fact that King's obsession with the Pacific ... cost us dear in the Battle of the Atlantic.'[43] General Dwight Eisenhower was more forthright about King, writing in his diary in March 1942 that 'the one thing that might help win this war is to get someone to shoot him. He is the antithesis of cooperation, a deliberately rude person which means he is a mental bully.'[44]

In March 1943 eighty-two ships and nearly 500,000 tons of shipping were sunk because of U-boat attacks, mostly in the Gap.[45] Approximately half the sinkings involved tankers that were crucial to the war effort in both the European and North African theatres of operations. These losses were unsustainable, and Admiral King was compelled to convene the Atlantic Convoy Conference in Washington, if only to short-circuit the clamour for a centralized command structure.[46]

Previously, and throughout 1942, Joubert clearly recognized the urgent need for a unified Allied command, but he soon came to realize that because of Admiral King this would never occur. As a result of King's recalcitrant attitude, senior members of Roosevelt's administration proposed that Slessor take control of all Atlantic maritime aircraft to be used in the U-boat campaign. Both Stimson, the American Secretary for War, and Robert Lovett, the Assistant-Secretary of State for Air, favoured the idea of Slessor taking command of all Allied air forces involved in the Atlantic area. But Slessor was wise to the impossibility of this proposal succeeding and considered that it was a non-starter. On 18 May he wrote to Portal:

> It was no good merely nominating some chap who was acceptable to both sides, calling him C.-in-C. Ocean Air Command and giving him the responsibility, unless they also gave him the powers effectively to exercise command which involved moving squadrons from A to B. I did not see King agreeing, for instance, to my coming to the conclusion on the operational statistics that a U.S. Naval squadron was not pulling its weight in the Caribbean and should be moved to Iceland. I think that is where it would break down – in practice it would mean going to the U.S. Chiefs of Staff about it, and then how would we be much better off than we are now?[47]

On 19 May King decided to form the 10th Fleet, a force which would now comprise all the USAAF and US Navy's anti-submarine aircraft under one command. These aircraft, which included 120 VLR Liberators, would be responsible for patrolling all the waters strictly under American jurisdiction. No discussion took place with either the Royal Navy or Coastal Command. Furthermore, King never acknowledged the existence of Coastal Command at any point.[48] Slessor considered that King resented the existence of the RAF as an autonomous upstart service that knew nothing about war at sea.[49] He also believed that King's deployment of the 10th Fleet was a poor use of air power. During several months there had been virtually no threat by U-boats to the American convoys in waters under American jurisdiction.[50] By comparison, Coastal Command, assisted by an experienced squadron of Canada's Eastern Air Command, based in Newfoundland, succeeded in closing the 'Air Gap' in late May with the comparatively modest number of forty-eight VLR Liberators.[51]

Slessor visited Washington in June and met King to request the transfer of two additional squadrons of USAAF Liberators to be deployed in England to continue operations in the Bay. King initially warmed to the idea. However, he eventually revoked the decision because the Liberators would then be used in offensive roles, rather his favoured strategy of using the aircraft in a defensive convoy escort role.

In Washington, both Generals Marshall and Arnold started to have deep suspicions of King's motives, and his use of his Liberators. Given King's continued belief in the 'Pacific First' priority, it was becoming clear that he was hoarding his increased allocation of Liberators for bombing operations in the Pacific that would, in any event, be the responsibility of the USAAF rather than the Navy.

Slessor wrote after the war that King never understood the subject of the fight against the U-boat. He cited correspondence in which King wrote to Marshall stating that 'The submarines can be stopped only by wiping out the German building yards and bases', adding 'the escort of convoys is not just one way of handling the submarine menace; it is the only way that gives any promise of success. The so-called patrol and hunting operations have time and again proved futile.'[52] King wrote these words in his memoirs after the war.[53] Clearly, he had not recalled that bombing U-boat pens in the Biscay ports ended in failure, whereas attacking U-boats in the transit area of the Bay of Biscay was an unqualified success.

Coastal Command's maritime offensive role, 1943

Most of Slessor's time at Coastal Command was devoted to the defeat of the U-boat menace. However, nearly 50 per cent of Coastal's squadrons were carrying out other maritime roles. The U-boat campaign was focused on trade defence and ensuring the critical transatlantic lifelines continued to operate by preventing Allied shipping from being sunk. However, a significant number of aircraft were concentrated on an offensive strategy at sea, and particularly on the maritime blockade of Germany. In essence, this meant attacking ships, the so-called 'blockade runners', that were proving vital to maintaining the Axis war effort. In *Central Blue* Slessor described offensive operations against ships carrying iron ore off the coast of Spain and in the coastal shipping lanes off the Norwegian coast. Other identified ships that were attacked were carrying raw materials from the Far East, including rubber from Japanese-occupied Malaya.

In raids on Dutch ports Coastal's fighter-bomber and torpedo aircraft were often accompanied by Fighter Command aircraft. During 1943 the port of Rotterdam was subjected to repeated raids that affected its ability to unload iron ore cargoes destined for onward movement by barge or rail to the Ruhr's iron and steel foundries. This compelled the Germans to switch Swedish ore imports to Bremen or Emden, a far more inconvenient route. Consequently, imports into Rotterdam declined by 60 per cent and effectively closed a large part of the port's activity. Slessor concluded that 'the abandonment of Rotterdam as the principal importing terminal of his [the German] North Sea shipping route was a serious blow to him'.[54]

An assessment of Slessor at Coastal Command

The air historian Henry Probert wrote of Slessor in 1991 that he was best remembered by many as the Commander-in-Chief of Coastal Command at the climax of the Battle of the Atlantic and at a time when that battle was far from won. He added:

> he was fortunate in that many of the techniques of naval/air warfare had at last been learnt and the long-range aircraft needed to cover the mid-ocean gap would soon be available, and his own experience both with the Royal Navy and the Americans did much to improve the co-operation between sea and air forces on each side of the Atlantic. The great turning point in the Battle came in May, when shipping losses fell dramatically, and from then on – though Coastal Command could never relax – the U-boats were held on the defensive ... although he remained at Northwood for less than a year he is widely considered the best of Coastal Command's war time Commanders-in-Chief.[55]

In 1990 Jack Slessor's grandson, Major Anthony Slessor, on the staff at Fortress headquarters, Gibraltar, was stopped in the street by a Canadian couple seeking directions. The gentleman noted the nametag on Slessor's uniform and enquired if he was related to Jack Slessor. The affirmative answer elicited effusive praise and genuine affection from a man who had been a young pilot in one of the Canadian squadrons engaged in the Battle of the Atlantic – testament to the reach of Jack Slessor's 'Nelson touch'.[56]

A new assignment, January 1944

In the first week of January 1944 Slessor met Archibald Sinclair, the Secretary of State for Air. Sinclair asked Slessor if he would go to the Mediterranean to take over Air Chief Marshal Sir Arthur Tedder's command of the RAF in the Mediterranean and the Middle East. With some reluctance Slessor agreed. He had hoped to stay on at Coastal Command during the build-up to Overlord. But he also knew 'that the back of the real job – the defeat of the U-boat – had been broken'.[57] During Slessor's time as Commander-in-Chief, eighty-four U-boats had been destroyed by Coastal Command.[58]

On 14 January he left for Gibraltar and Algiers 'to start a very different sort of job', adding, 'I could at least not complain of lack of variety in my war experience'.[59]

Chapter 12

Hitler's Third Front

The Southern Snare: the Mediterranean Allied Air Forces, Italy and the Balkans, January 1944–March 1945

The Mediterranean Allied Air Forces (MAAF) Command was established in December 1943 replacing the Mediterranean Air Command (MAC), an Anglo-American joint air force that had been under the command of Air Chief Marshal Sir Arthur Tedder during the closing stages of the North African campaign, through to the invasion of Sicily and finally into southern Italy.

In forming Anglo-American/Allied air forces, the commanders were drawn from either the USAAF or the RAF with deputies appointed from the other's air force, in accordance with the convention established during the Casablanca Conference. This arrangement was implemented to ensure joint Anglo-American agreement in the areas of policy, strategy and tactics. In mid-January 1944 Lieutenant General Ira Eaker was appointed as Commander of the MAAF, with Air Marshal Sir John Slessor as his deputy. Eaker had previously served as the Commanding General of the USAAF's Eighth Air Force in England, and Slessor knew him well from his time as ACAS (Policy) in 1942. Over the next fifteen months Slessor was to make a significant contribution to the Allied operations not only in Italy but also in the Balkans, and even on 'special duty' operations in attempting to drop much-needed supplies to the beleaguered Poles during the Warsaw uprising. However, he is probably best remembered for his direct involvement in Operation Strangle in central Italy between March and May 1944.

In addition to his position as Deputy Commander-in-Chief of the MAAF, Slessor had 'a second hat'. Under a directive from London, he was also Commander-in-Chief, Royal Air Force, Mediterranean and Middle East, and he had responsibility for a large geographic area east of longitude 20° East that included the Balkans, Greece, Cyprus, Egypt, Palestine, East Africa, Persia (now Iran), Iraq and Aden.[1]

The Mediterranean Allied Air Forces:
organization and structure

The formal decision to create the Anglo-American Mediterranean Allied Air Forces had been taken by the Combined Chiefs of Staff on 5 December 1943 during the Cairo Conference. It would eventually lead to the establishment of the largest military air command during the Second World War. It would comprise nearly 13,000 aircraft of varying types and over 420,000 personnel involved as aircrew, ground support and engineering echelons, and the administrative functions. Although the MAAF was organized as an Anglo-American entity, many other nationalities were incorporated through their respective air force squadrons that included (Free) France, Poland, Greece, Yugoslavia, Australia, New Zealand, Canada, South Africa and Rhodesia. At its inception the MAAF had personnel dispersed across three headquarters in Algiers, Tunis and Caserta in central Italy. However, over the ensuing months more of the operational aspects would be centralized at the Caserta headquarters, a former royal palace located 30 miles north of Naples.

The MAAF was a giant undertaking and coalition air warfare on this scale had never previously been attempted. During the first weeks of its establishment Eaker and Slessor spent valuable time with Sir Henry Wilson, Supreme Allied Commander, Mediterranean (SACMED) and Carl Spaatz, Commanding General[2] of the United States Army Air Forces, Europe (USAAFE), planning for an organizational structure that would operate efficiently and one which would ensure that the American and British staffs would work in a harmonious relationship. Many of the improvements resulted out of learning from earlier experiences of inefficiency during 1943 when there had been unnecessary duplication of functions by the British and American staffs, particularly in the areas of intelligence. The guiding principle was based on a policy of now establishing a joint Anglo-American operational staff group that would concentrate on intelligence, statistics, strategic and tactical planning, targeting and public relations. That organization, now based at Caserta, became the hub of all air operations in the Mediterranean. With its Anglo-American staff, the teamwork was excellent and resulted in a nice balance between British and American staff methods.[3] In marked contrast, administrative functions such as the command of the RAF and USAAF squadrons proceeded along the established national lines. Previously, there had been considerable problems when one of the Allies attempted to impose their administrative standards and practices on the other.[4]

Slessor wrote, 'it was fortunate that in the Mediterranean Allied Air Forces all the personalities concerned were able to get on well together ... we soon evolved an effective division of work between us … we naturally acted in the closest day-to-day co-operation and complete mutual understanding. I had in Ira Eaker an Allied Commander-in-Chief who was not only an old friend, but a splendid chap who stood on no dignities, trusted me to serve him loyally in the sphere where he was responsible and left me to get on with it and gave me all the help he could'.[5] It was all a very pleasant contrast to the difficulties Slessor had previously encountered when dealing with Admiral Ernest King and the US Navy during his time at Coastal Command.

The MAAF operated through three key roles: strategic, tactical and coastal operations:

(1) **Strategic Operations** were undertaken primarily through the American Fifteenth Army Air Force. Though it was based in southern Italy, its primary mission was to maintain the strategic offensive against Germany, together with the Eighth and Ninth Army Air Forces, based in England. These three American strategic air forces now had the range and capability to reach all areas of Italy, Germany, Romania and Bulgaria. At its peak the Fifteenth Air Force had eighty-five squadrons of heavy bombers (B-24s and B-17s), and twenty-two squadrons of fighters that were used to escort the bombers on their missions. The Fifteenth Army Air Force was commanded by Major General Nathan Twining, who had a dual reporting line, answering to Spaatz on strategic objectives such as Operation Pointblank[6], and to Eaker on specific strategic targets in Italy, and all other administrative matters.[7] Their squadrons were stationed at various airfields in the Foggia area of southeast Italy. During 1944 their bombers were involved in missions over central and northern Italy, extending north to central, southern and eastern Germany. They also conducted bombing missions over the Ploesti oil facilities in southern Romania, which were a vital source of fuel supplies for Germany's armed forces.

The Royal Air Force's 205 Group was also involved as a strategic component of the MAAF in strategic operations with nine squadrons of Wellingtons, Liberators and Halifaxes. For all strategic bombing missions in Italy, the strategic air force components were incorporated into the Mediterranean Allied Strategic Air Forces (MASAF).

(2) **Tactical Operations**. The American Twelfth Army Air Force provided the major component of the tactical air forces with fifty-three squadrons that were primarily responsible for providing close air support for ground forces and for air interdiction, which was to play such a decisive role during 1944. The RAF provided twenty-seven squadrons, including its Desert Air Force. Other national air forces that provided squadrons included the Australians,

Canadians, South Africans, Free French, Polish and the by now co-belligerent Italians. During May the tactical air forces fielded ninety-four squadrons of fighters, fighter-bombers and medium bombers that were stationed in the Naples area, Sicily, Brindisi and on the Mediterranean islands of Corsica and Sardinia.

(3) **Coastal operations** were primarily conducted by the RAF's squadrons against enemy ships using coastal routes, in addition to carrying out attacks on port facilities used for the storage of the enemy's supplies.

Stalemate in central Italy: Anzio, Cassino and the Gustav Line, January–May 1944

The initial hopes and plans that the Anglo-American Allied armies would advance rapidly northwards up the Italian peninsula foundered during the last two months of 1943. Italy was proving to be anything but 'the soft under-belly of Europe', with experienced and determined German troops holding a defensive line south of Rome, under the inspired and dogged leadership of Field Marshal Kesselring.[8] It became known as the Gustav Line, and it extended from Ortona on the Adriatic coast south-westwards to the town of Cassino and beyond to the Rapido and Garigliano rivers through the coastal plain to the Tyrrhenian Sea. The steep mountainous terrain gave the German defenders a distinct advantage, in addition to the atrocious weather conditions during the winter of 1943/1944. The air historian John Terraine wrote that in early 1944:

> the [Allied] armies found themselves trapped in battlefields either deep in snow, or deep in mud, or both, inescapably and ominously recalling the doomed landscape of the Western Front in 1916 and 1917. Soldiers and airmen suffered the depression of feeling that they were now caught in a secondary theatre where they would have to go on fighting and suffering casualties, but no longer for prime purposes.[9]

In an attempt to break the deadlock, the Allied High Command in the Mediterranean planned operation Shingle, an amphibious landing at Anzio, a coastal port located 30 miles south of Rome. The objective was to outflank the German defences with a simultaneous frontal attack on the Gustav Line by American forces of the Fifth Army across the Rapido and Garigliano rivers. The two Allied forces would then join up to advance towards Rome. The Anzio landings commenced on 22 January and were almost completely un-opposed by German forces. However, the Allied force failed to move inland in the first days, the commanders preferring to consolidate their forces on a narrow beachhead. Consequently, valuable time was wasted and the element of surprise was lost. General Kesselring rapidly redeployed his reinforcements south of Rome. Consequently, the Allied forces at Anzio remained hemmed into the narrow beachhead for a further four months. Churchill was to write later that he 'had hoped we were hurling a wildcat onto the shore, but all we got was a stranded whale'.[10]

Slessor was incredulous, writing to Portal five days after the landings:

> Here we are, with air superiority so complete as to be amazing ... I have not the slightest doubt that if we had been Germans or Russians landing at Anzio, we would have been in Rome by now and the whole right of the enemy line opposite the [American] Fifth Army would have crumpled.[11]

Slessor could not fathom why with 50,000 troops and 5,000 vehicles the force could not have succeeded against an opposition with less than half that strength. Despite the uncertainties of a possible major German counterattack, Slessor concluded that it was all an illustration of the maxim that a battle is lost only when the commander thinks it is, and in this case the commander, General Mark Clark, thought it was lost before it had started. Furthermore, the fact that the US Fifth Army had failed to break the Gustav Line only added to the sense of deep disappointment.

Monte Cassino Monastery: the moral dilemma

The sixth-century Benedictine monastery standing at 1,770ft above the Gustav Line commanded panoramic views of both the Liri valley to the southwest and the Garigliano valley to the south. This historic site had special religious and cultural significance and on 15 November 1943 General Eisenhower had notified the Allies' Fifteenth Army Group that the monastery had been added to the list of Italian monuments to be protected.

During the period between late December and early February the British, New Zealand and Indian troops who had been pinned down by both German artillery fire and snipers on the flanks of Monte Cassino were convinced that the monastery was a strongpoint that was being used by Panzer units. In this slow and depressing battle of attrition Eisenhower changed his mind, and on 29 December announced: 'If we have to choose between destroying a famous building and sacrificing our own men, then our men's lives count infinitely more and the building must go ... nothing can stand against a military necessity.'[12] With increasing losses, the New Zealand commander, General Bernard Freyburg, requested the MAAF carry out air raids to destroy the monastery.[13]

The official air historians Dennis Richards and Hilary St George Saunders wrote that the American generals Mark Clark and Ira Eaker expressed strong doubts about bombing the monastery, as did Slessor.[14] Slessor wrote later that 'we airmen were strongly opposed to it and only agreed as a result of irresistible (and justifiable) pressure from the Army'.[15] In the event, over 500 tons of bombs were dropped by 254 aircraft of the American Twelfth and Fifteenth Air Forces on 15 February, reducing the monastery to a shattered ruin that the Germans then, for the first time, used as a strongpoint.[16] The bombing did not enable the Allies to achieve a breakthrough on the Gustav Line. A month later, on 15 March, heavy bombing of the town of Cassino equally failed to dislodge the German troops. In writing to Portal in April Slessor emphasized that *'the bomber is not a battlefield weapon'*.[17] In the same letter Slessor referred to the battle for the Messines Ridge during the First World War where incessant heavy artillery bombardment, in addition to subterranean mines, failed to achieve the anticipated breakthrough. Slessor's prescient remarks should have also served as a warning for the Normandy campaign, four months later. The heavy bombing of Caen in July equally failed to dislodge the German forces and had the unfortunate and tragic effect of killing many innocent French civilians.[18]

The plan for air interdiction in central Italy

By early March all attempts to break the German defences on the Gustav Line had failed. To Slessor it was reminiscent of the static trench warfare on the Western Front during the First World War. On 11 February he wrote a memorandum to Brigadier General Lauris Norstad, the American Director of Operations at Caserta, as follows:

> There are now some seventeen German divisions in Italy south of Rome. I do not believe the Army – even with our support – will move them. But I think it more than possible that the Hun, by concentrating all this force so far south, has given us – the Air Forces – an opportunity. He has been able up to now just to support his smaller armies on the present line in spite of our air attacks on his communications. I find it hard to believe that, by increasing those forces, he has not put a load on his communications which they will not be able to stand if we really sustain a scientifically planned offensive *against the right places* in his L. of C. [Lines of Communication].[19]

Slessor's memorandum reflected his own thinking on air interdiction – the disruption of the enemy's supplies and movements behind the front line. This was very much Slessor's idea. During the early 1930s he had lectured on the concept at the Army's Staff College at Camberley, and his ideas on the interaction between ground and air forces were published subsequently in his book

Air Power and Armies.[20] However, in early 1944 his ideas had yet to be tested on a scale relevant to the size, technologies, capabilities and sophistication of modern warfare. Central Italy had become the crucible of experimentation for tactical air interdiction and would provide important learning experiences that would then be applied during the Battle of Normandy three months later with considerable success.

Prior to taking up his post at the MAAF, Air Chief Marshal Tedder, his predecessor in the appointment, recommended to Slessor that he should meet Professor Solly Zuckerman, who had served as Tedder's scientific adviser in the Mediterranean during 1943. Zuckerman held a strong view that success would come with sustained air attacks on the Italian rail system infrastructure: major railway centres, marshalling yards and large concentrations of loco-motives and rolling stock. Slessor met Zuckerman and had no argument with his ideas. Of course, none of this was new to Slessor since he had lectured and written on the same subject during the 1930s. However, Slessor also believed that there was no simplistic, empirical solution to air interdiction, and that one method should not be adopted to the exclusion of all others.[21] He con-sidered it vital to adapt 'one's thinking to the conditions at the time and to the developing capacity of aircraft and weapons, making full use of the flexibility of air-power to attack the enemy transportation system in the way that seemed most likely to be profitable in the conditions with which we were faced, and with the resources we had at our disposal'.[22]

Operation Strangle, 19 March–10 May 1944

On 19 March the air directive was issued that embodied air interdiction and came to be known as Operation Strangle. Its stated objective was 'to reduce the enemy's flow of supplies to a level which will make it impossible for him to maintain and operate his forces in Central Italy'.[23] Slessor knew that air interdiction went far beyond bombing railway infrastructure. Target selec-tion was expanded to include attacks against port facilities and shipping, bridges, tunnels, viaducts, road junctions and motor transport, and he hoped that 'German resources would wither below the tourniquet applied by the MAAF'.[24] However, after the first month of Strangle Slessor admitted to Portal that he had been over-optimistic. In his long letter to him on 16 April he added that 'we are not going to succeed in doing what I had hoped with some confidence we should do, namely, make it impossible by the end of April for the Hun to maintain an army of seventeen odd divisions south of Rome'. The adverse weather conditions during that first month had been a limiting factor in carrying out interdiction missions. Furthermore, the Germans had been resourceful in building up their reserves of fuel, ammunition, rations and fodder to the forward depots. With the situation of stalemate on the Gustav Line, Slessor noted *'we are not forcing him to expend fuel or ammunition'*.[25]

In the first few weeks of Strangle, as interdiction sorties focused on railway infrastructure, it was becoming increasingly obvious that it was not preventing German supply movements. In frustration Eaker wrote to General Devers, the Deputy Supreme Commander of the Allied Force in the Mediterranean, as follows:

> All our experience in attacks on communication in this theater has shown that even the most successful bombardment of a marshalling yard does not cut traffic for more than a few hours. Attacks on marshalling yards are valuable because they destroy concentrations of goods, rolling stock and repair facilities. We have found that a more permanent way to cut lines is by attacks on bridges and viaducts which are more difficult to repair.[26]

Eaker took issue with Zuckerman's dismissal of attacks on choke points such as bridges and viaducts as being 'uneconomical and difficult targets [that] in general do not appear to be worth attacking'.[27] Both Eaker and Slessor considered the best way to choke off supplies to the front was through the complete, simultaneous and continuous cutting of all German supply lines in an interdiction zone north of Rome.

As the weather improved in late April and early May, the Allied tactical air forces increased their attacks on supply routes south of a line extending from Spezia to Rimini. Their sorties were now focused on a wide range of targets. The squadrons of medium bombers (B-25 Mitchells and B-26 Marauders) based in Sardinia and Corsica attacked bridges and viaducts, while the fighters and fighter-bombers based in southern Italy (Spitfires, P-47 Thunderbolts, P-51 Mustangs and Beaufighters) attacked ships, motor vehicles, trains and road junctions. These sorties were now having considerable success but not because of cutting supplies, the original objective for Strangle. Nearly thirty years later the RAND aviation analyst F.M. Sallager published a comprehensive analysis of Strangle which concluded that it never succeeded in preventing the flow of German supplies to the front.[28] The report revealed that, in many cases, the German supply inventories actually increased, and nowhere did they reach critically low levels. However, the report concluded that whereas supply denial had not succeeded, by mid-May air interdiction had comprehensively denied German mobility on the battlefield.[29] Between 15 March and 10 May the tactical air forces flew 21,688 sorties in the interdiction zone between Spezia and Rome.[30] Richards and Saunders credited Slessor with his ability to ensure that Strangle proceeded: 'he succeeded in

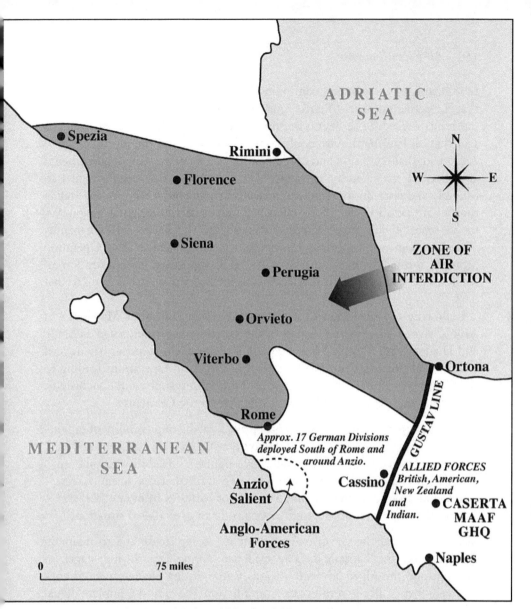

Operation Strangle, Central Italy, 15 March–10 May 1944.

blending the two opposing designs [the attacks against rail infrastructure versus bridges, viaducts, roads and motor transport] into a single plan'.[31]

On 11 May the Allies finally launched their major ground offensive, known as operation Diadem, across the Gustav Line. Forces in the Anzio beachhead broke out and joined up with the forces travelling north through the Liri valley towards Rome. Air interdiction continued throughout the Diadem period. Slessor commented that German mobility was paralysed by their enormous losses in motor transport and the catastrophic conditions of the roads.

In following up the advance, continuing Diadem, he wrote further, 'they found that the actual numbers of tanks, guns and vehicles wrecked or burnt out on the roads exceeded the claims we had made', adding, 'Lord Trenchard has said that all land battles are confusion and muddle, and the job of Air is to accentuate that confusion and muddle in the enemy's Army to a point when it gets beyond the capacity to control.'[32] That point had been reached in Strangle and later during Diadem, proving that air interdiction in the Italian theatre of operations had been effective. The impact of air interdiction was to be repeated just three months later during the Battle for Normandy. The American war historians Craven and Cate concluded that 'Operation Strangle formed without question the most significant demonstration of Anglo-American tactical air cooperation in the Second World War up to that date.'[33]

Following the liberation of Rome in early June, Generals Marshall and Arnold visited Caserta and discussed the success and challenges of Strangle and Diadem with Slessor. He gave them a comprehensive paper, the text of which is included in *Central Blue*, entitled, 'Notes on Operations leading to the Capture of Rome' that, amongst his other observations and conclusions, addressed the importance of tactical mobility to the Germans:

> Above all, perhaps, the enemy was deprived, by the impossibility of rapid and coherent movement, of that flexibility which has always been such an admirable quality in German defensive fighting, his ability to pick up a battalion here, the contents of a leave train there, a machine-gun *abteilung* from one division and a couple of batteries from another, and fling them in as an improvised battle group to save a local situation.[34]

Slessor respected the German Army's ability to improvise and to maintain flexibility on the battlefield. The evidence during the closing stages of Strangle and the Allied advance towards Rome during Diadem proved conclusively that of all the results of air interdiction, the almost complete denial of the enemy's mobility was foremost.

Operation Anvil: differences of opinion between the American and British Chiefs of Staff

During the Tehran Conference in November 1943 the Combined Chiefs of Staff reached agreement to prepare for an invasion of southern France, to be known by the codename Operation Anvil, to coincide with operation Overlord, the planned invasion of Normandy in June 1944. But significant differences remained between the British and Americans on the future strategy in the Mediterranean. Whereas the Americans strongly favoured Anvil as the more direct assault on Western Europe, the British continued to favour an active campaign through the Balkans.

Slessor continued to argue for keeping up the pressure on the Germans in Italy in the hope that the Allies would persist in advancing at pace, driving the German defending forces into the Alps. At that point the Allied armies could then turn east towards Austria and the Balkans. As he wrote, 'what I really hankered after was to see the Anglo-American forces on the Danube before the war came to an end'.[35] But this was not to be. First, the Germans put up very strong resistance in northern Italy during the second half of 1944, and second, Anvil (later renamed Dragoon) took place in August 1944 and by then the matter was settled.

But none of this meant that the Allies would not continue to pursue active involvement in the Balkan region. Any action that tied down German forces in the Balkans would inevitably prevent their redeployment to Western Europe.

Yugoslavia and Slessor's involvement in the establishment of the Balkan Air Force

The Balkan region that comprised Yugoslavia, Albania, Macedonia and Greece was occupied by eighteen German divisions in addition to garrison battalions of Hungarians and Bulgarians.

Since 1941 the British government through the Special Operations Executive (SOE) had maintained links with partisan groups in the area. In Yugoslavia the British had initially backed partisan forces organized by General Mihailović, who was supported by the exiled King Peter and his government in Cairo. However, a rival group of partisans under Josip Broz 'Tito' became more significant. Like Mihailović, Tito wanted to defeat the German forces, but in any post-war settlement he was seeking to install a Communist government in Belgrade. The two partisan groups became active enemies and in effect caused an internal civil war during the German occupation. But it soon became evident that Mikhailović was actively collaborating with the Germans. At this point it was abundantly clear that, as Slessor wrote, 'if we want to kill Germans in the Balkans the man to back was Tito'.[36] Despite his Communist background, backing Tito was seen as an expedient solution and at the time Slessor recalled that 'we were all starry-eyed about the prospects of friendly co-existence with Communist states in the better world that was to come'.[37]

Recognizing the threat that Tito posed, German special forces made a failed attempt in late May to capture him at his headquarters at Drvar, in the Dinaric Alps. Tito had a narrow escape and was evacuated to Bari in southern Italy. Slessor met him there in early June and was favourably impressed by this Moscow-trained Communist leader. He always felt he was a Yugoslavian patriot first, and a Communist second.[38] Tito's partisan groups had already been receiving much-needed air drops of military equipment from the MAAF that included rifles, machine guns, mortars and ammunition. However, Slessor believed that there was a bigger need for air support to assist the partisans. In a signal he sent to Portal he wrote:

> the best service we in this theatre can perform for Overlord is really to create hell in the Balkans by every means, air, land, and sea that can be made available without embarking on major bridgeheads that have to be covered and supplied ... it appears reasonably certain that if the Balkan satellites were knocked out, the effect on German strategy would be catastrophic. [39]

Slessor's request did not go unheeded. Portal was strongly supportive of air operations in the Balkans. Consequently, the Balkan Air Force was formed as a component of the MAAF and came directly under the command of the RAF. Its specific remit was to provide air cover and support for all activities in the region. Slessor wrote 'seldom can there have been a more thoroughly cosmopolitan force', drawn as it was from eight national air forces. It was initially composed of fighter and light bomber squadrons that had been taken from the MAAF's desert and coastal air forces but was expanded to include transport squadrons that were required for supply drops. In December 1944 the Balkan Air Force had twenty-four squadrons comprising fighter and transport squadrons from the new (co-belligerent) Italian air force; Yugoslavian, British, South African and Greek squadrons; plus American squadrons involved in supply drops. It was a success story that demonstrated just what could be achieved by a force of multinational squadrons operating within a highly organized and well-led air force controlled and directed by experienced, judicious commanders.

The Tragedy of Warsaw, 1 August–23 September 1944

On 23 June 1944 the Soviet forces opened Operation Bagration, their major ground offensive westwards. Over the following six weeks they advanced from Belorussia to the Polish frontier. The German forces were now on the defensive and had retreated behind a broad front that extended from Lithuania in the Baltic area to Odessa in western Ukraine. The Polish government in exile based in London, also known as the 'London Poles', had for some time been planning an uprising in Warsaw through their covert Home Army, under the direction of General Bor, and timed to coincide with the anticipated arrival of

Soviet forces. The details of these plans were not shared with the British, who had no idea of how and when this might occur.

On 1 August the Polish uprising led to their occupation of central Warsaw as they started to drive the German defending forces from the city. They hoped that Soviet forces would join them. However, the Soviet forces chose to stop their advance and maintain their front line on the banks of the river Vistula to the east of central Warsaw. Consequently, the Home Army came under retaliatory attacks and became increasingly threatened by encirclement. It was at this point that Slessor became directly involved. He wrote later in *Central Blue* that what followed 'gave me, I think, the worst six weeks in my experience'.[40]

In London General Sosnkowski, Commander-in-Chief of the Polish Army, made strong requests for immediate Allied help. In particular, he had four demands for immediate air operations: the bombing of German strongholds in Cracow, Lodz and specific areas in Warsaw; the deployment of fighter squadrons manned by Polish aircrew that would land at selected airfields in Warsaw and then provide close air support to their ground forces; a Polish parachute brigade to be deployed as reinforcements; and finally, a continuous supply by air drop of heavy machine guns, anti-tank weapons, ammunition and grenades.[41]

Slessor clearly recognized the immense risks involved in providing any aid for the uprising in Warsaw. He considered that the Polish government in exile had ignored the self-evident fact that Warsaw was separated from Italian airbases by 750 miles, most of which was over enemy-held territory. Set against this, he also recognized the importance of maintaining good political relationships between Britain and Poland. All air operations would be risky, but air supply would offer the best form of cooperation.

Inevitably, Slessor agreed very reluctantly to authorize a small number of Polish flight crews from 1586 Flight of the MAAF to make the supply drops. All seven aircraft returned without loss and some of the supplies reached the Polish ground forces. The fact that this modest operation was a success only engendered a sense of false optimism. Subsequent 'special duty' supply flights were not so fortunate. On five consecutive nights in mid-August seventeen out of the ninety-three heavy bombers dispatched failed to return. The losses continued throughout August and September and, as Slessor recalled, 'on twenty-two nights during the two months of Warsaw's agony, that had cost us thirty-one heavy aircraft missing out of 180 dispatched – a loss rate overall of more than seventeen percent'.[42]

During this period the Russians deliberately held back from advancing into central Warsaw to help the beleaguered Poles. It was a cynical ploy that ultimately led to the Polish Home Army being decimated by the Germans. It was perfectly obvious to Slessor that the Russians would only support militias and partisans who were committed to the Soviet cause. Slessor summed it up when he wrote, 'I am not a vindictive man, but I hope there may be some very special hell reserved for the brutes in the Kremlin who betrayed Bor's army, and the fruitless sacrifice of some 200 airmen [Poles, South Africans and British] of 205 Group and 334 Wing.'[43] As Henry Probert observed, 'the cold treachery of the Russians in Poland would condition Slessor's thinking for the rest of his days'.[44]

During December, and following the exodus of German forces from Greece, Slessor witnessed first-hand the emerging ideological divide between the West and the Communists. Whereas the British and American governments fostered the installation of a pro-West government in Greece under the leadership of George Papandreou, the Greek Communist movement and its militia, known as ELAS, rose to attack key targets in Athens. The resulting civil war was to rumble on for five years and was the first example of the proxy wars that were to characterize East–West relations during the ensuing forty-five years of the Cold War. It also marked the point at which British power and influence in the region was replaced by America's emergent and ultimately dominant role in international politics. Slessor was to confront these realities in the post-war era, and particularly during his time as Chief of the Air Staff in the early 1950s.

In late 1944, and with the assurance of victory in Europe, Slessor was considering his next career move. Portal had already offered him the position of Air Member for Personnel (AMP), which Slessor knew would be a considerable challenge as the Royal Air Force contracted from its wartime peak of over a million personnel to adapt to the realities of the post-war era. This worthy and dutiful ambition almost came undone. In his otherwise newsy letter from HQ MAAF to Hermione on 15 November 1944, Jack wrote, 'The great worry now is Leigh Mallory [fellow Haileyburian and younger brother of George, the famous mountaineer who died on Everest] – he left U.K. 60 hours ago and hasn't been heard of since. Doris [Mallory's wife] is with him. It's beginning to look very black indeed I'm afraid.'[45]

Leigh-Mallory was on his way to take over the RAF's Southeast Asia Command (SEAC). Slessor had already been suggested for the post but did not want it because of the pain he suffered in a foot from hot weather. Nevertheless, he accepted that if they called on him to replace Leigh-Mallory, he would go. 'Perhaps poor old Trafford will turn up,' Slessor continued, 'I hope to God he does But [sic] if he does it will be a miracle I'm afraid.'[46]

Air Chief Marshal (temporary rank) Trafford Leigh-Mallory did not turn up, at least not alive. He and Doris were killed on the first leg of their trip out to Southeast Asia, crashing into the French Alps in bad weather. Portal offered Slessor the opportunity to take command of SEAC. Slessor paused to consider the new offer, but on balance preferred the AMP position that would give him considerable influence over key decisions for the future of the Royal Air Force. Portal acquiesced and Keith Park took over SEAC instead.

Slessor left the MAAF on 15 March 1945. He was given a ceremonial farewell from Marchionese airfield, near Naples, as his civilianized Mitchell bomber was given an escort of American fighters for its final take-off for England. Slessor had spent fifteen months in Mediterranean operations, the longest time of his three commands during the war.

He took up his new appointment at the Air Ministry as the Air Member for Personnel at Adastral House, on the junction of Kingsway and Aldwych. This would be the third occasion that he had worked at this address since the late 1920s: initially as an assistant to Lord Trenchard during his time as Chief of the Air Staff, and later as the Deputy Director of Plans during the pre-war years.

Chapter 13

A Time to Think

RAF Reorganization for Peacetime; and Commandant, Imperial Defence College, 1945–1949

Freed from the obligations of the operational commands that he had held for four years, Slessor could now use his time at the Air Council, and later at the Imperial Defence College, to think strategically about the role of the Royal Air Force in the early post-war years. As Air Member for Personnel (AMP) on the Air Council between April 1945 and December 1947, he would plan and implement the demobilization of 700,000 aircrew and the repositioning of the Royal Air Force to meet the challenges of the post-war era. Sir James Barnes, the Permanent Under-Secretary at the Air Ministry in 1947, noted that 'Slessor had made his mark on every aspect of the Air Council's work. His wide knowledge of the Air Force and the other Services, and his outstanding energy have not only been addressed to the work of his own Department but freely and unselfishly [helped] his colleagues in dealing with difficulties that were strictly not his own.'[1]

The Tizard Report, 'Future Development in Weapons of War', June 1945

In late 1944 the British Chiefs of Staff requested the government's technical warfare committee to produce a report that would provide them with a forecast of anticipated military developments for up to twenty years into the future. The report, entitled 'Future Development in Weapons of War', was produced by a team of eminent scientists headed by Sir Henry Tizard.[2]

Although Tizard and his team had no direct access to the latest developments in atomic weapons (the Manhattan Project at Los Alamos, New Mexico), the report predicted accurately that atomic weapons would have a devastating effect and change the course of warfare. In June 1945 the top-secret report was circulated to senior military commanders a month before the first detonation of an atomic bomb in New Mexico. It concluded that 'the only answer we can see to the atomic bomb is to be prepared to use it ourselves in retaliation. The knowledge that we were prepared to do this might well deter an aggressive nation.'[3] This early pronouncement of nuclear deterrence theory was subsequently acted on by politicians in post-war Britain. Sir James Barnes asked Slessor to comment on the Tizard Committee Report. Slessor agreed with most of the Committee's conclusions and correctly predicted that 'the rocket-propelled atomic bomb would revolutionize warfare and render obsolete all hitherto known methods of waging it ... clearly the most vital question in the world today and one which this country must solve or perish'.[4]

Although Slessor never claimed to be the first strategist to use the term atomic deterrence, he was to become the principal architect that moved deterrence from a concept to a reality. He ensured Britain would have a workable and independent nuclear deterrent. Slessor recognized the strategic value of the atomic bomb but considered it as an essentially political weapon. Demonstrating the means and the will to use nuclear weapons would compel an adversary to realize that any unprovoked attack would result in unacceptable and appalling destruction on its homeland. However, there was a significant time gap of a decade before that milestone was reached. Austerity in Britain, and the consequent budget restrictions, slowed the pace at which projects could proceed. From late 1946 onwards defence expenditures were subject to a 'Ten Year Rule', which stated that no major war was anticipated before 1957.[5] However, no serious examination was made to forecast the international situation, and the potential impact of budget restrictions on national security. These decisions were taken for political and financial rather than military reasons.[6]

The conventionally armed RAF bomber squadrons of the late 1940s and early 1950s were not a credible deterrent to the Soviet threat. As early as August 1946 Slessor had argued for a long-range jet bomber.[7] Whatever influence Slessor may have had on Air Ministry thinking, the Air Staff issued design specification B.35/46 in January 1947 for a long-range, four-engined jet bomber capable of flying at 500 knots, reaching altitudes of 50,000ft with a range of 1,500 miles, and delivering a 10,000lb bomb.[8] It took eight years for the first of this bomber type, the Valiant, to enter squadron service in 1955.

Clement Attlee was the first British leader to consider a policy of nuclear deterrence. At a cabinet meeting in August 1945 he stated that 'the answer to an atomic bomb on London is an atomic bomb on another great city'.[9] The perceived threat from Soviet Russia was recognized even in the closing phases of the Second World War. Many senior British political and military leaders understood that Stalin's Russia represented the new threat to the security of western Europe. Britain had fought through over six years of the Second

World War at a cost of near bankruptcy. The American Cold War historian Andrew Pierre wrote that 'wealth accumulated over decades had been rapidly consumed. Over one-quarter of overseas investments had been sold off to pay for war supplies; external debt had risen to 440% of the pre-war figure; and exports had gone down by 30%.'[10] Despite austerity, Attlee's Labour government gave the highest priority to defence expenditure. In 1948 defence took the largest slice of public expenditure at 19 per cent compared with education (9 per cent), welfare (8 per cent) and health (5 per cent).[11] The economic historian David Edgerton wrote that 'by peacetime precedents, post-1945 Britain was extraordinarily militarised'.[12]

Slessor was well aware of the dilemma of creating a credible defence against the Russian threat at a time of austerity. He considered the futility of a strategy of attempting to build up prohibitively expensive conventional forces to match the large Soviet forces stationed in central and eastern Europe. He sent his friend, the military theorist and historian Basil Liddell Hart, a paper on preventing war with Russia in September 1947 in which he wrote:

> It is inconceivable on any realistic basis of strategy that a field army on traditional lines could possibly be used against Russia. Does anyone seriously imagine that we are going to defeat Russian armies in Western Europe, or invade Russia, with 3 or 13 or 30 corps of the Territorial Army? ... But until the day comes [replacement of manned aircraft by the robot weapon and the push button] our primary aim must be the Air Force which alone can produce the counter offensive capable of overcoming Russia's inaccessibility and the only form of strength which at least is likely to deter Russia from aggression; and which must be the main agent of our survival in the event of war.[13]

Five years later that paragraph was to become the central theme of the Chiefs of Staff's 1952 Global Strategy Paper (GSP), largely written by Slessor. He recognized the importance of developing a modern strategic 'air atomic' counterforce. However, he also considered that Britain could not defend itself against the Soviet Union alone. Both of Slessor's books, *The Great Deterrent* and his *Strategy for the West*, expounded a consistent theme, namely the importance of the Anglo-American relationship for the defence of Britain during the Cold War.[14] In *The Great Deterrent* Slessor wrote, 'it does not make sense to discuss British strategy except as part of a combined Anglo-American strategy'.[15]

However, between mid-1946 and late 1947 the Anglo-American 'special relationship' came under considerable strain. Many in America were surprised by the landslide victory for Attlee's Labour government in July 1945. There was a widely held suspicion that socialism, like Communism, was a threat to the American way of life. In March 1946 Lord Inverchapel, the British Ambassador in Washington, wrote to Attlee that 'many Americans were then inclined to jump to the conclusion that a socialist Britain would tend to align with a communist Russia rather than with capitalist America ... All this leads to a feeling there is a danger of us being placed in a position of a mere breakwater between the United States and Russia.'[16] In this febrile atmosphere, Congress passed the Atomic Energy Act in mid-1946. This was better known as the McMahon Act, named after Senator Brien McMahon, the sponsor of the legislation. The Act prevented the passing of nuclear information to any foreign country or foreign individual, thereby retaining an American monopoly on nuclear energy and atomic weapons. Attlee felt the United States were guilty of a breach of faith.[17] Feeding this resentment was the fact that Britain had already given the US unfettered access to its own atomic research. At wartime meetings between Churchill and Roosevelt in 1943 and 1944, agreements had been finalized to continue with collaboration and the exchange of information on nuclear research and development after the war.[18]

In the context of Britain being frozen out of any future collaboration on nuclear energy and weapons development, Margaret Gowing, the official historian of British nuclear energy in the post-war period, wrote in 1974: 'If Britain wanted to be sure of being covered by an atomic deterrent, she had no option but to make it herself.'[19] In January 1947, at a special meeting of the Cabinet's GEN 163 Committee, the decision was taken to develop the British atomic bomb. At that meeting Ernest Bevin, the Foreign Secretary, stated that 'we could not afford to acquiesce to an American monopoly of this new development'.[20] However, there were senior politicians who thought that seeking defence through American [nuclear] cover would be a more acceptable solution. In December 1947 Lord Tedder, Slessor's predecessor as CAS, sent a memorandum to his fellow Chiefs of Staff in which he wrote: 'It would be complete subservience to American policy, and it would render us completely impotent in negotiation with Russia or other countries.'[21] The idea of 'leaving it to the Americans' was also a challenge that Slessor was to confront during his tenure as CAS.[22]

In setting the context of early post-war thinking, the historian Sir Lawrence Freedman commented: 'it was a natural decision to build the atomic bomb. Britain was a great power; great powers have great weapons and therefore Britain should have it.'[23] There was an additional reason: one of trust in America's motives. Attlee told his biographer after his retirement that 'we had to bear in mind that there was always the possibility of [the Americans] withdrawing and becoming isolationists once again. The manufacture of the bomb was therefore at that stage essential to our defence.'[24]

Despite the problems with the Anglo-American relationship at the political and diplomatic level, personal relationships between the RAF and the recently formed USAF senior commanders continued to be close and cordial. However, Slessor was to discover how difficult it would be to re-establish the close working relationship that the RAF and the United States Army Air Forces had enjoyed during the Second World War. In correspondence with Charles Cabell, the head of USAF intelligence, Slessor commented that the continuing failure to get information on America's strategic war planning was a consequence of the 'legal iron curtain of the McMahon Act'.[25]

The Anglo-American relationship improved after late 1947. However, the rapprochement was driven by mutual need and the realization that America saw Britain as having valuable strategic assets at a time of increased tension with the Soviet Union. Key reasons for the improvement included Britain's geographic location, access to Britain's uranium allocations for America's build-up of a nuclear arsenal, and access to Britain's intelligence information.

Britain as an 'unsinkable aircraft carrier' put western Russian strategic targets within striking range of the USAAF's Strategic Air Command (SAC) bombers.[26] As early as June 1946 an informal agreement between Lord Tedder and Carl Spaatz, then Commanding General of the United States Army Air Forces, planned to make available to the USAAF four or five RAF air bases at times of acute international crisis, on a temporary basis.[27] The Berlin blockade between June 1948 and May 1949 set the precedent. That precedent led to permanent basing arrangements that continue to the present day. However, the basing of the SAC's atomic-capable B-29 'Silverplate' bombers would subsequently lead to acute concerns for Britain's exposure to Soviet nuclear attack during Slessor's time as CAS.

During the late 1940s America's ability to expand its nuclear weapons arsenal was limited by its access to uranium ore. A 'Declaration of Trust' between Britain and America, signed in 1944, outlined an agreement to share global access to uranium ore on an equal basis. The planned allocations for the years 1946–1952 gave Britain a surplus but left America with a critical shortage of uranium ore for expansion of its nuclear weapons programme. Keen to improve relations, Britain reallocated its ore reserves to the Americans as part of the 1948 'Modus Vivendi' agreement. That reallocation enabled the Americans to increase the size of their atomic weapons inventory.[28]

Intelligence was one of Britain's key assets. Britain retained an integrated intelligence structure staffed by experienced and well-trained personnel. In comparison, during the early post-war period the American intelligence community was highly compartmentalized. In addition, the lack of experienced officers was a concern. The CIA historian Michael Warner wrote that after 1945 'military intelligence capabilities were swept away in the haste for demobilization'.[29] USAAF commanders reduced their air reconnaissance groups by 80 per cent between August 1945 and July 1946.[30] The subsequent 'Eberstadt Report' published in January 1949 remarked on 'the loss of skilled and experienced [intelligence] personnel in wartime' and warned that 'those who remained have seen their organizations ruined by superior officers with no experience, little capacity and no imagination'.[31] Intelligence historian Richard Aldrich wrote: 'the bottom line was that Washington still did not have proper centralised intelligence', adding 'Britain's intelligence contribution was important in helping to offset the growing post-war imbalance of the "special relationship".[32] America was keen to share intelligence with the British. A number of bilateral intelligence-sharing agreements were finalized between 1946 and 1950: BRUSA, covering communications intelligence [COMINT] (March 1946); UKUSA, covering signals intelligence [SIGINT] (June 1948); the RAF/USAF Target Intelligence Treaty (1948); and the Attlee/Truman agreement whereby Britain agreed to join America in 'coordinated overflights of the Soviet Union' (1950).[33]

Slessor had a deep appreciation of the value of intelligence from all sources and the need for reliable coordinated intelligence. He had seen the positive results of reliable intelligence during the later stages of the Second World War, notably during operation Strangle in central Italy in early 1944 and later in northwest Europe during the Transportation and Oil Plans of late 1944 and 1945.[34] In August 1946 Slessor delivered a lecture at the Thunderbolt Conference to military leaders at the Army Co-operation School at RAF Old Sarum in which he spoke of the shortcomings of getting reliable intelligence during the earlier stages of the Second World War. He advocated the integration of information gathered from a variety of sources, and insisted that it 'must be based on a system of military, scientific and industrial intelligence'.[35] Correspondence in 1945 between Slessor and Stuart Menzies, head of the Secret Intelligence Service (SIS) and referred to as 'C', revealed their degree of agreement on how the future organizational structure of the intelligence services would operate in the post-war era.[36] Slessor continued to have good working relationships with the other intelligence chiefs, including Kenneth Strong, the head of the Joint Intelligence Bureau (JIB).[37] In appreciating the need for information on an adversary's key strategic sites, Slessor strongly advocated the use of air reconnaissance. Richard Aldrich credited Slessor as one of the most forward-thinking in the [intelligence] area and underlined his prescient observation in July 1945 of the need for 'an efficient secret service' and for the development of 'a long-range, stratospheric Photo Recce [sic] aircraft'.[38] However, the rigid control of Iron Curtain borders together with Russia's vast landmass posed a major challenge to intelligence gathering. Reconnaissance aircraft capable of overflying key sites in Russia and its satellite states were in short supply or still in the development stage. The first American jet-powered strategic reconnaissance aircraft, the RB-45C Tornado, entered service with the SAC in 1948.[39] The British equivalent, the PR3 Canberra, only started entering squadron service with 540 Squadron in November 1952.[40]

Commandant of the Imperial Defence College,
January 1948–November 1949

Slessor took up the position of the Commandant of the Imperial Defence College in January 1948 during the two years immediately prior to being appointed as CAS. This prestigious institution was attended by 'outstanding medium-rank officers in all three Services, British and Commonwealth, where they were introduced to those inter-Service and national issues that would concern them if they reached high rank'.[41] For nearly two years Slessor was able to escape the pressures of the administrative duties of a senior air commander. This was an ideal preparation for Slessor's subsequent role as CAS. The air historian Henry Probert commented that this time 'gave him the opportunity to think deeply about strategic problems of the post-war world and the roles of air power in the nuclear age'.[42]

In 1948 Slessor conducted a lengthy lecture tour of United States military staff colleges and participated in talks with senior Pentagon officials.[43] Two lectures that he gave during that tour were published subsequently in his book, *The Great Deterrent*. Both lectures gave an insight into Slessor's thinking and evolving strategy to confront the Soviet threat. At his lecture at the War College, he said:

> Our [British] policy is to give first priority to that form of force which affords the most obvious deterrent to attack by Russia. It has therefore been laid down that the first priority is to be afforded to defence research; after that to the Air Force – and particularly to the long-range striking force ... I have no doubt of our ability to defeat it [Russia] in a cold war as well as in a hot one, should that come; the way to avert the shooting war is to win the cold one.[44]

Because Slessor saw the atomic bomb primarily as a political weapon, he was concerned about American ideas of using nuclear weapons for a future war-fighting strategy. In his lecture 'The Chance of War' to the Air War College, he cautioned his audience about talk of a so-called 'preventive war' against

Russia while America still had the advantage of a nuclear monopoly. The USAF's senior commanders – LeMay, Vandenberg, Power, Kenney and Twining – had all privately supported the concept.[45] Apart from political and moral considerations, Slessor considered this kind of thinking was wrong and would only increase the chance of war occurring. He stated:

> I have heard it argued – usually by Americans – that war is inevitable sooner rather than later. Russia has not yet got the atom bomb but when she has, in addition to her great military strength in conventional arms, she will be undefeatable and irresistible and a mortal threat to Western civilisation.

He expressed the importance of empathizing with the Russian perception of war being inevitable. He believed that the Russians expected to be attacked sooner or later, saying 'there would be some excuse for a Russian who reads the American Press imagining that it is only a question of time before the USSR is attacked. The atom bomb was a shock to them, and they are still frightened of it.'[46]

The psychological impact of the threat of an atomic war would have the effect of deterring the Russians. However, from the British standpoint, throughout the late 1940s very little attention was given to a detailed plan of how and where to attack key Soviet targets. Margaret Gowing wrote:

> Until 1951 there had been very little serious study of the military implications of atomic weapons or their future development. Until then military calculations had taken account only of the British atomic bomb as a deterrent ... and even military calculations surrounding the production of the first atomic bombs were rough and ready. There had been no discussions about future types of atomic weapons and their uses.[47]

Attlee's government gave 'super priority' to the development of the atomic bomb. The same priority was not afforded to the development of the jet-powered bombers that would be later known as the V-force. The priority did not even exist within the RAF's own immediate plan.[48] Consequently, development of the V-force did not proceed at the pace required. During the late 1940s greater emphasis was being given to the expansion of fighter squadrons and the development of defensive guided missile projects. The first Soviet atomic test in August 1949, known in the West as 'Joe-1', led to a fundamental shift in perception and a clear recognition of the urgent need to develop Britain's airborne nuclear deterrent using atomic air power. On becoming CAS in January 1950, Slessor was to have a significant influence on Britain's defence policy.

Chapter 14

The Pinnacle

Chief of the Air Staff, January 1950–December 1952

During his first year as CAS, Slessor faced five formidable challenges: the emergent threat to Britain from a Russian nuclear-armed bomber force; the lack of control over the use of the USAF's Strategic Air Command bombers based in Britain; the start of the Korean War; the continuing difficult issues with the Anglo-American relationship; and the constant campaign to obtain budget approval for the V-force of long-range jet bombers.

The perceived Soviet threat

Throughout Slessor's time as CAS, Britain was highly vulnerable to the Soviet threat. It had not yet developed its own atomic weapon nor a bomber to deliver it. Britain depended on American nuclear cover without having any influence over how, and when, it might be used. Between 1950 and 1955 this was a major concern. Slessor reflected on this fact later when he wrote:

> If we were to leave it to any Ally, however staunch and loyal, the monopoly of an instrument of such decisive importance in the stupendous issues of war and peace, we should sink to the level of a fourth-rate power. In peace we should lose our influence in Allied policy and planning; in war we should have little influence on the direction of Allied strategy.[1]

Following the 1948/1949 Berlin Crisis, the SAC bombers remained at their bases in the south Midlands and East Anglia. Ernest Bevin, the Foreign Secretary, had initially welcomed the USAF presence, but there was no comprehensive written agreement in place, secret or otherwise.[2] The Russian leadership would have considered American bombers based in Britain as a nuclear threat to its homeland. The Russian Tu-4s, a reverse-engineered copy of the American B-29, had entered service with the Russian Long-Range Air Force in 1949. Known in the West by the NATO codename 'Bull', the Tu-4 had the operational capability to attack British targets, possibly with atomic bombs, as early as 1950.[3] Fear of an atomic attack started to enter the national consciousness. In March 1950 and again in February 1951 Churchill, then

Leader of the Opposition, saw Britain as a prime target for a Russian atomic attack. In Parliament he stated:

> We must not forget that by creating the [American] atomic base in East Anglia we have made ourselves the target, and perhaps the bullseye of a Soviet attack ... if Russia had 50 [atomic bombs] and we got those 50, fearful experiences, far beyond anything we have endured, would be our lot.[4]

Slessor was concerned that there was still no clearly written joint agreement covering the use of SAC bombers from air bases in Britain. The Americans took an intransigent position. They refused to share their strategic air plans with their British allies – a notable contrast to the close, cooperative and open relationships during the Combined Bomber Offensive of the Second World War. The issue centred on sovereignty: the Americans wanted unrestricted freedom of action to use their nuclear weapons where and when they wished, whilst the British were concerned about their vulnerability to a Soviet atomic attack.

The Korean crisis, December 1950

The issue came to a head in late 1950. With his typical foresight and strategic vision, Slessor had already considered the possibility of an American overreaction to a crisis elsewhere in the world drawing Britain into a major conflict.[5] From mid-1950 onwards this scenario became a distinct possibility. Slessor was highly concerned by General MacArthur's prosecution of the Korean War. He predicted correctly that MacArthur's proposal to advance north of the 38th Parallel into North Korea might escalate the war by drawing the Communist Chinese, and possibly the Russians, into a wider and deeper conflict.

Slessor warned both Attlee and his Foreign Secretary, Bevin, of the dangers of Britain supporting MacArthur's proposal to advance into North Korea. However, despite Slessor's warnings, Bevin agreed to MacArthur's plan. He was keen to maintain good relationships with Washington.[6] The historian Peter Lowe wrote:

> Slessor intellectually was the ablest of the chiefs of staff and he revealed courage and shrewd judgement in his appraisals of Korea. Undoubtedly, he provided the leadership which soon carried the defence chiefs into increasingly urgent warnings of escalation within Korea.[7]

Slessor's prediction became a reality in late October 1950 when an initial force of 120,000 Chinese Communist troops massed across the Yalu river and pushed the UN forces into retreat.[8] In an atmosphere of rising international tension, the US Joint Chiefs of Staff (JCS) alerted LeMay and other air commanders that 'the current situation in Korea has greatly increased the possibility of general war'.[9] This crisis also alerted the British government to the possibility of global war, and the likelihood of SAC bombers based in Britain being used to attack targets in Russia. In late November Truman held a press conference in which he did not rule out the use of atomic weapons to regain the initiative.[10]

With the real possibility of the crisis escalating into global war, Attlee met Truman in Washington in early December. Attlee was concerned about the direct threat this posed to Britain. He received no clear information or plan on the potential use of the British-based SAC bombers. Truman gave Attlee a 'verbal assurance that the US government would not consider using the atomic bomb without consulting the United Kingdom'.[11] However, the subsequent communiqué issued by the American side after their meeting contained only vague platitudes, and made no mention of 'consultation'.[12] On Attlee's return to London, Slessor and the other Chiefs of Staff were 'left in the dark ... and had little grasp of the outcome of the Truman-Attlee talks'.[13] In December 1950 Slessor, with the other Chiefs of Staff, requested Lord Tedder, then head of the British Joint Service Mission (BJSM) in Washington, to approach the American Joint Chiefs of Staff (JCS) to gain a clear understanding of America's plans to use its British-based bombers in the event of war.[14] Tedder failed to get any further information from the Americans. Subsequently, Air Marshal William Elliot, Tedder's replacement at the BJSM, also failed to make any progress on this issue. In desperation, Slessor produced a paper for the COS committee which addressed his so-called 'stop lines', the scenarios under which nuclear war might be initiated in response to Soviet aggression in Europe.[15] The paper was sent to Elliot to discuss with the JCS. Slessor was attempting to flush out the American position.[16] However, the JCS did not change their stance: they would not disclose their war plans to the British.

The JCS position should be considered in the context of the McMahon Act. The Act prohibited American citizens, either military or civilian, from having any discussion with foreign representatives that were related to nuclear issues. Any violation could lead to prosecution that could result in a sentence of 'life imprisonment or death'.[17] Moreover, the revelation that Alan Nunn May and Klaus Fuchs, both British atomic physicists, had passed secrets to the Russians only served to reinforce an American perception of the fragility of British atomic security.[18] American politicians and senior military commanders were always suspicious of Attlee's post-war Labour government. Professor Ken Young, a British political scientist who has studied Anglo-American Cold War issues, wrote 'U.S. officials worried that some Labour ministers were unduly sympathetic to Soviet interests.'[19]

Elliot met the JCS in September 1951. During the course of their discussions Nathan Twining, the Deputy Chief of Staff of the USAF, commented 'our people are so het up over the Soviets that we must use the [atomic] bomb'.[20] In a letter to his American friend George Fielding Eliot, Slessor wrote: 'we are in the atomic front line and you are still a hell of a long way from it, and the experience of the Korea panic last winter does make us wonder a bit what you are liable to do in another really critical situation'.[21] No amount of dialogue from Slessor, Elliot or Oliver Franks, the British ambassador in Washington, moved the JCS from their intransigent position. Out of frustration, Slessor and the other Chiefs of Staff sent a message to Elliot to pass on to the JCS. It read:

> The United Kingdom is not an American aircraft carrier conveniently anchored off the coast of Europe. We are their only really solid ally – in the long run as indispensable to them as they are to us – and we intend to be treated as such. And in this matter, more perhaps than in any other strategic matter, we insist on having an agreed policy thought out in advance.[22]

The rejection of requests, undue delays and obfuscation on the American side dogged the relationship between the British COS and the American JCS until the end of Attlee's government in October 1951. Slessor expressed his concern on the prevailing attitude held by the majority of the American public in 1951: that atomic bombs should be used to deal with Russia. Slessor and his fellow Chiefs of Staff wrote a report in December 1951 that addressed the concern:

> There is a widespread, though not universal, belief in the quite mythical idea that the atomic bomb by itself is a panacea, a means by which Russia could be brought to its knees and the rule of law could be restored in the world without having to endure perhaps twenty years of the present sort of 'cold' war ... without having to send American troops to fight once more on European soil; and without any very unpleasant consequences to anyone else.[23]

Few historians have concentrated on the fraught period of Anglo-American relations in late 1950 and early 1951. The British historians Peter Lowe and Ken Young, and more recently Alex Shaw, are exceptions.[24] Most of the historiography overlooked both Slessor's role and influence in the British policy on Korea and his insistence on attempting to clarify America's war plans for SAC bombers based in Britain in late 1950.

The evolution of the Global Strategy Paper, 1952

In early 1950, and immediately prior to the Korean War, the American policy document NSC-68 called for a substantial rearmament programme to meet the perceived Soviet threat.[25] The [American] Medium Term Defence Plan reflected NSC-68 policy and formed the basis of the NATO force goals agreed in Lisbon by the North Atlantic Council in February 1952. In summary, it established a clear 'division of labour' between (NATO) Allies that allowed the United States to develop its nuclear war plans without Allied interference. Meanwhile, the European Allies were encouraged 'to develop ground forces for the defence of Europe'.[26] It called for NATO members to build up a conventional force of 9,000 aircraft and 96 army divisions by 1954 to meet the perceived Soviet threat from eastern and central Europe. Slessor understood that the impossibly large expenditures on conventional defence would have a detrimental impact on the general economies of Western Europe. Western European NATO members were still in a fragile economic state after the war and, furthermore, had suffered a further recession between 1950 and 1952. In November 1951 Slessor wrote:

> Over-expenditure on rearmament, leading to the ruin of the economy of Western Europe, would be to play the Communist game and to present Russia with a bloodless victory gained at the sole cost of playing upon the nerves of the Free World.[27]

Despite these setbacks, Slessor persisted with the quest to establish a credible British nuclear deterrent. The return of a Conservative government in October 1951, with Churchill as Prime Minister, was welcomed by many in the armed forces. In addition, the Truman administration and most Americans were pleased to see Churchill returned. Churchill visited Truman in Washington in January 1952. In the atmosphere of a much-improved relationship, the JCS gave Churchill a comprehensive briefing on America's advances in nuclear weapon technology, the build-up of their nuclear arsenal and their war plans.[28]

In light of these revelations, Churchill considered that a fundamental re-appraisal of Britain's defence policy was long overdue. He instructed the COS to develop a paper, outlining their ideas, to address the issue. During April 1952 the COS produced what later became known as the Global Strategy Paper (GSP). Slessor took a dominant role in writing the key sections of the GSP, and it contained many of the ideas that he had developed since 1945.

In summary, the GSP made three important points. It placed deterrence at the centre of British defence policy. It talked of the need to prepare for a long Cold War. Finally, it considered that the NATO force goals agreed in Lisbon were unrealistic and unacceptable.[29] The GSP was written as much for American politicians as it was to reappraise Britain's defence policy.[30] To emphasize this point, Churchill sent Slessor to Washington in July 1952 with the intention of getting the American Chiefs of Staff to agree to an Anglo-American nuclear deterrence policy. Slessor presented the GSP to the American JCS in July 1952. He argued for a fundamental change of NATO strategy, stating that the 'force goals' were an 'economic impossibility, a logistic nightmare and strategic nonsense'.[31]

Cold War historians have acknowledged that the GSP represented a turning point in the way that nuclear deterrence was now placed at the centre of British defence policy. In writing about the GSP, the American historian Andrew Pierre wrote that Britain 'was the first nation to base its security planning almost entirely upon a declaratory policy of nuclear deterrence' and that it should rank as 'a classic amongst military documents', giving credit to Slessor for its authorship.[32] Baylis and Macmillan contended that the GSP 'remains perhaps the best known, the most often discussed and also the most highly regarded defence document of the post-war period'.[33] The GSP was accepted and approved by Churchill and the Cabinet in June 1952. Moreover, the decision was taken to obtain V-bombers in quantity and their production was officially given 'super-priority'.[34]

However, the strategy expressed in the GSP was at variance with American strategic policy. The JCS saw the policy change as an indication that the British were reneging on their NATO (conventional) force goal commitments previously agreed in Lisbon in February 1952.[35] The JCS took a dim view of the planned reduction of British troop numbers in western Europe, while at the same time planning to build up the RAF's V-force and expand their atomic weapons production.[36] However, Nathan Twining, Deputy Chief of the USAF's Air Staff, told Slessor privately that 'they shared the British view'.[37] Air Vice-Marshal Tony Mason wrote in 1994 that 'no [NATO] partner, not even the USA, could meet the specified requirements [of force goals] after the start of the Korean War. The force goals were never attained and deferred indefinitely in April 1953.'[38]

Thinking on the subject of nuclear deterrence was also changing in America. In early 1953 Charles Murphy, an influential New York columnist who was also a USAF reservist and air power apologist, wrote succinctly that the British initiative gave 'substance to the abstractions and theories on air power ... an actuality, feared by Soviet Russia, and therefore a potent instrument for military and diplomatic action'.[39] By late 1954 Eisenhower's 'New Look' programme followed GSP thinking on the employment of nuclear weapons for deterrence.[40] However, a historiographic debate surrounds the influence of the 1952 GSP on Eisenhower's 'New Look' 1954 policy. Both Slessor and Alastair Buchan, a leading writer on defence studies in the post-war period, maintained that the 'New Look' was 'a function of the ideas planted by the GSP in 1952'.[11] Irrespective of the differing viewpoints, both Baylis and Freedman considered that the fact remains that both policies 'grew from the same reasoning'.[42] That the GSP was presented to the JCS in July 1952 cannot have failed to influence the future 'New Look' American thinking on defence policy and the role of nuclear deterrence that was announced in February 1954.

Air intelligence and reconnaissance 'Special Duty': Operation Jiu Jitsu, April 1952

In the quest to develop an effective deterrence policy, Slessor was cognizant of the urgent need for targeting information of Russia's key strategic sites. Slessor played an active role in expanding air reconnaissance operations known by their acronyms, ranging from IMINT (imagery intelligence from the electromagnetic spectrum that includes photographs, infrared and radar imagery in addition to maps, reports, navigation data, etc.) to SIGINT (intelligence-gathering by the interception of signals, whether communications between people (communications intelligence (COMINT) or electronic signals not directly used in communication (ELINT)).

Until the early 1950s both the British and the Americans had relied on captured Luftwaffe wartime photo imagery, much of it retrieved during operation Dick Tracy, for their intelligence assessments of western Russia. In addition, they also relied on HUMINT, human intelligence derived from espionage and agent activity; this included projects such as Wringer and Dragon Return that involved the debriefing of returning German prisoners of war, scientists and refugees.[43] Amongst other information obtained, these programmes revealed some useful material on Russian rocket research and developments.[44]

A secret strategic photographic reconnaissance conference held at RAF Benson in October 1950 concluded that the existing photoreconnaissance (PR) aircraft in the RAF – the Mosquito, Spitfire and Lincoln – were unsuitable for gathering data over the Russian landmass. These obsolescent aircraft were limited by their speed, range and altitude. Only the PR 31/46, a photoreconnaissance variant of the Canberra, could meet the criteria. But this was still in the development phase and did not enter service until late 1952.[45] Additional challenges to image-gathering over Russia's northern latitudes included the fact that it was often covered by cloud, and for much of the year the snow-covered terrain made photo interpretation difficult. However, ongoing research and development in Britain and America on such areas as navigation, radar mapping and optical resolution ultimately resolved the challenges of gathering IMINT over northern Russia.

Gathering air intelligence over an adversary's territory was, and still is, always considered a highly provocative act, with potentially serious political repercussions. The shooting-down of a US Navy Privateer off the Latvian coast in April 1950 and the resulting strong Soviet protests at a time of international tension led Truman to forbid further Russian overflights.[46] As discussed earlier, Attlee and Truman had concluded an agreement 'to undertake periodic overflights of the Soviet Union to locate its airbases and disposition of its long-range bomber forces that could conduct atomic surprise attacks on the West'.[47] A squadron of RB-45C Tornado reconnaissance aircraft were deployed for this purpose to RAF Sculthorpe in Norfolk during January 1950.[48]

To circumvent Truman's restriction on overflights, Hoyt Vandenberg, Chief of Staff of the USAF, contacted William Elliot at the BJSM to see if RAF aircrew would fly rebadged 'RAF' Tornados on reconnaissance operations.[49] Slessor agreed. He saw this as an opportunity for gathering much-needed target intelligence. It also had the benefit of improving the RAF/USAF relationship. Curtis LeMay, the SAC commander, was keen to get target intelligence for his expanding force of bombers. Target sets included airfields, submarine pens, nuclear facilities, rocket sites, command and control centres, aircraft factories and key transportation hubs.

Six RAF flight crew, led by Squadron Leader John Crampton, were sent to America for training and familiarization with the Tornado.[50] The plan for Operation Jiu Jitsu would involve simultaneous overflights of the Soviet Union by three aircraft to gather SIGINT and IMINT on air bases located in western Russia and Ukraine. Slessor was directly involved in the operation. He prepared a highly restricted, top secret briefing note for Churchill, Lord Alexander and Lord Cherwell in early February 1952. In the note he explained the importance of having target intelligence prior to the outbreak of war for any counterforce operations. He wrote:

> If Russia wished to disable this country, her best chance would be to strike a crippling blow with atom bombs ... the Air Defence Committee

have concluded that if 50 atom bombs could be allocated for a counter-offensive against Russian airfields, the weight of the attack could be halved. This counter-offensive, if it is to be effective, must take place immediately on the outbreak of war ... accurate results can only be achieved if radar photographs are available to ensure the identification of the target.[51]

Despite his initial reservations, Churchill approved the Jiu Jitsu 'special duty' operation on 24 February. This was a high-risk operation but the overflights were a success. The international political consequences of the shooting-down of a Tornado would have been disastrous. Such an incident might well have also led to demands for the resignations of both Churchill and Slessor. Churchill's agreement, however reluctant, is the clearest evidence of his trust and respect for Slessor's judgement and influence. A further overflight operation, Jiu Jitsu II, took place in May 1954.

A report written prior to that operation described the first 1952 overflights as follows: 'During the moonless night of 17/18 April 1952, three aircraft flew over Russian territory simultaneously and valuable results were obtained on 20 out of 35 long range airfields.'[52] In addition to the IMINT (radar imagery), important SIGINT information was gathered. On the conclusion of the Jiu Jitsu I operation, Slessor sent a telegram to Elliot at the BJSM in Washington in which he referred to the overflights in coded language, writing that 'Vandenberg was expecting more details of the "little party" held recently and suggesting "further festivities" later in the year'.[53] The Jiu Jitsu I operation marked the start of a new association between the RAF and the USAF, and later with the CIA in its U-2 Aquatone programme. That association would continue until 1960.[54]

Moving from theory to practice: Slessor as architect of the airborne nuclear deterrent

One of Slessor's greatest challenges during his three years as CAS was the continual pressure that he needed to exert on politicians to persevere with the build-up of the V-force against the background of post-war austerity. Defence took the largest part of public expenditure during the period 1950–1952, averaging 30 per cent, or nearly 10 per cent of GNP.[55] On his first day as CAS, Slessor sent a position note to Arthur Henderson, the Secretary of State for Air, on the poor state of Bomber Command. It read: 'The provision for the Royal Air Force over the period 1950–1953 leaves the Service in no position to meet its commitments in the event of war ... the conception of the "visible deterrent" – a powerful first-line to discourage aggression is no longer tenable, if ever it was. It is a policy adopted in the last cold war from 1937 to 1939 when it was completely ineffective.'[56]

The RAF's front-line force had declined from a peak of 55,000 aircraft in 1945 to little more than 1,000 in 1947.[57] By 1949 Bomber Command had only twenty squadrons of obsolescent Lincolns and Lancasters, with a front-line strength of no more than 140 aircraft.[58].

Slessor was committed to building up the new generation of four-engined jet bombers that would be capable of reaching targets in western Russia and the eastern European satellite states. He suggested the name 'V-force' during an Air Council meeting. The name was based on the wing shape of the three variants. He stated that his own preference was 'to establish, so to speak, a "V" class of jet bombers'.[59] The three bomber types that evolved from the original B.35/46 design specification became better known as the Vickers Valiant, the Avro Vulcan and the Handley Page Victor. Some historians have doubted the reliability and credibility of the deterrence value of the V-force. Vincent Orange criticized Slessor's plan for nuclear deterrence using the British bombers. He wrote:

> Slessor ignored the fact that post-war bombers were even more vulnerable to ground fire than they had been until 1945 ... an economic and military folly for a nation as impoverished and short of skilled labour as Britain – of producing three different types of immensely complex and expensive bombers to do the same job. All three V-bomber types were excellent flying machines but would have been 'easy meat' for Soviet fighters and missiles ... American bombers were faster ... and were equipped with more electronic devices.[60]

These conclusions were both incorrect and highly speculative. Slessor strove to ensure that Britain would have a credible deterrent. He made the decision to approve all three types of V-bomber, stating: 'He would have been a very bold man who could have selected the best of the three V-bombers, until we tried out all three we couldn't say which was the best.'[61] He was repeating the tried and tested experience of the 1930s when the RAF was evaluating long-range bombers – the Manchester, Stirling and Halifax.[62] Duncan Sandys of the Ministry of Supply agreed, asserting that 'in equipping an air force, as in racing, it is risky to put all your money on one horse, or to try to guess the winner too long before the race'.[63] In terms of performance, all three types and marks of the V-force were comparable in their speeds to American bombers at 40,000ft.[64] Paul Graham wrote: 'All three V-bomber variants compared favourably with their contemporaries of other nations, and in some respects were markedly superior, the Vulcan for example was famed for its "fighter-like" handling, especially at high altitude.'[65] Andrew Brookes, an air historian who served as a Victor pilot during the Cold War, wrote that dependent on either day or night-time attack, between 50 and 90 per cent of the V-force would have reached their targets.[66] The V-force carried sophisticated electronic countermeasures equipment (ECM) capable of jamming communications to Soviet fighter interceptors.[67] In the mid-1960s, with the increase in the effectiveness of the Russian defence network, Vulcans and Victors changed their tactics. If deterrence failed, they would have flown at low level to avoid radar detection and then have launched their 'Blue Steel' stand-off weapons up to 100 miles from their targets.[68]

Slessor's quest to build up the V-force during his time as CAS was hampered by both Labour and Conservative politicians, who argued that the highly expensive strategic bomber force should be left to the Americans. Even in the year before Slessor became CAS, his friend Liddell Hart considered that the cost of the new jet bomber force would be prohibitively expensive. Some senior RAF commanders agreed. Sir George Pirie, Air Member for Supply and Operations (AMSO) in 1949, commented to Liddell Hart, 'let them [the USA] develop the bombers'.[69]

Peter Hudson, who worked in the secretariat at the Air Ministry, commented that during 1950 Slessor developed an ambitious plan for the role, deployment and build-up of up to 240 V-bombers.[70] However, defence budget restrictions during the final two years of Attlee's Labour government frustrated his efforts. Ironically, the shock of the Korean War fundamentally changed thinking on previously restricted defence expenditures. Attlee's government approved a comprehensive rearmament programme that started in late 1950. Parliament voted an additional £100 million immediately for defence and for a three-year build-up that would ultimately cost £5.2 billion.[71] The defence build-up included an order for twenty-five Valiants in early 1951.[72] Though the Valiant had not yet made its test flight, the Labour government recognized the urgent need for its early production and entry into Bomber Command. However, it would be nearly four years before the first Valiants entered service in January 1955.

Budget restrictions in a period of austerity continued to be a challenge, despite the fact that Churchill's Conservative government had given 'super-priority' status to the build-up of the V-force in 1952.[73] Slessor expressed real concern about a reduction, or even cancellation, of the V-force build-up. To alleviate budget problems at a time of austerity, there was a persistent idea held by some Conservative ministers who continued to believe that strategic nuclear bombers should be left to the Americans. At times, even Churchill and Lord Alexander, the Defence Minister, questioned the wisdom of continuing with the V-force programme.[74] On 11 January 1952 the first Valiant prototype crashed after a flight trial for an engine shutdown and relight. Churchill wrote a minute to Norman Brook, Secretary of State for Air, stating:

> Thank you for your explanation issued to the Press about the crash of the prototype 'Valiant'. I am glad the crew escaped. I suppose we have lost quarter of a million pounds. This is a heavy blow to all that line of Air thought who argue that Britain should plunge heavily on the largest class of Air bombers. The Americans will do this, and also have the things to carry. We should concentrate **not entirely** but far more on the fighter aircraft to protect ourselves from destruction. I am not at all comforted by the assertion that you are going to make a lot more 'Valiants' even though you may avoid repetition of this initial disaster.[75]

Despite the obvious pessimism, the unfortunate crash did not seriously slow down the production schedule. The design faults were rectified and the second Valiant prototype became available for testing in April. Slessor now had a mandate to proceed with the build-up of the British strategic nuclear bomber force. Slessor's decision to proceed with all three different models was vindicated during the 1960s. The Valiant was found to have metal fatigue problems. The change of tactics for a nuclear attack on Soviet and Eastern European targets to a low altitude approach to avoid a new generation of Soviet surface-to-air missiles proved to be beyond the Valiant's structural capabilities and it was withdrawn from the strategic V-force operations when its airframe was found to be unsuitable for dealing with low-level turbulence and manoeuvring.

Slessor had to fight for the continuation of the V-force build-up. Both Churchill and Lord Alexander repeatedly expressed their doubts, wanting perhaps to slow down or even cancel the V-force, and considered 'leaving strategic bombing to the Americans'. Slessor felt compelled to write to Alexander, stating:

> In connection with our bomber programme, the Prime Minister has more than once referred to the same thing [leaving it to the Americans]. The influence of Atomic Air Power is a fundamental factor in the Chiefs of Staff Global Strategy policy. The provision for a Medium Bomber Force in the R.A.F. share of the new rearmament programme is far from excessive. I am convinced that it would be absolutely fatal for us to adopt the line that we can leave all long-range Bomber operations to the Americans.[76]

Slessor subsequently met his old mentor Lord Trenchard and shared his concern that 'he didn't trust our [political] masters about the bomber force'. Slessor feared that the V-force build-up might have been cancelled as an act of political expediency at a time of national austerity. Shortly after writing to Alexander, he sent a personal letter to Trenchard on 3 October: ' I'm still afraid that if the Treasury push really hard, the eyes of the Cabinet will turn, not to teeth and spectacles, and housing and welfare generally, but to the bomber force as a means of saving money.'[77]

On that same day Britain detonated its first atomic bomb in the Monte Bello islands off northwest Australia in the culmination of Operation Hurricane. Britain now joined America and the Soviet Union as an atomic power. With national prestige restored, Churchill would certainly have seen the advantage of the nuclear weapons programme, together with the development of the V-force. However, Slessor remained suspicious of political motives.

Slessor also warned of the danger of this complacency. On his last day as CAS, Slessor wrote to Churchill:

Tomorrow I am leaving the employed list of the R.A.F. after nearly 38 years in the Air Service and shall have no more share in the responsibility for shaping our military programmes. Whilst it is clear that the Chiefs of Staff themselves understood the importance of the bomber in British policy, I have sometimes felt that it is not universally recognised as the vital thing it is ... Are we to leave all this to our American Allies? We can never aspire to match them in numbers. But we have an unparalleled contribution to make in quality and fighting value, in battle experience, in technique, design and invention. The British four-jet bombers now flying are the best in the world.[78]

Chapter 15

Forecasts Come to Fruition

Sage, Writer and Broadcaster, 1953–1965

During his last year as CAS, Slessor had ensured the V-force programme would continue. All three prototypes of Britain's new V-force bombers – the Valiant, Victor and Vulcan – made their first flights. Furthermore, after five years of nuclear research and development, Operation Hurricane had delivered Britain's first test of an atomic weapon in October of that year. Slessor had left a significant legacy for his CAS successors.

The political historian Anthony Seldon wrote, 'it is ironical that it was only after Slessor's departure in December 1952 that his thoughts were crystallized into policy statements, the more so as none of the three Chiefs of Staff who served during 1953–4 possessed the creative minds of Slessor's calibre'.[1] Seldon wrote further that 'it is of note that Ministers as a whole did not play a significant role in the evolution of this [nuclear deterrence] strategy. The important work and thought was put in by senior officers of the Services, notably Slessor ... and the supporting scientists.'[2] As we shall see later, not all historians agreed with this view.

In retirement Slessor was now able to concentrate on writing about strategies to deal with the challenges of the Cold War. He wrote numerous articles throughout the 1950s. He also wrote three books between 1953 and 1957, gave lectures in both Britain and America, and appeared on television and radio programmes. The discussion of deterrence and the use of atomic and then hydrogen weapons had entered the national consciousness. His publications during the 1950s demonstrated his qualities as a first-rate strategic thinker. John Baylis wrote in 1977 that 'Slessor's post-war publications laid the intellectual foundation for further study ... which are now the main organizing concepts of contemporary strategic thought.'[3] The key themes that Slessor addressed in his writing and lectures during the 1950s included strategic deterrence through air power, his criticism of the American approach to massive retaliation and graduated deterrence, the likelihood of more limited wars, and his forecast of the way the Cold War would develop.

On leaving his post as CAS, Slessor delivered his first public lecture at Chatham House in March 1953, just three months into his retirement. His subject was the place of the bomber in British policy. This matter had achieved particular importance following America's detonation of the first hydrogen bomb only six months earlier. He believed that the atomic, and particularly the hydrogen, bombs had 'levelled the playing field' between Russia and Britain. He wrote: 'it is the bomber that could turn the vast spaces that were Russia's prime defence against Napoleon and Hindenburg and Hitler into a source of weakness rather than strength'.[4]

His first book, *Strategy for the West* was published in 1954. It was well received in Britain and America and summarized much of the thinking that he had included in the Global Strategy Paper (GSP).[5] Professor John Groom wrote that 'his thoughts were so influential in British and US policy making circles'.[6] Slessor made a strong plea to his readers to recognize that 'the great deterrent' had abolished total war.[7] Not everyone agreed with Slessor's ideas. Bernard Brodie criticized him, stating that 'the essential idea ... was that everything must now rest on the principle of deterrence. No line of thinking, let alone of action, must be permitted to impair the value of [nuclear] deterrence.'[8] Slessor had always argued that thermonuclear air power was the ultimate sanction and only to be used 'when great nations were mortally threatened. It is by its nature an unlimited instrument.'[9]

To dispel the impression that he was automatically in support of the American approach to massive retaliation, Slessor argued that 'no one suggests that we should immediately drop a hydrogen bomb on Moscow the moment there is a frontier incident, for instance, on the border of the Soviet zone. That is one of the reasons why we have conventional forces in Germany.'[10] Brodie had clearly ignored the fact that Slessor had argued in *Strategy for the West* that, instead of total war, there would be many smaller localized wars that would need to be fought with conventional weapons. With his typically prescient observation, Slessor wrote:

> I think that this generation will see more 'Koreas' elsewhere in the world ... if they come, they should be regarded as tactical episodes in the real world war of our time [the Cold War], which it will be in our interest to isolate and keep localised, as unquestionably it was in Korea ... we should not achieve our object by deliberately blowing up a small, localised campaign into World War III.[11]

That final remark underlined the essential difference between his thinking and that of John Foster Dulles, American Secretary of State. Dulles gave a speech in January 1954 that stressed the importance of a 'great capacity to retaliate, by means and at places of our own choosing'.[12] The 'all or nothing' approach of massive retaliation could turn minor and limited hostilities into major conflict.[13] Dulles subsequently modified his views, but he did not rule out the use of nuclear weapons through a policy of 'graduated deterrence' in limited peripheral wars.[14] This distinct difference between Slessor's more selective approach on the use of nuclear weapons and America's massive retaliation policy was a theme Slessor returned to address in his lectures and articles throughout the mid-1950s.[15]

In Eisenhower's 'New Look' era, weapons development had entered the age of 'nuclear plenty'.[16] Smaller nuclear weapons were now being manufactured in volume for intended tactical use in battlefield conditions. Eisenhower announced at a press conference in March 1955 that he could see 'no reason why they [smaller nuclear weapons] shouldn't be used just exactly as you would use a bullet or anything else'.[17] Churchill had bluntly rejected the 'New Look' claim two years earlier, stating 'this represents a fundamental difference between public opinion in the USA and England'.[18] In one of his lectures at the Royal United Services Institute, Slessor stated: 'If we place too much emphasis on the atomic deterrent for a purpose for which it is not suitable the effect may be exactly the reverse.'[19]

The concept of graduated deterrence was taken up in a public debate at Chatham House between Rear Admiral Sir Anthony Buzzard and Slessor in November. Buzzard supported a graduated deterrence policy 'so that we can use our atomic weapons tactically without provoking the strategic use of hydrogen weapons'.[20] He argued that this policy would compel the Russians 'to accept our distinctions in the use of nuclear weapons'.[21] Conversely, Slessor replied that a declared policy of graduated deterrence for a war in Western Europe would hand the advantage to the Russians. They would control the way the war was fought as they advanced into Western Europe. Furthermore, he doubted whether West Germans would care about the finer distinction between 'tactical' and 'strategic' nuclear weapons. Either way, West Germany would be left as a 'radioactive desert' while the Russian homeland would remain intact.[22] Twenty-five years later Professor Sir Lawrence Freedman agreed with Slessor's line of reasoning. In his view the descriptors 'tactical' and 'strategic' in the context of nuclear weapons were 'useless terms'. He wrote: 'To a German the most "tactical" of nuclear weapons is strategic in its local consequences.'[23] To underline his point, Freedman referred to NATO's military exercise Carte Blanche of June 1955. This revealed that 'in a real war 355 tactical nuclear weapons would have been used, 1.7 million West Germans would have been killed with a further 3.5 million injured'.[24] Graduated deterrence was never accepted in Britain as a strategic concept.

However, Slessor and his fellow Chiefs of Staff did not rule out the role of smaller atomic weapons. They considered that in other parts of the world 'it might be necessary to use the atomic bomb in a localized war, but only as last resort'.[25]

In his many articles and lectures Slessor often predicted correctly the nature and course that the Cold War would take over the following three decades. He wrote: 'The prospect before us is not a sudden flare-up into atomic Armageddon but prolonged endurance [of the Cold War].'[26] His qualities as a Cold War prophet were captured in a lecture he gave at Oxford in 1955, where he discussed Russia's political and military strategy in terms that reflected Sun Tzu's maxim of 'knowing your enemy':

> If the Soviets are satisfied that they are blocked in Europe they will follow traditional Russian policy by seeking soft spots elsewhere. And that must be in Asia – Persia, perhaps, or Afghanistan, but more likely in Southeast Asia or the Far East somewhere ... we must not lean too heavily on the assumption that our particular brand of democracy is at all suitable for Asian peoples.[27]

In the event, instead of nuclear war, significant limited wars were fought over the three decades following the mid-1950s. The Vietnam War and the Soviet invasion of Afghanistan were notable examples.

However, Slessor had his detractors. Vincent Orange did not consider that Slessor had any new insights to offer in his lectures, commenting:

> He [Slessor] relished the rare opportunity to lecture at Oxford in 1955 ... merely repeating himself to whoever on either side of the Atlantic would offer him a platform. His analysis is simple and shallow, as if the world were divided into two armed camps. He shows little awareness of changes since 1945.[28]

This disparaging critique is at least forthright, unlike the overworked barbs peppering Professor Orange's text whenever he felt obliged to acknowledge positives and presents them grudgingly girded with unconvincing caveats. This animus for Jack Slessor is distinctly rare amongst servicemen, politicians and historians. As Dr Noble Frankland wrote in 2006, when Orange's book was published, 'The first step of a biographer should be to catch the mores and conditions of the age in which his subject lived', and he should 'without sycophancy, look up rather than down to him'. Noble Frankland considered Orange to have neglected these literary obligations. Frankland went on to regret that Orange referred to 'Commanders and Commanders-in-Chief as "Heads" as though they were school masters rather than those upon whom the lives of men and the fate of nations depended'.[29] It is dispiriting that Vincent Orange, who had himself spent three years as an RAF serviceman, was insensitive to such propriety.

Slessor's long-term forecast of the future course of the Cold War was optimistic. He gave a lecture at the RAF Staff College, Andover in 1953 in which he commented, 'this war cannot go on indefinitely. Militant communism as a political theory will become obsolete.'[30] His prediction became reality thirty-six years later with the fall of the Berlin Wall. Slessor's appearance on television and radio programmes inevitably took the form of discussion around – and his defence of – the policy of nuclear deterrence. In April 1954 he appeared on a panel discussion in *Panorama*, the BBC's current affairs programme. It aired only six weeks after the detonation of America's 15-megaton hydrogen bomb over Bikini Atoll. That test shot brought home to an apprehensive British public the immense destructive power of the hydrogen bomb – a thousand times more powerful than the atomic bomb used at Hiroshima. The radioactive fallout contaminated 11,000 square miles of the South Pacific. Despite this grim news, Slessor told a large television audience that a third world war was unlikely. He commented that 'the existence of these fearful weapons in the armouries of the world is a reason for real hope and encouragement, because I believe that it has spelt the end of total war ... I don't believe either side will force a war.'[31]

Slessor had no time for American rhetoric that called for 'rollback' of the Communist frontier. He wrote:

> We have no God given mission to destroy Communism ... we must accept that our opponents have their own rights, hopes and fears ... and there must be a reciprocal programme of 'Live and Let Live' ... It means accepting the status quo for many years 'until the forces of sanity that are at work in the world will assert themselves'.[32]

Michael Howard elaborated on that prediction in a Chatham House lecture in 1998, saying: 'Few policies, either political or military, have ever been so triumphantly vindicated.'[33]

In 1951 the American Joint Chiefs of Staff considered that the British nuclear deterrent force was a strategic irrelevance.[34] By 1956 both Valiant and Vulcan bombers were operational in Bomber Command.[35] As the reality of Britain's nuclear deterrent drew closer, the USAF was becoming ever more interested in involvement through a joint nuclear strike force.[36] In August 1956 senior RAF and USAF officers agreed the terms of reference for a joint strike force at the Encircle Conference in London.[37] In September 1956 Slessor wrote in *The Times* aviation supplement, 'Now that the Anglo-

American alliance is so close, and surely permanent, it only makes sense that we pool our resources ... In the military sphere the present role of air power is to gain time for the forces of sanity to assert themselves in the political and economic spheres.'[38]

In 1957 Britain had reached the point when she could justifiably claim to have created a credible airborne nuclear deterrent.[39] All three aircraft of the V-force, the Valiant, Vulcan and Victor, were operational. In addition, the Grapple programme delivered Britain's first test of a hydrogen bomb.[40] The Anglo-American relationship improved significantly when Harold MacMillan replaced Anthony Eden as Prime Minister after the débâcle of the Suez Crisis. Eisenhower and MacMillan met for high-level talks in Bermuda in February 1957. Correspondence between the two men reveals the approval of the supply of [American] nuclear bombs and release gear to the RAF under the designated Project 'Emily'.[41] Agreements were also reached for the resumption of U-2 Aquatone reconnaissance flights from Britain which had been suspended by Eden in May 1956.[42]

During this time Slessor also continued to keep up with correspondence to the senior military commanders and intelligence chiefs and maintained his personal contacts with friends and confidants that included Liddell Hart. In the wake of reactions to the Sandys 1957 Defence White Paper, Dermot Boyle, CAS at that time, wrote to Slessor for advice on how to deal with the threat of amalgamation of the three services. Politicians from both sides of the political spectrum were in favour of amalgamation as a cost-cutting measure. Slessor responded by advising Boyle that:

> The basic yardstick should be one of function. The function of the RAF, and of the new navy arising from the White paper, is primarily the application of air power ... against the enemy and in support of land forces. If they have any sense, they will leave the missile and nuclear support to the air forces, shore-based or seaborne ... Amalgamation would be appropriate in the area of flight training, engineering expertise ... in time we might even come to having a common staff college.[43]

By the by, the 'staff college' prediction would become a reality forty years later in 1997.

In one particular letter, Kenneth Strong, head of the Joint Intelligence Bureau, commented to Slessor on America's misplaced fear of a perceived 'gap' in bombers and missiles between NATO and the Warsaw Pact. The USAF and major aerospace manufacturers were happy to talk up the 'gap'. Eisenhower later spoke of his concerns about the 'military-industrial complex'.[44] Reports of wildly exaggerated numbers of Soviet missiles and bombers had started to appear in the American press.[45] Strong informed Slessor that the alarmist stories were without foundation. However, he also wrote that the USSR had launched its first intercontinental ballistic missile (ICBM) in May 1957.

Slessor's quest to reforge the Anglo-American relationship with a joint strike force was about to be realized. The catalyst for this goal came with Russia's *Sputnik 1* satellite launch in October 1957. Baylis wrote: 'Ironically, it was the "Sputnik" satellite which created the circumstances that finally transformed rhetoric [of a joint strike force] into reality'. [46] That event alerted the Americans to the fact that the Russians were ahead in ICBM development. They were now vulnerable to a Russian atomic missile attack. The news sent shockwaves through the American government, the military and the general public. At a meeting in late October Eisenhower informed MacMillan that the McMahon Act would be repealed, thereby opening the door for joint nuclear collaboration.

In June 1958, during a visit to Washington, Macmillan also managed to persuade Eisenhower to sign a new agreement on the employment of nuclear weapons in Britain to come under joint control.[47] Finally, a bilateral agreement entitled 'Cooperation on the Uses of Atomic Energy for Mutual Defence Purposes' was signed in July 1958. It enabled the finalization of arrangements for the joint strike force. By November 1958 the V-force consisted of a front-line complement of 144 aircraft, of which 104 were Mark 2 Victors and Vulcans.[48] It would eventually build to a peak of 180 aircraft, with a front-line operational strength of 156 aircraft in June 1964.[49] These numbers were small compared to America's global SAC complement of nearly 1,700 bombers.[50] Despite this disproportionate ratio, the USAF senior air historian Alfred Goldberg wrote: 'The V-bombers added a new dimension to British military power. Comparable to the best American bombers, the B-52 and B-58, except in range, and superior in some respects, the V-bombers were eventually moulded into a small but élite strategic bombing force.'[51]

Freedman commented that by the late 1950s 'the [British atomic and later hydrogen] bomb had come along, the V-bombers had come along, and we had influence on the Americans'.[52] Young wrote: 'This larger political agenda had been laid out by Macmillan in July 1957.'[53] At a defence committee meeting Macmillan stressed the need for Britain to:

Retain our special relationship with the United States and, through it, our influence in world affairs, and, especially, our right to have a voice in the final issue of peace or war [and] to enable us, by threatening to use our independent power, to secure United States cooperation in a situation in which their interests were less immediately threatened than our own.[54]

Slessor's quest for an interdependent Anglo-American nuclear strike force had finally been fulfilled.

* * *

Nineteen years after Slessor's death, Sir Michael Howard, the eminent military historian and Slessor's close friend, delivered a lecture entitled 'Sir John Slessor and the Prevention of War' to the Air League at Chatham House. It was an assessment of Slessor's innovative approach in dealing with the realities and threats at the start of the nuclear age. In a comprehensive analysis of the evolving doctrine of nuclear deterrence, Howard described how Slessor dealt with the challenges he faced during his time as CAS. His persistence and influence led to a fundamental shift in British strategic defence policy. Howard praised Slessor, who 'had thought through and had persuaded many (though not all) of his service colleagues and political masters to accept a doctrine of nuclear deterrence that was to provide the basis for all strategic thinking until the end of the Cold War'.[55]

Nonetheless, Howard did not always agree with all of Slessor's thinking. He gave examples of flaws in his deterrence argument. Why, in a deteriorating and serious confrontation, would Slessor support, in any circumstances, a nuclear first strike in defence of vital interests? Surely Britain itself would be deterred from such a move for the very reasons Slessor had espoused in his own defence thinking. Would we not be ourselves deterred from striking the first blow by fear of Soviet nuclear retaliation? As Howard pointed out, 'Here Slessor was less than convincing ... it must be said that [he] had lost touch with reality ... there could be no comparison between the aftermath of a thermonuclear attack and the German blitz of 1940.' But Slessor was not alone in holding these views. Howard later described studies of the ever more confusing and 'abstruse level of the nature of deterrence' as proposed by nuclear strategy theorists such as Brodie, Kahn, Kissinger, Schelling and others.[56] Debates on the paradoxes of nuclear weapon strategies came to dominate thinking amongst political scientists and nuclear deterrent theorists, on both sides of the Atlantic, throughout the Cold War. Slessor continued to be active in those discussions through the 1950s and 1960s.

Howard concluded his lecture by paying his own personal homage to Slessor:

In the mid-fifties some of us founded what was to become the International Institute for Strategic Studies to provide an informed and critical forum to debate the whole issue of deterrence and arms control, and Jack became one of our earliest Council members. He was a regular attender at our seminars, discussions and conferences, and never for a moment tried to pull rank. He always expressed himself with force and precision, but listened courteously to dissenting voices, made thoughtful interventions in discussions and, without ever abandoning his principles, allowed himself to be moved along by the arguments. He never made you feel a fool, but if you disagreed with him, it was wise first to think through exactly what you were going to say. He was always the voice of experience, realism and sanity, and he kept us all on track. Although he would himself have hotly denied it, he was indeed a truly great man. His contribution to the winning of the war had been outstanding. No less was his contribution to the subsequent keeping of the peace.[57]

Epilogue

In 1969 Sir John Slessor wrote his last book. It was entitled *These Remain. A Personal Anthology: Memories of Flying, Fighting and Field Sports.* He dedicated the book to his five grandchildren, 'on whom we can rely for the future greatness of the country'.[1] The book covers his recollections of growing up as a young child in Edwardian Oxford, his time at Haileybury College, and his experiences during the First and Second World Wars. But he also wrote about his pastimes: field sports, including foxhunting, fly-fishing and shooting. The book brings out more of Slessor's personality than any of his previous books, including *Central Blue*. It reveals that Slessor was a proud Englishman, proud of the legacy of the British Empire, even though by the mid-1960s it had largely gone. At 73 years of age, Slessor felt he was too old and out of touch with current affairs. But this was unconvincing. He had lost none of his acute interest in global affairs. In the last chapter, entitled 'A Look at the Future', he offered an incisive analysis of Britain and its place in the world during the 1960s.

His prediction made in the early 1950s that nuclear weapons would abolish general war had (so far) been vindicated. After the Cuban Missile Crisis of October 1962 the prospect of an all-out nuclear war had receded. Both the Soviet Union and NATO would avoid any direct clash.[2]

Slessor revealed his strong philanthropic feelings and convictions in supporting aid to the third world. 'We must meet our moral obligations – which will serve our own interest – but devoting the appropriate share (and it is a big one) of our human and material resources to relieving the distress and forwarding the economic and political development of less fortunate peoples overseas.'[3]

In European affairs Slessor stated that 'we [Britain] should not be satisfied until we have secured our proper place and seen that the beginnings of a true Atlantic Community [are achieved]'. As we enter the third decade of the twenty-first century, we now know that Slessor's aspirations of fifty years ago were never fully achieved.

But he ended his chapter on the years to come with an optimistic note on the future of Great Britain: 'I have enough faith in youth to believe they will not fail us, and Britain will again be Great.'[4]

Between 1966 and 1969 Slessor wrote a long series of handwritten notes to leave with his family. The notes are intimate and revealing and shed some light on some of his innermost thoughts and feelings. He emphasized that he had never been an ambitious man and he was never one of those people who, throughout their service careers, have always been determined to get to the very top. Nonetheless he wrote, 'I hoped I should get to high rank – in later years. I hoped I should be CAS and, to be frank, I always felt that I was professionally qualified to do so, more than most. But it would not have broken my heart if I had not – I suppose I had a wider range of interests outside the Service than many of my contemporaries.'

Slessor was appointed as Chief of the Air Staff (CAS) on 1 January 1950. In the five years since the end of the Second World War the international situation had deteriorated significantly. The Soviet Union under Stalin showed every indication of becoming more belligerent towards the West. The Berlin Crisis in 1948 gave every indication of a major war. In 1949 the Soviet Union tested its first atomic weapon. Slessor realized that he was being appointed as CAS at an acutely dangerous time for Britain during those early years of the Cold War.

Jack Slessor was also a deeply religious man, and the Slessor Family papers have revealed a hand-written prayer, psalm and hymn he prepared on being appointed as CAS. It is surely a rare example of a deep religious faith amongst the senior British military leaders. It read as follows:

Oh God my father, grant me the strength and courage to face bravely the high demands made upon me in the coming time. Let me always remember the high responsibilities that I bear to our country, and to the men in the Air Force. Strengthen my soul and help it to triumph over my nerves. Grant me a sound judgement and a valiant heart and help me to bring our country and the world to a safe haven, for Jesus' sake.[5]

He also included the hymn written by St Francis of Assisi entitled 'Oh now make me the instrument of your peace', and the 23rd Psalm, 'The Lord is my Shepherd. I shall not want.'[6]

Fortunately, and despite all the threats, and the war in Korea which included the involvement of Chinese troops and Soviet pilots, the world situation never escalated into a global atomic war, which would have had serious repercussions for the survival of Britain.

Interestingly, he mentioned that towards the end of his third year as CAS he was asked if he would stay on for a further year under the Conservative government. But he found serving under Churchill so difficult that he was reluctant to do another year of it. 'I have been able to live my own life, and had a very active and interesting life, since 1953.'[7]

Slessor's predecessor had been Tedder and he was elevated to a peerage. There was some expectation that Slessor too would achieve similar glory. It was not to be. The debonair Field Marshal Alexander was Secretary for Defence when Slessor retired and they were not close. But this concerned Slessor little. He did write in family papers that such an elevation would have put him in a position to further some of the causes dearest to his heart but he was content to retire from the lights of London and Strand on the Green to the arcadian delights of Somerset and the village of Rimpton.

There were other opportunities for twilight glory. Jack was asked if he would accept the appointment of Commandant of the Police Staff College at Bramshill. He declined, firmly advancing the view that future commandants should be top-class police officers, not retired senior military officers with no experience of policing. When asked if he would be prepared to have his name put forward for the governor generalship of Australia, Jack again refused, this time reluctantly, and on this occasion because he had always suffered a degree of sensitivity about his reliance on his cane to mitigate his gammy legs; he thought the governor general, as the Queen's representative, should be someone who could participate in the myriad ceremonial duties with a spring in his step. With Somerset's lord lieutenancy occupied by Lord Hylton over a protracted period, that too was not an option, although the matter of his cane might have again put him off. He did, however, do a stint as Somerset's high sheriff.

Jack continued to write, lecture and be interviewed but he knew in his heart that the time had come to hand over to the young bloods following him. Like so many of that generation who looked up into the dusk of twilight years, he knew he had done his bit to the best of his ability, but other pressures crowded in. A country increasingly moving to the left with regards to socialism and empire retraction was not easy. The application of transparency upset the ruling class. Hierarchical givens were being overturned. The certainties were no longer certain. Jack's personal and political sensibilities were also pushed aside by the early death of his adored Hermione.

Throughout the 1950s and 1960s Slessor continued to be admired by many of his contemporaries. As just one example, Emanuel Shinwell, who was Minister of Defence in Attlee's government during part of Slessor's time as CAS, wrote later:

The RAF has provided in its short life a tradition among its top-ranking officers which is impressive and unique – quite different from the type of men who run the Army and Navy. Among the RAF officers whom I met at this period I recall Jack Slessor, forceful, vigorous, and blessed with an obstinate determination to get what he wants. It was for this reason sometimes difficult to get on with him, for compromise was not a word he easily accepted. I regard him, however, as one of the most brilliant men in the RAF.[8]

In 2002 Jack's grandson, Anthony, was attached from the Army to the RAF Tactical Headquarters just prior to the Second Gulf War. David Walker, AOC 1 Group, introduced Anthony at a Group conference and ended that introduction with: 'Relation?' 'Grandson,' Anthony replied. The AOC turned to the rest of the audience and said, 'For anyone genuinely interested in our Service, you need to read about Jack Slessor.'

Appendix A

John Slessor's Air Force Career

	Promotions	Appointments
14.06.15		Brooklands
06.07.15	2nd Lieutenant RFC	
19.08.15		Gosport
15.09.15	Lieutenant RFC	23 Squadron, Suttons Farm
14.11.15		17 Squadron, Middle East
20.09.16		4 Squadron, Northolt
01.12.16	Temporary Captain RFC	
01.02.17		58 Squadron, France
02.05.17		5 Squadron, France
15.02.18		HQ 28 Wing (Artillery and Infantry)
03.07.18	Temporary Major, RAF	Central Flying School
14.05.19		14 Squadron
17.07.19		201 Squadron
21.08.19	Unemployed list	
24.02.20	Permanent Commission as Flight Lieutenant	1 Flying Training School, Netheravon
04.05.21		20 Squadron, India
25.01.23		Directorate of Staff Duties, Air Ministry
05.05.24		3 Course, RAF Staff College
01.01.25	Squadron Leader	
04.05.25		OC 4 Squadron, Farnborough
01.10.28		Directorate of Operations and Intelligence, Air Ministry
01.10.30		School of Army Cooperation
21.01.31		RAF Instructor, Army Staff College, Camberley
01.01.32	Wing Commander	
13.03.35		OC3 (Indian) Wing
17.05.37	Group Captain	Deputy Director of Plans, Air Ministry
22.12.38		Director of Plans, Air Ministry
01.09.39	Air Commodore	

21.10.40	Air Vice-Marshal (Temporary)	Special Duty in the USA
10.01.41	Air Vice-Marshal	
12.05.41		AOC 5 Group, Bomber Command
06.06.42		Assistant Chief of Air Staff (Policy)
05.02.43	Air Marshal (Acting)	AOC-in-C, Coastal Command
14.01.44		Deputy Air C-in-C, Mediterranean Allied Air Forces and C-in-C RAF Mediterranean and Middle East
05.04.45		Air Member for Personnel
01.01.46	Air Chief Marshal	
01.01.48		Commandant, Imperial Defence College
01.01.50		Chief of the Air Staff
08.06.50	Marshal of the Royal Air Force	
31.12.52		Appointment relinquished

Source: Amended from Air Commodore Henry Probert, *High Commanders of the Royal Air Force* (London: HMSO, 1991), Appendix, pp. 118–19.

Appendix B

Summary of Pre-war Expansion Plans, 1934–1939

Scheme	Date Submitted	Royal Air Force				German Air Force (estimated)			Remarks
		Total Striking Force (bombers)	Total Fighter Command	Total RAF incl. Overseas	Due for Completion	Striking Force	Total GAF	Due for Completion	
A	July 1934	500	336	1,252	March 1939	–	–	–	The first pre-war expansion.
C	March 1935	840	420	1,804	March 1937	800/950	1,512	March 1937	The result of Sir John Simon's and Mr Eden's visit to Hitler in Berlin.
F	Nov. 1935	1,022	420	2,204	March 1939	840/972	1,572	March 1937	Further German expansion and the Abyssinian war.
H	Jan. 1937	1,631	476	2,770	March 1939	1,700	2,500	March 1939	Withdrawn after consideration by cabinet.
J	Oct. 1937	1,442	532	3,031	June 1941	1,458	3,240	Dec. 1939	The first scheme based on estimates of minimum overall strategic requirement.
K	Jan. 1938	1,360	532	2,795	March 1941	1,350	2,700	Summer 1938	The 'emasculated J'.
L	April 1938	1,352	608	2,863	March 1940	1,950	4,400	April 1940	After Austria.
M	Oct. 1938	1,360	800	3,185	March 1942	–	–	–	After Munich, The first 'all-heavy' programme.

Source: J.C. Slessor, *Central Blue*, facing p. 184.

Glossary of Terms

AAF – US Army Air Forces, until 1947 it was not an autonomous single service but still a part of the US Army.

AASAC – Anglo-American Standardization of Arms Committee, the obfuscating title given to Anglo-American conversations in 1940.

AASF – Advanced Air Strike Force of Bomber Command deployed to France in 1940.

ABC – American-British secret staff conversations held in Washington between January and March 1941, prior to America's entry into the war.

ACAS – Assistant Chief of the Air Staff of the Royal Air Force (RAF).

ADC – Aide de Camp – the junior personal assistant to a senior officer.

AMP – Air Member for Personnel (RAF).

AMSO – Air Member for Supply and Organization in the RAF.

Anvil – Codename for Allied plans for an operation to invade southern France. Renamed Dragoon and put into effect in August 1944.

Aquatone – CIA project to overfly Russia using high-altitude U-2 spy planes between 1956 and 1960.

Argument – The Allied bombing offensive between 20 and 25 February 1944 that specifically attacked the Luftwaffe's fighter force in order to clear the way for Allied air superiority in the forthcoming invasion. Of peripheral interest, it occurred in the middle of the Luftwaffe's 'Baby Blitz' on southern England – Operation Steinbock, January–May 1944.

ASV – Air-to-Surface Vessel radar, the maritime adaptation of the H2S land surveillance radar (see also (LR)ASVIII).

ATP Agreement – The Arnold-Towers-Portal Agreement which rejigged US aircraft allocations in light of the US entry into the war.

AVM – Air Vice-Marshal of the RAF.

AVRO Lancaster – Heavy bomber developed from the AVRO Manchester. With four Merlin engines, it had a faster cruising speed and higher ceiling, and most importantly, double the Manchester's range. It entered service in 1941 and was one of the best heavy bombers of the Second World War.

AVRO Manchester – The forerunner of the far more successful Lancaster. The Manchester was powered by two Rolls-Royce Vulture engines which were prone to overheating and unreliable. The Manchester initially entered service in 1940 with 207 Squadron, based at Waddington.

AWPD/42 – The American Air War Plans Division/42: the plan for simultaneous bombing offensives against Germany and Japan, should the Soviet Union sue for peace with Germany.

B-17 – Boeing 'Flying Fortress', a long-range and well-armed heavy bomber. Mainstay of the US Eighth Air Force in the UK.

B-24 Liberator – heavy bomber built by the Consolidated Aircraft Corporation. Used extensively in an anti-submarine role during the Battle of the Atlantic. The introduction of the Very Long Range (VLR) Liberator was instrumental in closing the 'Atlantic Gap' where hitherto U-boats had been able to lurk without fear of aerial attack.

B-29 – Second World War vintage strategic bomber used against Japan in 1945. It was used to drop the atomic bombs on Hiroshima and Nagasaki. B-29s were stationed in the UK in the 1940s and early 1950s as part of the American SAC bomber force. The nuclear-armed B-29 was known as the 'Silverplate' version.

B-29 (RAF) – Known as the 'Washington', it was used by the RAF as a 'stop-gap' measure between 1950 and 1953, before the delivery of the British Canberra and Valiant jet bombers. Reconnaissance variants remained in service until 1957.

Bagration – The operational codename for the Soviet offensive from Belorussia into Poland between June and August 1944.

BE2 – Early First World War biplane (introduced in 1912) developed by the Royal Aircraft Factory in Coventry. It had two crew, although the observer's cockpit was often used to hold reserve fuel.

BEF – British Expeditionary Force, troops sent to France in 1940 to counter the German invasion of the Low Countries and France.

BJSM – British Joint Service Mission, based in Washington. Enabled dialogue with American service chiefs on matters of joint military concern.

Bolero – Codename for the build-up in Britain of forces and logistics required to precede an early invasion of Europe, then named Roundup. Renamed Overlord and leading to D-Day in June 1944.

Bristol Blenheim – Light bomber, which entered service in 1935. It was of limited capability.

Bristol F.2 – First World War fighter biplane introduced in 1916 to replace the BE2. It remained in service into the 1930s.

BRUSA – Bilateral British-United States communications intelligence agreement established in 1948.

CAS – Chief of the Air Staff of the RAF.

CBO – Combined Bomber Offensive by the RAF and US Eighth Air Force.

CCS – Combined Chiefs of Staff (Anglo-American).

CIA – Central Intelligence Agency (US).

CIGS – Chief of the Imperial General Staff (commander of the British Army).

C-in-C – Commander-in-Chief.

COMINT – Communications intelligence.

COS – Chiefs of Staff of the British armed forces.

Diadem – The operation to break through the German Gustav line in central Italy.

Dick Tracy – A joint Anglo-American operation carried out in 1945 to retrieve Luftwaffe air reconnaissance photo-images that were acquired over western Russia between 1941 and 1944, and referred to as GX material. The operation also recovered maps and target material. All data proved useful for early Cold War targeting of Russian strategic sites.

Dragon Return – A British HUMINT operation to interrogate returning German scientists, prisoners of war and refugees for relevant information on Russian military installations that included aircraft factories, rocket sites and airfields. The Americans ran a similar operation called **Wringer**.

Dragoon – Codename for Allied operations to invade southern France and put into effect in August 1944. Originally named **Anvil** during the planning stages.

Drumbeat – The German U-boat offensive in 1942 off the US eastern seaboard, along with operation **Neuland** in the Gulf of Mexico.

ECM – An aircraft's electronic countermeasures used to jam an adversary's communications and radar, and avoid/evade attacking aircraft and missiles.

ELINT – Non-communicative emissions such as radar or radio telemetry from an adversary's electronic devices.

Fairey Battle – Light bomber, which was obsolescent by 1939. It suffered severe losses during the Battle of France.

GEE – A British navigation system developed in the early 1940s, working on the principle of measuring the time delay between two pulses of radio signals to produce a navigational fix with an accuracy of several hundred metres at ranges of up to 350 miles from transmitting stations in eastern England.

GEN-163 – Atomic sub-committee of the British Cabinet in the mid-1940s.

GHQ – General Headquarters in field operations.

Grapple – The British H-bomb test programme carried out between May 1957 and September 1959 near the Christmas and Malden Islands in the southwest Pacific.

GSP – UK 1952 White Paper entitled 'Defence Policy and Global Strategy' but more widely referred to as the 'Global Strategy Paper'.

Gymnast – Plans for the invasion of Vichy-held North Africa. Subsequently renamed **Torch** and put into action in November 1942.

H2S – The first airborne ground-scanning system that was developed by the British during the Second World War to identify targets for bombing, particularly at night-time or when there was heavy cloud cover over the target.

Handley Page Hampden – Medium bomber, in service from 1936 to 1943. It was of limited capability.

Hawker Henley – Light bomber, which was obsolescent by 1939.

HUMINT – Human intelligence derived from espionage/agent activity and interrogation.

Hurricane – The British operation to test its first atomic bomb during October 1952 in a lagoon within the Monte Bello Islands, northwest of Australia.

ICBM – Intercontinental ballistic missile with a minimum range of 3,400 miles. The first ICBM was launched from the Tyuratam missile site in Kazakhstan in August 1957.

IMINT – Image intelligence. Comprises visible spectrum photo-images (PHOTINT) but also imagery from other parts of the electromagnetic spectrum: radar and infra-red.

JCS – Joint Chiefs of Staff (US). Senior uniformed leaders of the armed services who advise the Secretary of Defence and the President on military matters.

JIB – Joint Intelligence Bureau (1945–1964) headed by Kenneth Strong. The bureau undertook a centralizing role that worked with all sections of British intelligence.

Jiu Jitsu – Codename given to overflights of the Soviet Union in April 1952 (Jiu Jitsu I) and May 1954 (Jiu Jitsu II). RAF aircrew flew three American RB-45C Tornado aircraft over key strategic sites in the western Soviet Union and obtained valuable radar imagery (IMINT) and signals intelligence (SIGINT)

JPC – Joint Planning Committee, UK military planning group.

(LR)ASVIII – Improved long-range ASV radar operating in the 10cm range. During most of 1943 it was undetectable by U-boats (see also ASV).

MAAF – Mediterranean Allied Air Forces.

MASAF – Mediterranean Allied Strategic Air Force. A heavy bomber force based on several airfields in the La Foggia area of southeast Italy. It concentrated on targets in northern Italy, southern Germany and Romania.

McMahon Act – The Atomic Energy Act of 1946, sponsored by Senator Brien McMahon. It prohibited the passage of all information relating to nuclear research and development to any foreign country or foreign individual. It went through several amendments in the early 1950s before its effective repeal in 1958. Congress modified the Atomic Energy Act in June 1958 and America and Britain again began sharing nuclear research under the Mutual Defence Agreement of that year.

NATO – North Atlantic Treaty Organization formed in 1948. Its fifteen member states in 1955 were the US, Canada, Britain, Turkey and eleven European countries.

Neuland – German U-boat offensive in 1942 in the Gulf of Mexico (see also Drumbeat).

New Look – Named after Christian Dior's 'New Look' fashion revolution, this was an US defence policy that shifted the focus of military expenditure away from large conventional forces and towards one of nuclear deterrence. Devised primarily by Secretary of State John Foster Dulles, it initially threatened nuclear retaliation in response to Communist aggression anywhere in the world. Eisenhower was also concerned by the burgeoning defence expenditures that would have inhibited growth in the domestic civilian sectors. He saw 'New Look' as an ideal solution to the budget challenges of the mid-1950s. There is a historiographic debate on how much influence the 1952 British GSP might have had on the 1954 'New Look' Policy.

Oboe – A British blind bombing system based on radio transponder technology. Like Gee, it worked on the principle of measuring the time lapse between the transmissions of a signal from a land base in England to reach an aircraft, and from which the Oboe operators could direct the aircraft on to the target.

Overlord – Codename for the Allied invasion of Normandy in June 1944.

Pointblank – Codename for the operation designed to cripple German fighter capability and numbers prior to the invasion of Normandy.

RAF – Royal Air Force.

RB-45C – Also known as the Tornado. A four-engined, medium jet bomber modified for high-altitude reconnaissance, it entered service with the SAC in 1948. Reconnaissance versions were deployed to RAF Sculthorpe in April 1950. Rebadged (RAF) RB-45Cs were used in April 1952 and again in May 1954 during the Jiu Jitsu overflight operations.

RDF – Radio Direction Finding was the earliest development of what would later be known as radar.

RE8 – First World War biplane introduced in 1916 as a two-seater bomber and reconnaissance aircraft. It was designed by the Royal Aircraft Factory.

RFC – Royal Flying Corps, the army regiment which subsequently unified with the Royal Naval Air Service in 1918 to form the independent RAF.

Roundup – Plans for an early invasion of northern France in 1942/1943.

SAC – Strategic Air Command (USAF). Headquartered at Offutt, Nebraska, with General Curtis LeMay as commanding general between 1948 and 1957. SAC's bombers in the late 1950s and 1960s numbered up to 1,700 aircraft (B-47s, B-52s and B-58s).

Shingle The operation codename for the Allied landing at Anzio, south of Rome.

SIGINT – Electronic signals intelligence comprising both communications (COMINT) and non-communicative emissions, such as radar or radio telemetry, from an adversary's electronic devices (ELINT).

SIS – Secret Intelligence Service (*aka* MI6) headed by 'C', Sir Stuart Menzies during the Second World War. Responsible for foreign HUMINT operations.

Sledgehammer – Plans for an early watered-down invasion of Europe between Boulogne and Le Havre; in effect a raid to establish a bridgehead which, if successful, could be reinforced for a breakout.

SOE – Special Operations Executive, the clandestine Allied forces inserted into theatres of operation to liaise with resistance groups engaged in guerrilla warfare.

Strangle – Air interdiction operation in central Italy between March and May 1944

SWC – The Anglo-French Supreme War Council was established to oversee joint military strategy at the start of the Second World War, particularly during the period of the Phoney War.

Ten-Year Rule – A control on defence budgeting brought in by Attlee's post-war Labour government in late 1946. The intention was to control phasing of defence expenditures with the expectation of no major war before 1957. It had the unfortunate consequence of slowing down the development of the new generation of jet bombers requested by the Air Ministry in January 1947.

Torch – Invasion of Vichy-held North Africa.

Tu-4 – Known under the NATO codename 'Bull', the Russian Tu-4 was a reverse-engineered copy of the American B-29. It was manufactured by Tupolev and entered service in 1949 with the Soviet Long-Range Air Force

(LRAF). Tu-4s were capable of dropping atomic bombs and were seen as a distinct threat to Britain in the early 1950s. They had the range to reach British targets from western Russia or the Baltic states.

U-2 – Manufactured by Lockheed, the U-2 was an American ultra-high-altitude spy plane used by the CIA to overfly the Soviet Union and China between 1956 and 1960. It was also known as the 'Dragon Lady'. British pilots flew some of the U-2 missions.

UKUSA – A 1948 bilateral agreement covering Anglo-American signals intelligence.

ULTRA – Codename for the breaking of the German ciphers at Bletchley Park, Buckinghamshire, which gave invaluable intelligence to the Allies.

USAAF – United States Army Air Forces, 1941–1947. At this time it was not an autonomous single service but still a part of the US Army, comprising several American air forces deployed separately in different operational theatres.

USAF – United States Air Force. Founded in September 1947, successor to the USAAF.

Valiant – The first of the V-force bombers to enter service, in January 1955. It was manufactured by Vickers and the first flight took place on 18 May 1951. It was used during the **Grapple** programme to drop Britain's H-bomb over Malden Island, 350 miles south of Christmas Island, in May 1957.

VCAS – Vice Chief of the Air Staff, RAF.

V-force – Britain's three strategic jet bombers (Valiants, Vulcans and Victors). Named 'the V-force' by Air Marshal Sir John Slessor on account of the wing shapes of the aircraft.

Victor – Manufactured by Handley Page, it first flew in December 1952 and entered service in November 1957. Ultimately it was re-roled into an in-flight refuelling aircraft.

VLR Liberator – The Very Long-Range B-24 Liberator was designed by the Consolidated Aircraft Corporation for maritime operations.

Vulcan – Manufactured by AVRO, it first flew on 30 August 1952 and entered service in 1956. With its distinctive delta wing, it was highly manoeuvrable at both high and low altitudes. It only saw action in Operation Black Buck (the bombing of the runway at Port Stanley airport) during the 1982 Falklands Conflict.

Westland Wapiti – Biplane in service on the Northwest Frontier just before the Second World War. It entered service in 1927 and still operated in India up to 1942.

Wolf Pack – A German U-boat tactic used against Allied convoys in the North Atlantic. The U-boats were deployed in numbers to engage in massed, organized attacks against convoy vessels so overwhelming their escort warships. It was remarkably successful during the period between 1939 and early 1943.

Wringer – An American HUMINT operation to interrogate returning German scientists, prisoners of war and refugees for relevant information on Russian military installations that included aircraft factories, rocket sites and airfields (see also **Dragon Return**).

The Casablanca Directive on the Bomber Offensive

Approved by the Combined Chiefs of Staff at their 65th Meeting, on 21 January 1943.

1. Your primary object will be the progressive destruction of the German military industrial and economic system, and the undermining of the morale of the German people to a point where armed resistance is fatally weakened.

2. Within that general concept, your primary objectives, subject to the exigencies of weather and of tactical feasibility, will for the present be in the following order of priority:

    a. German submarine construction yards.

    b. The German aircraft industry.

    c. Transportation.

    d. Oil plants.

    e. Other targets in enemy war industry.

The above order of priority may be varied from time to time according to developments in the strategical situation. Moreover, other objectives of great importance either from the political or military point of view must be attacked. Examples of these are:

(1) Submarine operating bases on the Biscay coast. If these can be put out of action, a great step forward will have been taken in the U-boat war which the C.C.S. have agreed to be a first charge of our resources. Day and night attacks on the bases have been inaugurated and should be continued so that an assessment can be made as soon as possible. If it is found that successful results can be achieved, these attacks should continue whenever conditions are favourable for as long and as often as necessary. These objectives have not been included in the order of priority, which covers long-term operations, particularly as the bases are not situated in Germany.

(2) Berlin, which should be attacked when conditions are suitable for the attainment of specially valuable results unfavourable to the morale of the enemy or favourable to that of Russia.

(3) You may be required, at the appropriate time, to attack objectives in Northern Italy in connexion with amphibious operations in the Mediterranean theatre.

(4) There may be certain other objectives of great but fleeting importance for the attack of which all necessary plans and preparations should be made. Of these, an example would be important units of the German fleet in harbour or at sea.

(5) You should take every opportunity to attack Germany by day, to destroy objectives that are unsuitable for night attack, to sustain continuous pressure on German morale, to impose heavy losses on the German fighter force and to contain German fighter strength away from the Russian and Mediterranean theatres of war.

(6) When the Allied Armies re-enter the continent, you will afford them all possible support in the manner most effective.

(7) In attacking objectives in occupied territories, you will conform to such instructions as may be issued from time to time for political reasons by His Majesty's Government through the British Chiefs of Staff.

Source: Slessor, *Central Blue*, pp. 668–9.

Notes

Introduction

1. *The Times*, 17 November 1979.
2. Alethea Turner, *The Backbone* (Pentland Press, 1993).
3. Sir John Slessor, *Central Blue* (London: Cassell & Co. Ltd, 1956), p. 7.
4. Ibid, p. 204.
5. John Baylis (ed.), *British Defence Policy in a Changing World* (London: Croom Helm, 1977), p. 170.

Chapter 1: Twilight, La Belle Époque

1. Arthur Kerr Slessor (1863–1931) married Adelaide Cotesworth (1869–1925) on 10 June 1896.
2. Slessor Family papers.
3. Lord Blake and C.S. Nicholls (eds), *The Dictionary of National Biography: 1971–1980* (Oxford, 1986), p. 783.
4. Slessor Family papers.
5. Sir John Slessor, *Central Blue* (London: Cassell, 1956), p. 3.
6. Vincent Orange, *Slessor: Bomber Champion* (London: Grub Street, 2006), p. 14.
7. The term 'Gilded Age' has been used by American historians and '*La Belle Époque*' by French historians to denote a period of four decades between the 1870s and 1914 of significant global growth with peace and prosperity.
8. 'Recollections' in Haileybury Archives, 1968; Orange, *Bomber Champion*, p. 15.
9. John Bew, *Citizen Clem: A Biography of Attlee* (London: riverrrun, 2016), p. 35.
10. Slessor, *Central Blue*, p. 2.
11. Ibid.
12. Ibid.

Chapter 2: The Kaiser's War

1. 'While Wilhelm did not actively seek war, and tried to hold back his generals from mobilizing the German army in the summer of 1914, his verbal outbursts and his enjoyment of the title of Supreme War Lord helped bolster the case for those who blamed him for the conflict.' https://www.history.com/topics/world-war-i/kaiser-wilhelm-ii (accessed 21 May 2020).
2. Slessor, *Central Blue*, p. 16.
3. James Hamilton-Paterson, *Marked for Death: The First War in the Air* (London: Head of Zeus, 2015), p. 1.
4. At the time of writing the Haileybury name is still in existence in Stepney as Haileybury Centre, a youth and sports facility serving the East End. Clement Attlee started volunteer

work there in 1905. He saw the realities of social inequality, which led him to join the Independent Labour Party in 1908.

5. Slessor, *Central Blue*, p. 6.

6. Ibid.

7. Ibid., p. 7.

8. Ibid., p. 2

9. Slessor, *Central Blue*, p. 24. The Fédération Aeronautique Internationale (FAI) is an internationally recognized qualification for competence in air sports.

10. Ibid., p. 8.

11. Ibid. Wings are awarded to pilots when they have achieved a significant standard after flight training. For recognition the winged insignia is then stitched on to the pilot's uniform.

12. BE2cs were constructed to Royal Aircraft Factory specifications at the Daimler Factory in Coventry.

13. Sutton's Farm went on to be expanded as RAF Hornchurch and played a key role in the Battle of Britain. During 1940 three squadrons of Spitfires (603, 41 and 264 Squadrons) were stationed there as part of 11 Group, Fighter Command.

14. Slessor Family papers: Jack Slessor's letter to his mother, 15 October 1915.

15. TNA AIR 1/522/16/15/38, 'Police Reports on Air Raids in England', 1915.

16. Slessor, *Central Blue*, p. 14.

17. Sir John Slessor, *These Remain: A Personal Anthology* (London: Michael Joseph, 1969), p. 45.

18. Ibid., p. 46.

19. Brigadier Andrew Roe, 'Air Power in Darfur, 1916: The Hunt for Sultan Ali Dinar and the Menace of the Fur Army', *Air Power Review*, Spring 2017, 20(1):11.

20. Ibid., p. 14.

21. Slessor, *Central Blue*, Appendix A, p. 648.

22. Ibid., p. 653.

23. Ibid., p. 650.

24. TNA AIR 1/2250, 'Reconnaissance Report, Lieutenant Slessor, 23 May 1916; J.A. Gillan, 'Darfur 1916', *Sudan Notes and Records*, 1939, 22(1):15.

25. Roe, 'Air Power in Darfur', p. 19.

26. Slessor, *These Remain*, p. 57; John Masters, *Fourteen Eighteen* (London: Michael Joseph, 1956), p. 72.

27. *The Times*, 7 August 1916: 'The Airmen's work in Darfur: Bombing the Sultan's Party'. On the first day of the Somme offensive the British Army suffered 57,480 casualties: 19,240 killed and 38,230 injured, captured or missing.

28. Roe, 'Air Power in Darfur', p. 9.

29. Anthony Slessor, pers. comm., February 2021.

30. Harry Tate was a popular music hall comedian of the time.

31. Slessor, *Central Blue*, p. 6.

32. Orange, *Bomber Champion*, p. 21.

33. Ibid.

34. Slessor, *Central Blue*, p. 19.

35. Ibid., p. 18.

36. Ibid., p. 19.

37. Ibid., p. 22.

Chapter 3: Amanuensis

1. Slessor, *Central Blue*, p. 45.
2. Russell Miller, *Boom: The Life of Viscount Trenchard* (London: Weidenfield & Nicholson, 2016), pp. 269–70.
3. Ibid., Preface, p. xii.
4. Ibid., p. 22.
5. Air Commodore Henry Probert, *High Commanders of the Royal Air Force* (London: HMSO, 1991), p. 1.
6. Ross Mahoney, 'Trenchard's Doctrine: Organisational Culture, the "Air Force Spirit" and the Foundation of the Royal Air Force in the Interwar Years', *British Journal of Military History*, February 2018, 4(2):143.
7. HANSARD HC Debates, 23 February 1920, vol. 125, col. 1,354, accessed 20 July 2015.
8. Michael A. Longoria, *The Origin of British Air Policing: An Historical View of Air Policing Doctrine: Lessons from the British Experience between the Wars, 1919–1939* (Air University Press, 1992), pp. 15–16.
9. Slessor, *Central Blue*, p. 46.
10. Phillip Meilinger, *Paths of Heaven. The Evolution of Air Power Theory* (Maxwell AFB, Alabama: Air University Press, 2001), p. 53.
11. Ibid., p. 56.
12. Ibid., p. 64.
13. Slessor, *Central Blue*, p. 70.
14. Ibid., p. 51.
15. Ibid., p. 53.

Chapter 4: Educating the Army

1. Phillip S. Meilinger, *Air War, Theory and Practice* (London: Cass, 2005), Ch. 3, 'John C. Slessor and the Genesis of Air Interdiction', p. 64.
2. Slessor *Central Blue*, p. 80.
3. Meilinger, 'Slessor and the Genesis of Air Interdiction', p. 67.
4. Slessor Family papers.
5. Slessor, *Central Blue*, p. 98.
6. Edward Smalley, 'Qualified but unprepared: Training for War at the Staff College in the 1930s', *British Journal for Military History*, November 2015, 2(1).
7. Slessor, *Air Power and Armies*. Part I: *Air Superiority* (Oxford: Oxford University Press, 1936), p. 3.
8. Meilinger, 'Slessor and the Genesis of Air Interdiction', p. 67.
9. Slessor, *Air Power and Armies*, p. 122.
10. Ibid., p. 167.
11. Ibid., p. 61.
12. Meilinger, 'Slessor and the Genesis of Air Interdiction', p. 67.
13. Ibid.
14. Slessor, *Air Power and Armies*, p. 214.
15. Ibid.
16. Slessor, *Central Blue*, p. 95.
17. Ibid., p. 98.
18. Smalley, 'Qualified but unprepared', p. 71.
19. Slessor, *Central Blue*, p. 83.

20. Ibid.
21. Slessor, *Air Power and Armies*, Introduction, p. i.
22. Tami Davis Biddle, *Rhetoric and Reality in Air Warfare* (Princeton: Princeton University Press, 2002), p. 99.
23. Slessor, *Air Power and Armies*, p. 9.
24. Meilinger, 'Slessor and the Genesis of Air Interdiction', p. 73.
25. Clayton K.S. Chun, *Aerospace Power in the Twenty-First Century* (United States Air Force Academy, July 2001, pp. 53–6.

Chapter 5: Rearming for War

1. HANSARD HC Debates, 8 March 1934, vol. 286, col. 2,078.
2. See Appendix B.
3. Malcolm Smith, 'The Royal Air Force, Air Power and British Foreign Policy, 1932–1937', *Journal of Contemporary History*, January 1977, 12(1):162.
4. British dead and injured in the First World War. https://archive.org/details/statisticsof mili00grea (accessed 9 July 2020).
5. Slessor, *Central Blue*, p. 155.
6. Biddle, *Rhetoric and Reality in Air Warfare*, pp. 108–9.
7. Terraine, *A Time for Courage* (London: Macmillan 1985), p. 32.
8. Ibid.
9. HANSARD HC Debates, 12 November 1936, vol. 317, cols 1081–55; also see Winston Churchill, *The Second World War*. Vol. I: *The Gathering Storm* (London: Cassell, 1939), pp. 60–80.
10. Slessor, *Central Blue*, p. 155.
11. Terraine, *A Time for Courage*, p. 25.
12. Reserves: the additional aircraft required as back up to the first line to allow for losses due to accidents or combat.
13. Slessor, *Central Blue*, p. 157.
14. Ibid., p. 158.
15. TNA AIR 2/2720, 3 September 1937; Slessor, *Central Blue*, p. 158.
16. Terraine, *A Time for Courage*, pp. 50–1.
17. Slessor, *Central Blue*, p. 184; Terraine, *A Time for Courage*, p. 51.
18. Charles Webster & Noble Frankland, *The Strategic Air Offensive against Germany, 1939–1945* (London: HMSO, 1961), vol. 1, p. 76.
19. Terraine, *A Time for Courage*, p. 51.
20. Slessor, *Central Blue*, p. 159.
21. G.C. Peden, Problems of Setting Strategic Priorities: The Inskip Defence Review of 1937–38. *RUSI Commentary*, 19 August 2010. https://rusi.org/commentary/problems-setting-strategic-priorities-inskip-defence-review-1937-38 (accessed 22 May 2020).
22. TNA AIR 8/226, 9 December 1937.
23. Philip Meilinger, *Air War, Theory and Practice* (Abingdon: Cass, 2005), p. 54.
24. Ibid.
25. Malcolm Smith, *British Air Strategy between the Wars* (Oxford: Clarendon Press), p. 184.
26. Webster & Frankland, *Strategic Air Offensive*, vol. IV, p. 98, appendix 5 'Aide Memoire' by Sir Thomas Inskip, 9 December 1937.
27. Terraine, *A Time for Courage*, p. 52.
28. Slessor, *Central Blue*, p. 160.

29. Ibid.
30. Ibid., pp. 166–7.
31. Ibid.
32. Ibid., p. 150, italics in the original.
33. TNA AIR 75/5, 'American Cooperation with Great Britain in the event of War with Germany. The Neutrality Act and War Debt Settlement', 13 November 1937.
34. David J. Gill, 'The UK's unpaid war debts to the United States, 1917–1980', 21 August 2018. https://ehsthelongrun.net/tag/debt/ (accessed 5 October 2020).
35. Brian Brinkworth, 'The Planning of British Aircraft Production for the Second World War', *Journal of Aeronautical History*, Paper 2018/09 (2018). https://www.aerosociety.com/media/10277/on-the-planning-of-british-aircraft-production-for-second-world-war-and-reference-to-james-connolly_2018-09.pdf (accessed 28 May 2020).
36. Malcolm Smith, 'Planning and Building the British Bomber Force, 1934–1939', *Business History Review*, Spring 1980, vol. 54(1):41.
37. Slessor, *Central Blue*, p. 164.
38. Ibid., p. 169.
39. Ibid., p. 170, italics in the original.
40. Webster & Frankland, *Strategic Air Offensive*, vol. I, p. 94.
41. Terraine, *A Time for Courage*, p. 80.
42. Ibid., pp. 95, 97.
43. Ibid., p. 101.
44. TNA AIR 2/2948, 'Answers to questions raised by D.D. Plans', 11 March 1938, and 'Douglas ACAS to Slessor (D.D. Plans)', 23 March 1938.
45. Webster & Frankland, *Strategic Air Offensive*, vol. I, p. 101 and footnotes.
46. Terraine, *A Time for Courage*, pp. 703–4, APPENDIX G.
47. HANSARD HC Debates, 21 June 1938, vol. 337, col. 936.
48. TNA AIR 19/39, Air Ministry Report, 'The Restriction of Air Warfare', 14 January 1938.
49. Ibid.
50. Ibid.
51. TNA AIR 20/22, Minute J.B. Abraham to C-in-C Bomber Command, 15 September 1938; see also AIR 41/5, Air Ministry Instructions of 15 September 1938.
52. Peter Gray, *Air Warfare: History, Theory and Practice* (London: Bloomsbury, 2016), p. 98.
53. Slessor, *Central Blue*, p. 114.
54. Ibid., p. 217.
55. Ibid., p. 225.
56. David Reynolds, *Summits* (London: Allen Lane, 2007), p. 93.
57. Ibid., p. 94.
58. Denis Richards, *The Royal Air Force, 1939–1945*. Vol. I: *The Fight at Odds*, p. 30. https://www.ibiblio.org/hyperwar/UN/UK/UK-RAF-I/UK-RAF-I-1.html (accessed 8 July 2020).
59. Reynolds, *Summits*, p. 7.
60. Terraine, *A Time for Courage*, p. 67.
61. Slessor, *Central Blue*, p. 223.
62. Ibid., p. 225.
63. Terraine, *A Time for Courage*, p. 69.
64. Sir Maurice Dean, *The RAF and Two World Wars* (London: Cassell, 1979), p. 76.
65. Webster & Frankland, *Strategic Air Offensive*, vol. I, pp. 129, 134.
66. Slessor, *Central Blue*, p. 206.

Chapter 6: The Curtain Rises

1. Slessor, *Central Blue*, p. 145.
2. Churchill, *Gathering Storm*, p. 311.
3. Terraine, *A Time for Courage*, p. 69.
4. Slessor, *Central Blue*, p. 147. The Joint Planning Committee (JPC) was an inter-service committee drawn from the Army, Navy and Air Force to provide input and advice to the Chiefs of Staff (COS). In 1939 the committee representatives were Brigadier John Kennedy (Army), Captain Vincent H. Danckwerts (Navy) and Slessor (Air Force).
5. Ibid., p. 146.
6. Terraine, *A Time for Courage*, p. 66.
7. Martin S. Alexander, 'Fighting to the Last Frenchman? Reflections on the BEF Deployment to France and the Strains in the Franco-British Alliance, 1939–1940', *Historical Reflections*, Winter 1996, 22(1):237.
8. Ibid., p. 238.
9. Slessor, *Central Blue*, p. 148.
10. Ibid., p. 147.
11. Maude Williams & Bernard Wilkin, *French Soldiers' Morale in the Phoney War* (Abingdon: Routledge, 2019), see Table 5.1 and Fig. 5.1.
12. Martin Alexander & William Philpott, *Knowing your Friends: Intelligence Inside Alliances, 1914 to the Cold War* (Abingdon: Routledge, 1998), p. 70.
13. Ibid., p. 72.
14. Alexander, 'Fighting to the last Frenchman', p. 242.
15. TNA AIR 2/2884, Slessor to Ludlow-Hewitt, 19 April 1939, and Slessor, *Central Blue*, p. 149.
16. Slessor, *Central Blue*, p. 252.
17. TNA AIR 41/40 AHB, Narrative, The RAF in the Bombing Offensive against Germany, p. 36; Webster & Frankland, *Strategic Air Offensive*, vol. I, p. 136.
18. Slessor, *Central Blue*, pp. 242–3.
19. Terraine, *A Time for Courage*, p. 66.
20. Slessor, *Central Blue*, p. 244.
21. Alexander, 'Fighting to the last Frenchman', p. 249.
22. Slessor, *Central Blue*, p. 262.
23. Ibid., pp. 264–5.
24. Ibid., p. 269.
25. Ibid., p. 276.
26. Churchill, *Gathering Storm*, p. 415. The naval historian John Roskill wrote that the naval representative on the JPC, Captain Vincent Danckwerts, was sacked for his candid advice on the Norway plans which did not accord with Churchill's views, and his departure served as an ominous warning to staff officers of the fate that awaited them.
27. Terraine, *A Time for Courage*, p. 115.
28. Slessor, *Central Blue*, pp. 237–8.
29. Alexander, 'Fighting to the last Frenchman', p. 254.
30. 'Schwerpunkt' literally means 'hard point' or 'difficult point' but is best translated as 'maximum weight of effort' or 'centre of gravity'. The original use of the term has been attributed to Clausewitz in *On War*, ed. and trans. Michael Howard and Peter Paret (Princeton: Princeton University Press, 1962), p. 59.

31. French air reconnaissance sorties had discovered the large columns of German trucks and tanks in the Ardennes. These reports were discounted at Gamelin's Vincennes general headquarters.
32. Weygand had had a distinguished career in the First World War. He was Marshal Foch's right-hand man throughout his victories in the final months of the war.
33. Slessor, *Central Blue*, pp. 286–7.
34. Ibid., p. 288. The destroyer was sunk by enemy action shortly afterwards.
35. Ibid., p. 289.
36. Julian Thompson, *Dunkirk: Retreat in Victory* (London: Pan Books, 2008), p. 82.
37. Slessor, *Central Blue*, p. 289.
38. Major L.F. Ellis, *The War in France and Flanders, 1939–1940* (London: HMSO, 1954), p. 82. https://www.ibiblio.org/hyperwar/UN/UK/UK-NWE-Flanders/UK-NWE-Flanders-5.html (accessed 26 June 2020).
39. Slessor, *Central Blue*, p. 291.
40. Ibid., p. 292.
41. John C. Cairns, 'Great Britain and the Fall of France: A Study in Allied Disunity', *Journal of Modern History*, December 1955, 27(4):398.
42. Slessor, *Central Blue*, p. 293.
43. Ibid., p. 294.
44. Ibid., p. 298.
45. Winston Churchill, *The Second World War*. Vol II: *Their Finest Hour* (London: Cassell, 1949), pp. 78–9.
46. Slessor, *Central Blue*, p. 299.
47. Churchill, *Finest Hour*, p. 79.
48. Cairns, 'Great Britain and the Fall of France', pp. 371, 373.
49. Thompson, *Dunkirk*, p. 47.
50. Terraine, *A Time for Courage*, p. 151.
51. Ibid.
52. Ibid.
53. Ibid., p. 153.
54. Cairns, 'Great Britain and the Fall of France', p. 378.
55. Ibid.
56. Ibid.
57. A reference to Air Ministry reservations about not wanting to be the first to 'take the gloves off' and now being under no illusions that the Germans did not apply a more civilized code for its western neighbours after the bombing of Rotterdam.
58. Slessor, *Central Blue*, p. 295. Heavy bombers refers to the Wellingtons and Whitleys, based in England.
59. Ibid.
60. Group Captain Alistair Byford, 'The Battle of France, May 1940: Enduring, combined and joint lessons', *Air Power Review*, Autumn/Winter 2011, 14(3):69–70.
61. Slessor, *Central Blue*, p. 297.
62. Ibid., p. 299.
63. Cairns, 'Great Britain and the Fall of France', p. 389.
64. Francis Joseph, *The Axis Air Forces: Flying in Support of the German Luftwaffe* (Oxford: Praeger, 2012), p. 59.
65. Alexander, 'Fighting to the last Frenchman', p. 262.

66. Churchill, *Finest Hour*, p. 211.
67. Ibid., pp. 219–20.
68. Churchill, *Gathering Storm*, p. 522.
69. Slessor, *Central Blue*, p. 303.
70. Ibid.
71. TNA AIR 75/5, Minute sheet, Slessor to Air Marshal Sir Richard Pierse (VCAS), 19 June 1940; Slessor, *Central Blue*, p. 303.

Chapter 7: Secret Emissary

1. David Reynolds, 'Lord Lothian and the Anglo-American Relationship, 1939–1940', *Transactions of the American Philosophical Society*, 1983, 73(1):15.
2. TNA AIR 2/7172, Msg. 2132 Air Attaché, Washington to Air Ministry, 13 February 1940.
3. TNA AIR 2/7234, Newall (CAS) to Sinclair, Secretary of State for Air, 11 March 1940.
4. Reynolds, 'Lord Lothian and the Anglo-American Relationship', p. 9.
5. TNA AIR 2/7234, Chief of the Air Staff to Secretary of State for Air, 11 March 1940.
6. Ibid., Minute 12 and Msg. S.5004/T.W.1. to Bomber, Fighter, Coastal Commands, 8 June 1940.
7. TNA AIR 8/443, 'Slessor quoted in Staff Conversations: Strategic Background for upcoming British- American Staff Talks', June 1940.
8. Richard G. Davis, *Carl A. Spaatz and the Air War in Europe* (Washington DC: Center for Air Force History, 1996), p. 44.
9. TNA AIR 75/5, 'Future Strategy Paper' by Air Commodore Slessor, June 1940; Slessor, *Central Blue*, p. 304.
10. TNA AIR 75/5, 'Future Strategy Paper'.
11. Ibid., 'Prime Minister's Memorandum on the Munitions Situation', June 1940.
12. Slessor, *Central Blue*, p. 298.
13. Ibid., p. 314.
14. TNA AIR 8/443, 'Memo on staff conversations with America', 28 June 1940.
15. Ibid., note: RDF: the acronym for 'Radio Direction Finding' (early name for radar).
16. TNA AIR 2/7251, Minute 5 (S.5185), ACAS (G) Air Commodore Richard Peck to A.I.(f), 3 July 1940.
17. Davis, *Carl A. Spaatz*, p. 47.
18. Slessor, *Central Blue*, p. 315.
19. https://spartacus-educational.com/2WWdonovanW.htm (accessed 5 August 2020).
20. Davis, *Carl A. Spaatz*, p. 48.
21. Slessor, *Central Blue*, p. 315.
22. Ibid.
23. Ibid., p. 316.
24. Ibid., p. 315.
25. Davis, *Carl A. Spaatz*, p. 48.
26. Ibid., p. 49.
27. TNA AIR 8/368, Letter, William Donovan to Newall, CAS, 17 August 1940.
28. Slessor, *Central Blue*, p. 316.
29. Douglas Waller, *Wild Bill Donovan* (London: Free Press, 2012), p. 61.
30. William T. Johnsen, *The Origins of the Grand Alliance: Anglo-American Military Collaboration from the Panay Incident to Pearl Harbour* (Lexington, Kentucky: University Press of Kentucky, 2016), p. 83.

31. TNA AIR 8/443, Lothian telegram to the Air Ministry describing his meeting with Roosevelt, 17 June 1940.
32. Ibid., Slessor memorandum on Staff Conversations with America, 28 June 1940.
33. TNA PREM 3/475/1, Standardization Conference, Slessor memorandum to War Cabinet and COS, 8 August 1940, pp. 33–4.
34. Joint Planning Committee memorandum, Standardization Conference 'Anglo-American Standardization of Arms', to the War Cabinet Chiefs of Staff, 8 August 1940.
35. TNA WO 193/311, Slessor to COS briefing on forthcoming meeting, 9 August 1940.
36. Johnsen, *Origins of the Grand Alliance,* p. 98.
37. TNA AIR 75/5, Air Ministry Report, 'Lessons of the War: Air Operations', 29 July 1940; Major Corvin J. Connolly, 'Marshal of the Royal Air Force Sir John Cotesworth Slessor and the Anglo-American Air Power Alliance, 1940–1945' (PhD thesis, Texas A&M University, December 2001), p. 77. http://www.dtic.mil/cgi-bin/GetTR%20Doc?AD=ADA39943520a 399435 (accessed 12 May 2016).
38. Johnsen, *Origins of the Grand Alliance*, p. 95.
39. TNA WO 193/311, AASC (Joint) First Meeting, 20 August 1940.
40. Johnsen, *Origins of the Grand Alliance*, p. 96.
41. TNA CAB 80/17 COS (40) 659, 24 August 1940; also, WO 193/311, Preparation for Aide Memoire for COS SA (40) 5.
42. TNA WO 193/311 COS (40) 667, Meeting between the COS and American Representatives, 26 August 1940.
43. Johnsen, *Origins of the Grand Alliance*, p. 98.
44. TNA CAB/66/11/42 WP (40) 362, also COS (40) 683, 4 September 1940 [Digital download]. https://discovery.nationalarchives.gov.uk/results/r?arrow=on&search_options= on&_q=Future+Strategy+1940 (accessed 12 August 2020).
45. TNA WO 193/311, (Joint) Second Meeting, pp. 6–7, 29 August 1940; Johnsen, *Origins of the Grand Alliance*, p. 99.
46. Johnsen, *Origins of the Grand Alliance*, p. 98.
47. TNA WO 1903/311, AASC (Joint) Third Meeting, p. 2, 31 August 1940.
48. Johnsen, *Origins of the Grand Alliance*, p. 103, author's italics.
49. J.R.M. Butler, *Grand Strategy.* Vol. 2: *September 1939–June 1941* (London: HMSO 1957), p. 343.
50. Johnsen, *Origins of the Grand Alliance*, p. 103.
51. Slessor, *Central Blue*, p. 318.
52. Ibid.
53. Ibid., p. 309.
54. Ibid., p. 318.
55. Ibid.
56. TNA AIR 75/64, Slessor memorandum on the British Supply Programme, 2 October 1940.
57. Johnsen, *Origins of the Grand Alliance*, p. 125.
58. TNA AIR 19/185, Arthur Purvis to FO, message PURSA no. 128, 4 October; Johnsen, *Origins of the Grand Alliance*, p. 125.
59. Slessor, *Central Blue*, p. 320.
60. Connolly, 'Sir John Cotesworth Slessor', p. 89.
61. TNA AIR 8/446, Air Ministry to Lord Lothian concerning Air Marshal Portal's visit to America, 10 October 1940.

62. Johnsen, *Origins of the Grand Alliance*, p. 125; TNA Air 19/185, Lothian to FO, 6 October 1940; Archibald Sinclair, Secretary of State for Air, to Beaverbrook, Minister of Aircraft Production; Sinclair to Prime Minister, 22 October 1940; and PREM 3/488/1.

63. TNA AIR 8/446, Slessor memorandum to Air Marshal Portal on American mission, 17 October 1940.

64. TNA AIR 19/185, Slessor to Secretary of State for Air and CAS, minute, 19 October 1940.

65. Ibid.

66. TNA PREM 3/488/1, Churchill to Secretary of State for Air and Chief of the Air Staff, 29 October 1940.

67. Slessor, *Central Blue*, p. 320.

Chapter 8: Clandestine Mission

1. Pan Am Clipper Flying Boats. https://www.clipperflyingboats.com/transatlantic-airline-service (accessed 8 September 2020).

2. Slessor, *Central Blue*, p. 320.

3. Ibid., p. 322.

4. Slessor Family papers.

5. Ibid.

6. *London Gazette*, 4 February 1941, no. 35065; Slessor Papers, Slessor to Hermione, 2 November 1940.

7. Johnsen, *Origins of the Grand Alliance*, p. 127.

8. Roosevelt's speech to the nation, 29 December 1941. https://millercenter.org/the-presidency/presidential-speeches/december-29-1940-fireside-chat-16-arsenal-democracy (accessed 24 August 2020).

9. ABC: the acronym stood for American-British Conversations, Washington, January–March 1941.

10. Slessor Family papers.

11. TNA PREM 3/475/4, 'War Cabinet Meeting: Anglo-American Issues, 21 November 1940'; and Johnsen, *Origins of the Grand Alliance*, p. 127.

12. Slessor, *Central Blue*, p. 324.

13. TNA AIR 75/63, Slessor to Morgenthau on aircraft production figures, 7 December 1940; Connolly, 'Sir John Cotesworth Slessor', pp. 99–100.

14. TNA AIR 19/185, Draft memorandum for CAS, 6 December 1940; Johnsen, *Origins of the Grand Alliance*, p. 127.

15. Slessor, *Central Blue*, p. 320.

16. TNA AIR19/185, Slessor to Portal, 1 January 1941; Slessor, *Central Blue*, p. 321.

17. Churchill, *Finest Hour*, pp. 499–500.

18. Slessor, *Central Blue*, p. 321.

19. Portal Papers, Christ Church College, Oxford: Portal to Churchill, Aircraft Production, 10 January 1940.

20. Slessor, *Central Blue*, p. 324.

21. Ibid., p. 325.

22. Johnsen, *Origins of the Grand Alliance*, p. 127.

23. TNA AIR 75/5, 'Future Strategy Paper', September 1940.

24. Churchill, *Finest Hour*, pp. 499–500.

25. TNA AIR 8/446, Providing America with Needed Information, 20 December 1940.

26. Slessor, *Central Blue*, pp. 326–36.

27. Ibid., p. 325.
28. Ibid., p. 327.
29. Ibid., p. 328.
30. Ibid., p. 330.
31. Jonathan Zeitlin, 'Flexibility and Mass Production at War: Aircraft Manufacture in Britain, the United States and Germany, 1939–1945', *Technology and Culture*, January 1995, 36(1):46–79, esp. p. 60.
32. R.J. Overy, *The Air War 1939–1945* (London: Europa Publications, 1980), p. 150.
33. War History Network. https://warfarehistorynetwork.com/2019/01/10/how-capitalism-won-wwii-this-is-capitalism-and-expert-rob-citino-explain/ (accessed 11 September 2020).
34. Slessor Family papers, Slessor to Hermione, 28 December 1940.
35. 'Ferry' is the aviation term for flying aircraft between locations and across the Atlantic, typically from factories to operational airfields or from home bases to deployed outstations. The use of ferry pilots (often women) allowed fighting aircrew to remain on active duty.
36. John D. Carter, 'The Air Corps Ferrying Command', in W.F. Craven & J.L. Cate (eds), *The Army Air Forces in World War II*. Vol. 1. *Plans and Early Operations, January 1939–August 1942* (University of Chicago Press, 1948), p. 313. https://www.ibiblio.org/hyperwar/AAF/I/index.html (accessed 24 August 2020).
37. TNA AIR 75/63, Slessor to Portal, 'Commentary on the American Situation', 4 December 1940; Slessor, *Central Blue*, pp. 335–6.
38. TNA AVIA 9/5, 'President to former Naval Person, Prime Minister's Personal Telegram', 29 May 1941.
39. Jeffrey Davis, 'Atfero: The Atlantic Ferry Organisation', *Journal of Contemporary History*, January 1985, 20(1):76, 91.
40. TNA CAB 80/24, Lothian to FO, 29 November 1940, and Annexe 1 to Chiefs of Staff CoS (40) 1,041, 5 December 1940.
41. ABC: American British Conversations.
42. Johnsen, *Origins of the Grand Alliance*, p. 132.
43. Connolly, 'Sir John Cotesworth Slessor', p. 114. Ismay was then Chief of Staff on the Defence Committee in Churchill's War Cabinet.
44. Slessor, *Central Blue*, p. 341.
45. James R. Leutze, *Bargaining for Supremacy* (Carolina: University of Carolina, 1997), p. 224.
46. Ibid.
47. Ibid.
48. Ibid.
49. See TNA AIR 75/5, 'Future Strategy Paper' and 'Prime Minister's Memorandum on the Munitions Situation', both authored by Slessor in June 1940.
50. Johnsen, *Origins of the Grand Alliance*, p. 137.
51. https://www.marshallfoundation.org. Editorial notes #2-363 January-February 1941 (accessed 9 September 2020).
52. Slessor, *Central Blue*, p. 347.
53. Johnsen, *Origins of the Grand Alliance*, p. 155.
54. Slessor, *Central Blue*, p. 353.
55. Leutze, *Bargaining for Supremacy*, p. 223.
56. Slessor, *Central Blue*, p. 352.
57. TNA AIR 8/447, Slessor to Portal: Need for Complete Frankness.

58. Portal Papers, Christ Church College, Oxford (Box 'C', File 4, No. 12c): Portal to Churchill, Release of Production figures to US', 3 February 1941.
59. TNA AIR 8/447, Beaverbrook to Portal, 14 February 1941.
60. Slessor, *Central Blue*, p. 308.
61. TNA AIR 8/447, Portal to Beaverbrook, 14 February 1941.
62. TNA AIR 8/447, Beaverbrook's response on Slessor, 21 March 1941.
63. *US Army in World War II: Strategic Plan for Coalition Warfare, January–November 1941*, ch. 3, p. 38. https://www.ibiblio.org/hyperwar/Dip/Conf/ABC/index.html (accessed 6 September 2020).
64. Johnsen, *Origins of the Grand Alliance*, p. 147.
65. Slessor, *Central Blue*, p. 358.
66. Ibid.
67. Ibid., p. 356.
68. Leutze, *Bargaining for Supremacy*, p. 245.
69. Ibid., p. 247.
70. Slessor, *Central Blue*, p. 356.
71. Mark M. Lowenthal, 'Roosevelt and the Coming of War: the Search for United States Policy, 1937–1942', *Journal of Contemporary History*, July 1981, 16(3):427.
72. Leutze, *Bargaining for Supremacy*, p. 253.
73. Ibid., p. 252.
74. Slessor, *Central Blue*, p. 364.

Chapter 9: Bomber Command

1. In Slessor's time as AOC 5 Group between April 1941 and March 1942, 61 and 144 Squadrons were at Hemswell, 83 and 49 Squadrons at Scampton, 97 and 106 Squadrons at Coningsby, 44 and 420 Squadrons at Waddington, 50 and 408 Squadrons at Lindholme, and 455 Squadron at Swinderby. Chris Ward, *5 Group Bomber Command: An Operational Record* (Barnsley: Pen & Sword, 2007), pp. 120–2.
2. Terraine, *A Time for Courage*, p. 85.
3. Ibid.
4. Slessor, *Central Blue*, p. 369.
5. Webster & Frankland, *Strategic Air Offensive*, vol. IV, p. 98, appendix 5, 'Aide Memoire' by Sir Thomas Inskip, 9 December 1937.
6. Orange, *Slessor: Bomber Champion*, p. 82.
7. Sir Arthur Harris, *Bomber Offensive* (Barnsley: Pen & Sword Military Classics), 2005, p. 39.
8. Webster & Frankland, *Strategic Air Offensive*, vol. IV, p. 133, Appendix 8 Directive (xiv), Freeman to Peirse, 9 March 1941.
9. Webster & Frankland, *Strategic Air Offensive*, vol. I, p. 241.
10. Ibid., p. 242.
11. Slessor, *Central Blue*, p. 376.
12. Webster & Frankland, *Strategic Air Offensive*, vol. IV, p. 135, Appendix 8 Directive (xiv), Freeman to Peirse, 9 March 1941.
13. TNA AIR 20/2795, Trenchard /Portal meeting, 2 June 1941.
14. Peter Gray, *The Leadership, Direction and Legitimacy of the RAF Bomber Offensive from Inception to 1945* (Birmingham War Studies, London: Bloomsbury, 2013), p. 176.
15. Ward, *5 Group Bomber Command*, p. 13.
16. Slessor, *Central Blue*, p. 372.

17. Ibid.
18. Martyn Chorlton, *The RAF Pathfinders* (Newbury: Countryside Books, 2012), p. 13.
19. Webster & Frankland, *Strategic Air Offensive*, vol. IV, pp. 140–1, Appendix 8 Directive (xvii), AVM Bottomley to Air Marshal Pierse, 30 August 1941.
20. Slessor Family papers, Cheltenham, 2017, accessed by Air Vice-Marshal Tony Mason.
21. Webster & Frankland, *Strategic Air Offensive*, vol. I, p. 135.
22. Slessor, *Central Blue*, p. 213.
23. Ibid., p. 371.
24. Terraine, *A Time for Courage*, p. 296.
25. Ibid.
26. Ibid., p. 298.
27. Slessor, *Central Blue*, p. 378.
28. Ibid.
29. Webster & Frankland, *Strategic Air Offensive*, vol. IV, pp. 142–3, Appendix 8 Directive (xx), AVM Bottomley to Air Marshal Pierse, 13 November 1941.
30. Webster & Frankland, *Strategic Air Offensive*, vol. I, p. 256.
31. Slessor, *Central Blue*, p. 396.

Chapter 10: Allied Strategic Priorities

1. Martin Gilbert, *Churchill: A Life* (London: BCA, 1992), p. 711.
2. Andrew Roberts, *Churchill: Walking with Destiny* (London: Allen Lane, 2018), p. 698.
3. Gilbert, *Churchill: A Life*, p. 711.
4. W.F. Craven & J.L. Cate (eds), *The Army Air Forces in World War II*. Vol. 3. *Europe: Argument to VE Day, January 1944 to May 1945* (University of Chicago Press, 1951), p. 243.
5. Slessor, *Central Blue*, p. 405.
6. Davis, *Carl A. Spaatz*, p. 75.
7. Ibid.
8. Ibid., and p. 93.
9. Each B-17G was armed with twelve .50 calibre (12.7mm) M2 Browning machine guns mounted in nine positions in the aircraft. The cumulative firepower of the machine guns was enhanced when flying the defensive box formation that could sometimes contain fifty-two aircraft.
10. Slessor, *Central Blue*, p. 430.
11. Davis, *Carl A. Spaatz*, p. 98.
12. TNA AIR 8/711, Slessor to Sinclair and Portal, 26 September 1942; Slessor, *Central Blue*, p. 431; Webster & Frankland, *The Strategic Offensive against Germany, 1939–1945*, Vol. I (London: HMSO, 1961), p. 358.
13. Davis, *Carl A. Spaatz*, pp. 84, 103; USAAF airfields in August 1942: Polesbrook, Molesworth, Alconbury, Chelveston, Podington, Underwood, Bovingdon.
14. TNA AIR 8/711, press cutting, October 1942.
15. Ibid., Portal to Sinclair, 28 October 1942.
16. Slessor, *Central Blue*, p. 432.
17. Webster & Frankland, *Strategic Offensive*, p. 359.
18. Ibid.
19. TNA AIR 8/711, Sinclair to Churchill, 23 October 1942; Webster & Frankland, *Strategic Offensive*, p. 360.
20. General H.H. Arnold, *Global Mission* (London: Hutchinson, 1951), p. 174.

21. Slessor, *Central Blue*, p. 398.
22. Ibid., p. 400.
23. Maurice Matloff and Edwin M. Snell, *Strategic Planning for Coalition Warfare, 1941–1942* (Center of Military History, United States, 1999), Appendix A.
24. Lowenthal, 'Roosevelt and the Coming of War', p. 432.
25. Slessor, *Central Blue*, p. 401.
26. Lowenthal, 'Roosevelt and the Coming of War', p. 423.
27. Ibid., p. 432.
28. Matloff and Snell, *Strategic Planning for Coalition Warfare*, pp. 98–114.
29. TNA CAB 88/1, 24 July 1942.
30. Slessor, *Central Blue*, p. 405.
31. Ibid., p. 406.
32. Ibid.
33. Ibid., p. 407.
34. Webster & Frankland, *Strategic Air Offensive*, vol. 1, p. 353.
35. Slessor, *Central Blue*, p. 411.
36. Davis, *Carl A. Spaatz*, p. 112.
37. Slessor, *Central Blue*, p. 434.
38. Ibid., p. 438.
39. OVERLORD: The Allied invasion of Western Europe through Normandy that began on 6 June 1944 .
40. Slessor, *Central Blue*, p. 439 and Appendix D, p. 668.
41. Ibid., p. 434.
42. Ibid., p. 443.
43. Philip Overy, *The Bombing War: Europe 1943–1945* (London: Allen Lane, 2013), p. 303.
44. Ibid.
45. Slessor, *Central Blue*, p. 443.
46. Ibid., p. 444.
47. Terraine, *A Time for Courage*, p. 394.
48. The Casablanca Conference. https://www.jcs.mil/Portals/36/Documents/History/WWII/Casablanca3.pdf (accessed 4 September 2020).
49. Slessor, *Central Blue*, p. 445.
50. Ibid.
51. https://www.jcs.mil/Portals/36/Documents/History/WWII/Casablanca3.pdf (accessed 4 September 2020).
52. Slessor, *Central Blue*, p. 446; TNA AIR 75/11, Slessor's handwritten Casablanca notes, 18 January 1943.
53. Overy, *The Bombing War*, p. 305.
54. Ibid.
55. Arnold, *Global Mission*, p. 203.
56. CCS 166/1/D, 'The Bombing Offensive from the United Kingdom', 21 January 1943.
57. Sebastian Cox, RAF Air Historical Branch, 'Exercise Thunderbolt: Objective Assessment of the Bomber Offensive or Air Staff View of History?' Paper presented at 'The RAF in a World Transformed, 1945–49', RAF Museum, Hendon, 29 September 2020. https://www.crowdcast.io/e/RAFM-Conference/4 (accessed 30 October 2020).
58. Cox, 'Exercise Thunderbolt'.

59. Slessor, *Central Blue*, p. 448.
60. Ibid., p. 434.

Chapter 11: Victory over the Atlantic

1. John Terraine, *Business in Great Waters: The U-boat War, 1916–1945* (London: Mandarin Paperbacks, 1990), p. 515.
2. TNA AIR 75/11, 'The Conduct of War in 1943', report by the Combined Chiefs of Staff, January 1943; Churchill, *The Second World War*. Vol. IV: *The Hinge of Fate* (London: Cassell, 1951), p. 619; https://www.jcs.mil/Portals/36/Documents/History/WWII/Casablanca3.pdf (accessed 4 September 2020).
3. Slessor, *Central Blue*, p. 465
4. Ibid.
5. Terraine, *Business in Great Waters*, p. 523; Terraine, *A Time for Courage*, p. 441.
6. Richards & Saunders, *Royal Air Force, 1939–1945*, vol. 1, p. 321.
7. TNA ADM 116/460, 4 December 1940.
8. John Buckley, 'Maritime Air Power and the Second World War: Britain, the USA and Japan', in Sebastian Cox & Peter Gray (eds), *Air Power History: Turning Points from Kitty Hawk to Kosovo* (London: Cass, 2005), p. 129.
9. Churchill, *Finest Hour*, p. 529.
10. John Buckley, 'Air Power and the Battle of the Atlantic', *Journal of Contemporary History*, January 1993, 28(1):146.
11. Ibid., 147.
12. Terraine, *A Time for Courage*, p. 406.
13. Buckley, 'Maritime Air Power', p. 133.
14. Terraine, *A Time for Courage*, p. 438.
15. Ibid.
16. Slessor, *Central Blue*, p. 465.
17. TNA AIR 14/3507, Harris to Churchill, June 1942.
18. Conducted by Mr Justice Singleton examining the most effective use of resources in the war against Germany, paying particular attention to Bomber Command.
19. Buckley, 'Air Power and the Battle of the Atlantic', p. 159.
20. Robin Brodhurst, *Churchill's Anchor* (Barnsley, Pen & Sword, 2000), p. 269.
21. TNA CAB 66/30, Churchill memorandum to Cabinet, WP (42) 483, 24 October 1942.
22. TNA CAB 86/2, Anti-U-boat Committee, 13 and 18 November 1942.
23. Buckley, 'Air Power and the Battle of the Atlantic', p. 159.
24. Slessor, *Central Blue*, p. 521.
25. Ibid., p. 508.
26. Terraine, *A Time for Courage*, p. 441.
27. Slessor, *Central Blue*, p. 510.
28. LRASVIII: Long-Range Air to Surface Vessel, version 3, working on a 10cm wavelength, and undetectable by U-boats until late 1943.
29. Terraine, *A Time for Courage*, p. 436.
30. Slessor, *Central Blue*, p. 511.
31. Ibid., p. 522.
32. Wolf pack: a tactic used by U-boats in which they patrolled in lines to scout for convoys. On receiving confirmation of the presence of a convoy, the U-boat group would then coordinate their attack.

33. Terraine, *A Time for Courage*, p. 448.
34. Ibid., p. 449.
35. Ibid.
36. Roberts, *Churchill: Walking with Destiny*, p. 777.
37. Slessor, *Central Blue*, p. 522.
38. Terraine, *A Time for Courage*, p. 448.
39. Ibid., p. 451.
40. The first 'happy time' referred to the appalling losses to U-boat attacks on shipping destined for Britain during the final months of 1940.
41. Jonathan Dimbleby, *The Battle of the Atlantic: How the Allies Won the War* (London: Penguin Random House, 2015), p. 256.
42. Slessor, *Central Blue*, p. 493.
43. Ibid., p. 441.
44. Dimbleby, *Battle of the Atlantic*, p. 253.
45. Slessor, *Central Blue*, p. 441.
46. Buckley, 'Maritime Air Power', p. 132.
47. Slessor, *Central Blue*, p. 490.
48. Buckley, 'Maritime Air Power', p. 130.
49. Slessor, *Central Blue*, p. 490.
50. Ibid. p. 532.
51. Ibid., p. 499. Slessor agreed to give up fifteen VLR Liberators to re-equip an experienced Canadian Anti-Submarine Warfare (ASW) squadron. During May 1943 Coastal Command had two squadrons comprising thirty-four VLR Liberators.
52. Ibid., p. 492.
53. Ernest J. King, *Fleet Admiral King: A Naval Record* (New York: W.W. Norton, 1952), p. 452.
54. Slessor, *Central Blue*, p. 477.
55. Probert, *High Commanders*, pp. 41–3.
56. Slessor Family papers.
57. Slessor, *Central Blue*, p. 556.
58. Ibid., p. 468.
59. Ibid., p. 556.

Chapter 12: Hitler's Third Front

1. Slessor, *Central Blue*, p. 558.
2. Ibid., 558–9.
3. Connolly, 'Sir John Cotesworth Slessor', p. 239.
4. Ibid.
5. Slessor, *Central Blue*, p. 558.
6. Designed to specifically attack German fighter numbers and capability prior to Overlord.
7. Pointblank Directive: the specific requirement to destroy the German air force and aircraft factories.
8. The term 'soft underbelly of Europe' was used by Churchill on several occasions in favouring an attack through Italy, which he considered as the weak point in the Axis defences.
9. Terraine, *A Time for Courage*, p. 585.
10. Winston S. Churchill, *The Second World War*. Vol. V: *Closing the Ring* (London: Cassell, 1952), p. 432.
11. Slessor, *Central Blue*, p. 562.

12. Connolly, 'Sir John Cotesworth Slessor', p. 254; Terraine, *A Time for Courage*, p. 589.
13. Richards & Saunders, *The Royal Air Force*, vol. 2, p. 358.
14. Ibid., p. 359.
15. Slessor, *Central Blue*, p. 577.
16. Ibid. In 1954 Slessor met General von Senger zu Etterlin, the former commander of 14 Panzer Corps. A devout Catholic, General Senger told Slessor that the monastery was not used by his troops prior to the bombing. Slessor believed there was no doubt that Senger spoke the truth.
17. Ibid., p. 573.
18. Anthony Beevor, *D-Day: The Battle for Normandy* (London: Viking, 2009), p. 269.
19. Slessor, *Central Blue*, p. 568.
20. Slessor, *Air Power and Armies*, ch. VII: Air Attack on Communications.
21. Slessor, *Central Blue*, p. 568.
22. Ibid.
23. Ibid., p. 570.
24. Portal Papers, Christ Church, Oxford (Box D, File 6, No. 3): letter, Slessor to Portal, 16 April 1944.
25. Ibid. Slessor's italics in the original.
26. F.M. Sallagar, 'Operation STRANGLE (Italy, Spring, 1944): A Case Study of Tactical Air Interdiction', Rand Corporation, R-185-PR, February 1972, pp. 32–3.
27. Ibid.
28. Ibid., Appendix 'A': German Records on Supply and Consumption of Ammunition and Fuel in the Tenth and Fourteenth Armies during STRANGLE and DIADEM.
29. Ibid., p. xiii.
30. Andrew Brookes, *Air War over Italy* (Hersham: Ian Allen, 2000), p. 84.
31. Richards & Saunders, *The Royal Air Force*, vol. II, p. 363.
32. Slessor, *Central Blue*, p. 583.
33. Craven & Cate (eds), *Army Air Forces in World War II*, vol. 3, pp. 388–9. https://www.ibiblio.org/hyperwar/AAF/III/AAF-III-11.html (accessed 5 December 2020).
34. Slessor, *Central Blue*, p. 584. *Abteilung* is a generic term for a detachment of troops from a military formation.
35. Slessor, *Central Blue*, p. 587.
36. Ibid., p. 592.
37. Ibid., p. 593.
38. Ibid., p. 592.
39. Ibid., p. 596.
40. Ibid., p. 612.
41. Ibid., p. 614.
42. Ibid., p. 620.
43. Ibid., p. 612.
44. Probert, *High Commanders*, p. 43.
45. Slessor Family papers, 15 November 1944.
46. Ibid.

Chapter 13: A Time to Think

1. Probert, *High Commanders*, pp. 44–5.
2. TNA AIR 2/21027, Tizard Committee to COS (45) 402(0), 16 June 1945.

3. Ibid., Tizard Report, paragraph 66.
4. Ibid., Minute from Slessor to VCAS, AMSO, AMT, 20 July 1945, paragraph 2.
5. Andrew Pierre, *Nuclear Politics: the British Experience with an Independent Strategic Force, 1939–1970* (London/New York: Oxford University Press), p. 71.
6. Alfred Goldberg, 'The Military Origins of the British Nuclear Deterrent', *International Affairs*, October 1964, 40(4):612.
7. TNA AIR 75/88, Sir John Slessor, 'Influence of Air Power on Strategy', lecture at Old Sarum, August 1946.
8. TNA AVIA 54/94, Design Branch Specification, B.35/46 Medium Range Bomber', January 1947.
9. TNA CAB 130/3 GEN 75/1, meeting, 28 August 1945.
10. Pierre, *Nuclear Politics*, p. 69.
11. http://www.ukpublicspending.co.uk/total_spending_1948UkmnCite (accessed 24 July 2016).
12. David Edgerton, 'War, Reconstruction, and the Nationalisation of Britain, 1939–1951', *Past and Present*, 2011, 210(6):34, and Appendix II.
13. Liddell Hart Papers, King's College, London (hereafter KCL): Slessor correspondence file, 1/644/unnumbered. 'What would you do if you were appointed Supreme Commander British Armed Forces with a directive (a) to prevent war with Russia, and (b) to be prepared to fight it if it came in five to ten years' time?' 6 September 1947, paragraph 7.
14. Sir John Slessor, *Strategy for the West* (London: Cassell, 1954).
15. Sir John Slessor, *The Great Deterrent* (London: Cassell, 1957), p. 78.
16. TNA PREM 8/703, Correspondence, Inverchapel to Attlee, 10 March 1946.
17. Alfred Goldberg, 'The Atomic Origins of the British Nuclear Deterrent', *International Affairs*, July 1964, 40(3):413.
18. John Baylis, *Anglo-American Defence Relations, 1939–1980* (London: Macmillan, 1981), Appendix 1 (the Quebec 'Tube Alloys' Agreement, 19 August 1943) and Appendix 3 (aide mémoire of conversation between President and Prime Minister at Hyde Park, 19 September 1944).
19. Margaret Gowing, *Independence and Deterrence. Britain and Atomic Energy, 1939–1952, Vol. 1: Policy Making* (London: Macmillan, 1974), p. 185.
20. TNA CAB 130/16 GEN 163, 1st Meeting, 8 January 1947.
21. TNA DEFE 5/6 COS (47) 254(0), 8 December 1947.
22. TNA AIR 8/1998, Churchill to Norman Brook (Secretary of State for Air), 17 January 1952; TNA AIR 75/117, Slessor to Lord Alexander, Defence Minister, 3 October 1952.
23. Sir Lawrence Freedman, 'The Origins and Development of the British Nuclear Deterrent Forces, 1945–1950. Concluding Review', *Royal Air Force History Society Journal*, 1990, 7:52.
24. Richard Gott, 'The Evolution of the Independent British Deterrent', *International Affairs*, April 1963, 39(2):240.
25. TNA AIR 75/92, Slessor to Charles Cabell, 25 January 1951.
26. TNA DEFE 20/1, Chiefs of Staff to Elliot, 24 August 1951.
27. Ken Young, 'No Blank Cheque: Anglo-American (Mis)Understandings and the Use of the English Airbases', *Journal of Military History*, October 2007, 71(4):1,139.
28. Gowing, *Independence and Deterrence*, pp. 266–72, Appendix 9 (The Anglo-American 'Modus Vivendi', 7 January 1948) and pp. 393–401, Appendix 10 ('Declaration of Trust', 13 June 1944).

29. Michael Warner, *The Collapse of Intelligence Support for Air Power, 1944–52: Two Steps Backward* (Washington DC: CIA, 2007), p. 3. https://www.cia.gov/library/center-for-the-study-of-intelligence/csi (accessed 9 December 2015).

30. Ibid., p. 4.

31. Ibid., p. 5. The Eberstadt Report resulted from hearings chaired by Ferdinand Eberstadt between 1948 and 1949. It was a study into better cooperation within the US intelligence community.

32. Richard Aldrich, *The Hidden Hand* (London: John Murray, 2002), pp. 85, 644.

33. Cargill Hall & Clayton D. Laurie (eds), *Early Cold War Overflights 1950–56: Symposium Proceedings Vol. I* (Washington DC: Office of the Historian, National Reconnaissance Office, 2003), p. 3.

34. TNA AIR 75/88, Thunderbolt Conference, Sir John Slessor, 'Influence of Air Power on Strategy', lecture at Old Sarum, August 1946, p. 8, paragraph 3.

35. Ibid., p. 8.

36. TNA AIR 75/92, Menzies to Slessor, 3 July 1945.

37. Huw Dylan, *Defence Intelligence and the Cold War: Britain's Joint Intelligence Bureau, 1945–1964* (Oxford: Oxford University Press, 2014), p. 22.

38. TNA AIR 2/12027, Slessor to VCAS, AMSO, AMT, 15 July 1945; Aldrich, *Hidden Hand*, pp. 66–7.

39. Peter B. Gunn, *Sculthorpe: Secrecy and Stealth. A Norfolk Airfield in the Cold War* (Stroud: History Press), p. 64.

40. Bruce Halfpenny, *The English Electric Canberra* (Barnsley: Pen & Sword, 2000), pp. 19, 51.

41. Orange, *Slessor: Bomber Champion*, p. 184.

42. Probert, *High Commanders*, p. 44.

43. Connolly, 'Sir John Cotesworth Slessor', p. 272.

44. Slessor, *Great Deterrent*, pp. 76, 85.

45. Jeffrey Record, 'Nuclear Deterrence, Preventive War, and Counter Proliferation', *Policy Analysis*, July 2004, 519:14. http://www.cato.org/publications/policy-analysis/nuclear-deterrencepreventive-war-counterproliferation (accessed 26 July 2016).

46. Slessor, *Great Deterrent*, pp. 89, 100.

47. Gowing, *Independence and Deterrence*, p. 437.

48. Ibid., p. 234.

Chapter 14: The Pinnacle

1. Slessor, *Strategy for the West*, p. 105.

2. Young, 'No Blank Cheque', pp. 1, 31.

3. TNA PREM 8/1383 COS(W)920, Slessor minute to COS, 'The Possible Implications of the U.S. Atomic Air Plan', paragraph 9, 27 January 1951.

4. HANSARD HC Debates, 28 March 1950, vol. 473, cols 133–89, and 15 February 1951, vol. 484, cols 623–70.

5. Slessor, *Great Deterrent*, pp. 98, 101.

6. Shaw, 'We have just about had it: Jack Slessor, the Foreign Office, and the Anglo-American Strategic Debate over Escalation of the Korean War, 1950–51', *Yonsei Journal of Modern Conflicts* [Korea], Winter 2014, 6(2):295. http://theyonseijournal.com/modern-conflicts-volume-6-issue-2-fallwinter-2014/ (accessed 12 May 2016).

7. Peter Lowe, 'An Ally and a Recalcitrant General: Great Britain, Douglas MacArthur and the Korean War, 1950–1', *English Historical Review*, July 1990, 105(416):632.

8. Max Hastings, *The Korean War* (London: Pan, 2010), p. 192.
9. Cargill Hall & Laurie, *Early Cold War Overflights*, p. 1.
10. Truman Papers, White House Press Conference, 30 November 1950. http://trumanlibrary.org/publicpapers/viewpapers.php?pid=985 (accessed 30 July 2016).
11. TNA DEFE 20/1, 'The U.S. Strategic Air Plan and Use of the Atomic Bomb', September 1951, paragraph 3; Young, 'No Blank Cheque', p. 1,148.
12. Young, 'No Blank Cheque', p. 1,145.
13. TNA AIR 75/117, minute from Elliot to Attlee (undated); Young, 'No Blank Cheque', p. 1,149.
14. TNA AIR 75/117, Chiefs of Staff to Tedder [BJSM], 11 December 1950, also PREM 8/1383, telegram, Tedder to MoD, 19 December 1950, and telegram, MoD to Tedder, 22 December 1950.
15. TNA DEFE 32/2 COS (51)106, 'The U.S. Strategic Air Plan and Use of the Atomic Bomb', September 1951.
16. Young, 'No Blank Cheque', p. 1,151.
17. John Baylis, 'The 1958 Anglo-American Mutual Defence Agreement: the Search for Nuclear Interdependence', *Journal of Strategic Studies*, 2008, 31(3):427.
18. TNA KV 2/2209, 'Klaus Fuchs files', online at http://www.nationalarchives.gov.uk/releases/2007/march/atom.htm (accessed 17 August 2016).
19. Ken Young, 'A Most Special Relationship: the Origins of Anglo-American Nuclear Strike Planning', *Journal of Cold War Studies*, Spring 2007, 9(2):5–31.
20. TNA DEFE 20/1, 'Summary of notes recorded by the secretary and deputy secretary of the JCS', 13 September 1951.
21. TNA AIR 75/107, Slessor, letter to George F. Eliot, 18 October 1951.
22. TNA DEFE 20/1, TNA Chiefs of Staff to Elliot, 24 August 1951.
23. TNA DEFE 32/2 COS (51) 741, Chiefs of Staff Report, 'A general War including the use of the atomic bomb in a localised war', paragraph 15, 13 December 1951.
24. Lowe, 'An Ally and a Recalcitrant General', pp. 624–53; Young, 'No Blank Cheque', pp. 1,133–67; Shaw, 'We have just about had it'.
25. Richard L. Kubler, *Laying the Foundations: the Evolution of NATO in the 1950s* (Santa Monica, CA: Rand, June 1990), pp. 50–5. https://www.rand.org/content/dam/rand/pubs/notes/2009/N3105 (accessed 30 July 2016).
26. Andrew Johnston, 'Mr Slessor goes to Washington: the Influence of the British Global Strategy Paper in the Eisenhower "New Look"', *Diplomatic History*, Summer 1998, 22(3):364.
27. TNA AIR 75/94, JS 11, 24 November 1951.
28. TNA DEFE 32/2 COS (51) 741, p. 14; Sir Lawrence Freedman, *The Evolution of Nuclear Strategy* (London: MacMillan, 1981), p. 79.
29. TNA AIR 75/120, 'Defence Policy and Global Strategy', report by the Chiefs of Staff, paragraphs 7, 10, 20, 21, 56, 92 and 139 (conclusions), 17 June 1952.
30. TNA 75/120, Handwritten note by Slessor (undated), 'I was sent to sell it [the GSP] to the US JCS.'
31. TNA AIR 75/120, Slessor's presentation of the Global Strategy Paper to the Joint Chiefs of Staff, 29 July 1952.
32. Pierre, *Nuclear Politics*, pp. 87, 308.
33. John Baylis & Alan Macmillan, 'The British Global Strategy Paper of 1952', *Journal of Strategic Studies*, 1993, 16(2):200.

34. Pierre, *Nuclear Politics*, p. 89.
35. Freedman, *Evolution of Nuclear Strategy*, p. 80.
36. Johnston, 'Mr Slessor goes to Washington', p. 379.
37. Ibid.
38. Air Vice-Marshal Tony Mason, *Air Power: a Centennial Appraisal* (London: Brasseys, 1994), p. 91.
39. Charles V. Murphy, 'Defence and Strategy', *Fortune* (January 1953).
40. Freedman, *Evolution of Nuclear Strategy*, p. 81.
41. Johnston, 'Mr Slessor goes to Washington', p. 366.
42. Ibid.; Baylis & Macmillan, 'British Global Strategy Paper', p. 221; Slessor, *Great Deterrent*, p. 145.
43. Aldrich, *Hidden Hand*, p. 192.
44. See Appendix C for terminology.
45. TNA AIR 14/3879, 'RAF Benson Strategic Photographic Reconnaissance Conference', 4 October 1950.
46. Paul Lashmar, *Spy Flights of the Cold War* (Stroud: Sutton Publishing, 1996), p. 42.
47. Cargill Hall & Laurie, *Early Cold War Overflights*, p. 3.
48. Gunn, *Sculthorpe: Secrecy and Stealth*, p. 64.
49. Lashmar, *Spy Flights*, p. 65.
50. John Crampton, 'RB-45C Overflight Operations in the Royal Air Force', in Cargill Hall & Laurie, *Early Cold War Overflights*, pp. 153–63.
51. TNA AIR 19/1126, Slessor sent the briefing note only to Churchill, Cherwell (Paymaster General) and Alexander (Minister of Defence), 'The Counter-Offensive against the Soviet Long-Range Bomber Force', 6 February 1952.
52. Ibid., note on Jiu Jitsu I, 22 February 1954.
53. Ibid., telegram from Slessor to Elliot (BJSM), undated.
54. Donald E. Welzenbach, 'The Anglo-American Origins of Overflying the Soviet Union: the Case of the "Invisible Aircraft"', in Roger D. Miller (ed.), *Seeing off the Bear* (Washington DC: Air Force & Museums Program, 1995), pp. 191–207 and Appendix I for terminology.
55. Annual abstract of Statistics No. 93 (HMSO, 1957); Antony Seldon, *Churchill's Indian Summer: the Conservative Government, 1951–1955* (London: Hodder & Stoughton, 1981), p. 332 and Appendix II.
56. TNA AIR 75/23, Slessor to Secretary of State for Air, 1 January 1950, paragraphs 1 and 3.
57. Paul Graham, 'RAF Nuclear Deterrence in the Cold War', *Royal Air Force Air Power Review*, Spring 2007, 10(1):50–75.
58. KCL, Liddell Hart Papers LH11/1949/10, personal communication between Liddell Hart and Air Marshal Sir George Pirie, AMSO, 15 March 1949.
59. Graham, 'RAF Nuclear Deterrence', p. 51.
60. Orange, *Slessor: Bomber Champion*, p. 235.
61. Andrew Brookes, *V-Force: the History of Britain's Airborne Deterrent* (London: Jane's Publishing, 1982), p. 67.
62. Webster & Frankland, *Strategic Air Offensive*, vol. I, p. 75.
63. Graham 'RAF Nuclear Deterrence', p. 53. Table 1.1: 'Statistics of Contemporary Bombers'.
64. Brookes, *V-Force*, pp. 108, 111.
65. Graham, 'RAF Nuclear Deterrence', p. 53.
66. Brookes, *V-Force*, p. 112.

67. Ibid., p. 106.
68. Ibid., pp. 125, 134–6.
69. KCL, Liddell Hart Papers, LH11/1949/10, Liddell Hart and Pirie, 15 March 1949.
70. Peter Hudson (Air Council, 1948–1951) in a lecture held at RAF Hendon, 11 April 2001, 'The RAF and Nuclear Weapons, 1960–1998', published in the *Royal Air Force Historical Society Journal*, 2001, 26:16.
71. Goldberg, 'Military Origins', p. 613.
72. Gowing, *Independence and Deterrence*, p. 235.
73. TNA AIR 8/1998, Churchill to Norman Brook (Secretary of State for Air), 17 January 1952.
74. TNA AIR 75/117, Slessor to Lord Alexander, Defence Secretary, 3 October 1952.
75. Ibid., Slessor to Lord Trenchard, 3 October 1952.
76. Ibid., Slessor to Churchill, 31 December 1952.

Chapter 15: Forecasts Come to Fruition

1. Seldon, *Churchill's Indian Summer*, p. 334.
2. Ibid.
3. John Baylis (ed.), *British Defence Policy in a Changing World* (London: Croom Helm, 1977), p. 170.
4. Air Marshal Sir John Slessor, 'The Place of the Bomber in British Policy', *International Affairs*, July 1953, 29(3):307.
5. Phillip Meilinger, 'The Historiography of Air Power: Theory and Doctrine', *Journal of Military History*, April 2000, 64(2):500.
6. John Groom, *British Thinking about Nuclear Weapons* (London: Frances Pinter, 1974), pp. 61–2.
7. Slessor, *Strategy for the West*, p. 15.
8. Bernard Brodie, 'Nuclear Weapons and Changing Strategic Outlooks' (Santa Monica: RAND, 27 February 1955), pp. 9–10. http://www.rand.org/pubs/papers/P0811.html (accessed 10 July 2016).
9. Sir John Slessor, 'The Great Deterrent and its Limitations', *Bulletin of Atomic Scientists*, May 1956, 12(5):140.
10. Anthony Buzzard, John Slessor & Richard Lowenthal, 'The H-bomb: Massive Retaliation or Graduated Response?' *International Affairs*, July 1956, 32(2):160.
11. Slessor, *Strategy in the West*, pp. 58–60.
12. Sir Lawrence Freedman, *Britain and Nuclear Weapons* (London: Macmillan, 1981), p. 4.
13. Slessor, *Great Deterrent*, pp. 145–6.
14. John Foster Dulles, 'Policy for Security and Peace', *Foreign Affairs*, April 1954, 32(3):360.
15. TNA AIR 75/58, 'Total or Limited War', notes for Slessor's lecture delivered at the US Army War College, January 1957.
16. James King, 'Nuclear Plenty and Limited War', *Foreign Affairs*, January 1956, 35(1): 238–56.
17. Freedman, *Evolution of Nuclear Strategy*, p. 78.
18. Johnston, 'Mr Slessor goes to Washington', p. 393.
19. Slessor, *Great Deterrent*, p. 144.
20. Buzzard, Slessor & Lowenthal, 'The H-bomb: Massive Retaliation or Graduated Response?', p. 148.
21. Ibid., p. 150.

22. Ibid., p. 160.
23. Freedman, *Britain and Nuclear Weapons*, p. 117.
24. Freedman, *Evolution of Nuclear Strategy*, pp. 109–10.
25. TNA DEFE 32/2 COS (51) 741, Chiefs of Staff Report, 'A general war including the use of the atomic bomb in a localised war', paragraph 7, 13 December 1951.
26. Slessor, *Strategy for the West*, pp. 21–2; Thomas Cleary, *Sun Tzu: Art of War* [translated] (London: Shambhala Publications Inc., 2005), p. 53.
27. Slessor, *Great Deterrent*, p. 196.
28. Orange, *Slessor: Bomber Champion*, p. 230.
29. Slessor Family papers, Dr Noble Frankland to John A.G. Slessor (Sir John Slessor's son), 2 December 2006.
30. TNA 75/58, Strategy: Total and Unlimited War, RAF Staff College, Andover, 6 September 1953.
31. TNA AIR 75/58, BBC transcript of *Panorama* programme 'The H-bomb', 13 April 1954.
32. Slessor, *Strategy in the West*, pp. 21, 27.
33. Michael Howard, 'John Slessor and the Prevention of War', Chatham House Lecture, 1998, later published in *Royal Air Force Historical Society Journal*, 1999, 19:132.
34. Stephen J. Ball, 'Military Nuclear Relations between the United States and Great Britain under the Terms of the McMahon Act, 1946–1958', *Historical Journal*, June 1995, 38(2):449.
35. Slessor's son John was to command a flight of Valiants and then a squadron of Vulcans. On Vulcans his allocated target was Kiev.
36. TNA AIR 20/11388, Air Vice Marshal Selway (BJSM) to Air Vice Marshal Earle, ACAS (Policy), 18 February 1956.
37. TNA AIR 2/18093, 'Encircle Conference', 8 August 1956; Young, 'A Most Special Relationship', p. 14.
38. Slessor, *Great Deterrent*, pp. 259–60.
39. Goldberg, 'Military Origins', p. 612.
40. TNA AIR 20/10811, '"Grapple": Value for future operations', undated.
41. E. Bruce Geelhoed & Anthony O. Edmonds (eds), *The Macmillan-Eisenhower Correspondence, 1957–69* (Palgrave MacMillan, 2005). MacMillan to Eisenhower, 22 March 1957. http://www.palgraveconnect.com/pc/doifinder/10.1057/9780230554825 (accessed 24 August 2016).
42. TNA AIR 19/286, Selwyn Lloyd to Eden (PM) Aquatone: U-2 Deployment to RAF Lakenheath, May 1956, and Appendix I for terminology.
43. TNA AIR 75/58, Boyle (CAS) to Slessor, 23 April 1957; Slessor to Boyle, 9 May 1957.
44. Dwight D. Eisenhower, 'Military-Industrial Complex Speech', 17 January 1961; *Public Papers of the Presidents, Dwight D. Eisenhower, 1960*, pp. 1,035–40. http://coursesa.matrix. msu.edu/~hst306/documents/indust.html (accessed 25 August 2016).
45. TNA AIR 75/58, Strong to Slessor, 8 August 1958; article by Joe Alsop, *New York Herald Tribune*, 1 August 1958.
46. Baylis, '1958 Anglo-American Mutual Defence Agreement', p. 433.
47. Ibid., p. 444.
48. TNA AIR 2/18093, 'V-force Operational Front-Line Strength', 18 November 1958.
49. Graham, 'RAF Nuclear Deterrence in the Cold War', p. 67; Pierre, *Nuclear Politics*, p. 156; Brookes, *V-Force*, p. 128.
50. Young, 'A Most Special Relationship', p. 30.

51. Goldberg, 'Military Origins', p. 617.
52. Lawrence Freedman, 'The Origins and Development of the Strategic Nuclear Deterrent Forces, 1945–1960', at the RAF and Nuclear Weapons Seminar held at the RAF Museum, Hendon, 11 April 2001, published in the *Royal Air Force Historical Society Journal*, 2001, 11:56.
53. Young, 'A Most Special Relationship', p. 29.
54. Ibid.
55. Professor Sir Michael Howard, 'John Slessor: The Prevention of War', *Royal Air Force Historical Society Journal*, 1999, 19:136.
56. Ibid., pp. 131–2; Nuclear strategists: Bernard Brodie, *Escalation and the Nuclear Option* (Princeton: Princeton University Press, 1966); Herman Kahn, *On Thermonuclear War* (Princeton: Princeton University Press, 1961); Henry Kissinger, *Nuclear Weapons and Foreign Policy* (New York: W.W. Norton, 1969); and Thomas C. Schelling, *The Strategy of Conflict* (Harvard: Harvard University Press, 1960).
57. Howard, 'John Slessor: The Prevention of War', p. 139.

Epilogue

1. Sir John Slessor, *These Remain. A Personal Anthology: Memories of Flying, Fighting and Field Sports* (London: Michael Joseph, 1969), Dedication.
2. Slessor, *These Remain*, p. 174.
3. Ibid., p. 180.
4. Ibid., p. 181.
5. Slessor Family papers.
6. Ibid.
7. Ibid.
8. Emmanuel Shinwell, *Conflict without Malice* (London: Odhams Press, 1955), p. 219.

Bibliography

Primary Sources

Books by Sir John Slessor
Air Power and Armies (Oxford: Oxford University Press, 1936).
Strategy for the West (London: Cassell, 1954).
The Central Blue (London: Cassell, 1956).
The Great Deterrent (London: Cassell, 1957).
What Price Coexistence? (London: Cassell, 1962).
These Remain: A Personal Anthology (London: Michael Joseph, 1969).

Selected Articles by Sir John Slessor
'The Place of the Bomber in British Policy', *International Affairs*, July 1953, 29(3):302–8.
'Air Power and World Strategy', *Foreign Affairs*, October 1954, 33(1):43–53.
'The Great Deterrent and its Limitations', *Bulletin of Atomic Scientists*, May 1956, 12(5):141–52.
Buzzard, Anthony, John Slessor and Richard Lowenthal, 'The H-bomb: Massive Retaliation or Graduated Response?' *International Affairs*, July 1956, 32(2):148–65.
'British Defence Policy', *Foreign Affairs*, July 1957, 35(1):551–63.

The Slessor Family papers: a comprehensive collection of memorabilia including personal notes, letters, photographs, and sketches, etc., kindly made available by Sir John's grandson, Anthony Slessor.
Liddell-Hart Papers, Kings College London: Slessor Correspondence file 1/644/unnumbered.
The Portal Papers, Christ Church College, Oxford: Slessor Correspondence with Portal and particularly during the Italian Campaign, 1944.
The National Archives (TNA), Kew: A wide range of material is archived under the AIR category and has been utilized extensively in researching source information for all aspects of air power during the period from the First World War through to the Cold War. AIR 75 (The Slessor papers) comprises a large and comprehensive collection of Slessor's correspondence between 1936 and 1960.
Other TNA sources consulted are: Cabinet Papers (CAB); Prime Minister's office (PREM); Foreign Office (FO); Ministry of Defence (DEFE); and Atomic Energy and Weapons (AB).

Secondary Sources

Books
Aldrich, Richard J., *The Hidden Hand* (London: John Murray, 2002).
Alexander, Martin S., *Knowing your Friends: Intelligence Inside Alliances, 1914 to the Cold War* (Abingdon: Routledge, 1998).
Arnold, General H.H., *Global Mission* (London: Hutchinson, 1951).
Baylis, John (ed.), *British Defence Policy in a Changing World* (London: Croom Helm, 1977).

Beevor, Anthony, *D-Day: The Battle for Normandy* (London: Viking, 2009).

Bew, John, *Citizen Clem: A Biography of Attlee* (London: riverrun, 2016).

Brodhurst, Robin, *Churchill's Anchor* (Barnsley: Pen & Sword, 2000).

Brookes, Andrew, *V-Force: The History of Britain's Airborne Deterrent* (London: Jane Publishing, 1982).

Brookes, Andrew, *Air War over Italy* (Hersham: Ian Allen, 2000).

Buckley, John, 'Maritime Air Power and the Second World War: Britain, the USA and Japan', in Sebastian Cox & Peter Gray (eds), *Air Power History: Turning points from Kitty Hawk to Kosovo* (London: Cass, 2005), ch. 6.

Butler, J.R.M., *Grand Strategy, vol. 2: September 1939–June 1941* (London: HMSO, 1957).

Chun, K.S. Clayton, *Aerospace Power in the Twenty-First Century* (United States Air Force Academy, July 2001, pp. 53–6).

Churchill, Winston S., *The Second World War. Vol. I: Gathering Storm* (London: Cassell, 1949).

Churchill, Winston S., *The Second World War, Vol. II: Their Finest Hour* (London, Cassell, 1949).

Craven, W.F. & J.L. Cate (eds), *The Army Air Forces in World War II, Vol. 3: Europe: Argument to VE Day, January 1944 to May 1945* (University of Chicago Press, 1951).

Davis, Richard G., *Carl A. Spaatz and the Air War in Europe* (Washington DC: Center for Air Force History, 1996).

Dean, Sir Maurice, *The RAF and Two World Wars* (London: Cassell, 1979).

Dimbleby, Jonathan, *The Battle of the Atlantic: How the Allies Won the War* (London: Penguin Random House, 2015).

Dylan, Huw, *Defence Intelligence and the Cold War: Britain's Joint Intelligence Bureau 1945–1964* (Oxford: Oxford University Press, 2014).

Ellis, Major L.F., *The War in France and Flanders, 1939–1940* (London: HMSO, 1954).

Freedman, Lawrence, *Britain and Nuclear Weapons* (London: MacMillan, 1980).

—, *The Evolution of Nuclear Strategy* (London: MacMillan, 1981).

Gilbert, Martin, *Churchill: A Life* (London: BCA, 1992).

Gowing, Margaret, *Independence and Deterrence: Britain and Atomic Energy, 1945–1952, Vol. 1: Policy Making* (London: Macmillan, 1974).

Gray, Peter, *The Leadership, Direction and Legitimacy of the RAF Bomber Offensive from Inception to 1945.* Birmingham War Studies (London: Bloomsbury, 2013).

Groom, A.J.R., *British Thinking about Nuclear Weapons* (London: Frances Pinter, 1974).

Hall, R. Cargill & Clayton D. Laurie (eds), *Early Cold War Overflights 1950–56, Vol. I: Memoirs* and *Vol. II: Appendices.* Proceedings of a symposium held at the Defence Intelligence Agency, Washington DC, February 2001. (Washington DC: Office of the Historian, National Reconnaissance Office, 2003).

Hall, R. Cargill & Jacob Neufeld, *The U.S. Air Force in Space 1945 to the Twenty-first Century.* Proceedings of the Air Force Historical Foundation Symposium, Andrews AFB, Maryland, 21–2 September 1995 (Washington, DC: USAF History and Museums Program, 1998).

Harris, Sir Arthur, *Bomber Offensive* (Barnsley: Pen & Sword Military Classics, 2005).

Hastings, Sir Max, 'Sir John Slessor', in Lord Blake and C.S Nicholls (eds.) *The Dictionary of National Biography, 1971–1980* (Oxford: Oxford University Press, 1986).

Howard, Sir Michael, *Captain Professor* (London: Continuum, 2006).

Johnsen, William T., *The Origins of the Grand Alliance: Anglo-American Military Collaboration from the Panay Incident to Pearl Harbour* (Lexington, Kentucky: University Press of Kentucky, 2016).

Lashmar, Paul, *Spy Flights of the Cold War* (Stroud: Sutton Publishing, 1996).

Leutze, James R., *Bargaining for Supremacy* (Carolina: University of Carolina, 1997).

Longoria, Michael A., *The Origin of British Air Policing: An Historical View of Air Policing Doctrine: Lessons from the British Experience between the Wars, 1919–1939* (Air University Press, 1992).

MacMillan, Harold, *Riding the Storm 1956–1959* (London: Macmillan, 1971).

Mason, Air Vice Marshal Tony, *Air Power: A Centennial Appraisal* (London: Brasseys, 1994).

Matloff, Maurice & Edwin M. Snell, *Strategic Planning for Coalition Warfare, 1941–1942* (Center of Military History, United States, 1999).

Meilinger, Phillip, *Paths of Heaven* (Maxwell AFB, Alabama: Air University Press, 2001).

Meilinger, Phillip, *Air War Theory and Practice* (London: Cass, 2005).

Miller, Russell, *Boom: The Life of Viscount Trenchard* (London: Weidenfeld & Nicholson, 2016).

Orange, Vincent, *Slessor: Bomber Champion* (London: Grub Street, 2006).

Overy, R.J., *The Air War 1939–1945* (London: Europa Publications, 1980).

Overy, R.J., *The Bombing War: Europe 1943–1945* (London: Allen Lane, 2013).

Pierre, Andrew J., *Nuclear Politics: the British Experience with an Independent Strategic Force 1939–1970* (London/New York: Oxford University Press, 1972).

Probert, Henry, *High Commanders of the Royal Air Force* (London: HMSO, 1991).

Reynolds, David, *From World War to Cold War* (Oxford: Oxford University Press, 2007).

Richards, Dennis & Hilary St George Saunders, *The Royal Air Force 1939–1945* (London: HMSO, 1954).

Roberts, Andrew, *Churchill: Walking with Destiny* (London: Allen Lane, 2018).

Seldon, Anthony, *Churchill's Indian Summer: The Conservative Government, 1951–1955* (London: Hodder & Stoughton, 1981).

Shinwell, Emmanuel, *Conflict without Malice* (London: Odhams Press, 1955).

Terraine, John, *Business in Great Waters: The U-boat War, 1916–1945* (London: Mandarin Paperbacks, 1989).

Terraine, John, *A Time for Courage* (London: MacMillan, 1989).

Waller, Douglas, *Wild Bill Donovan* (London: Free Press, 2012).

Ward, Chris, *5 Group Bomber Command: An Operational Record* (Barnsley: Pen & Sword, 2007).

Webster, Charles & Noble Frankland, *Strategic Air Offensive against Germany, 1939–1945.*, *Vol. I: Preparation* and *Vol. IV: Annexes and Appendices* (Uckfield: Naval & Military Press, 2006, reprinted edition).

Articles and contributed chapters

Aldrich, Richard J., 'British Intelligence and the Anglo-American "Special Relationship" during the Cold War', *Review of International Studies*, 1998, 24(3):331–51.

Aldrich, Richard J., 'Transatlantic Intelligence and Security Cooperation', *International Affairs*, 2004, 80(4):731–53.

Alexander, Martin S., 'Fighting to the Last Frenchman? Reflections on the BEF Deployment to France and the Strains in the Franco-British Alliance, 1939–1940', *Historical Reflections*, Winter 1996, 22(1).

Andrew, Christopher, 'Intelligence and International Relations in the Early Cold War', *Review of International Studies*, 1998, 24(3):321–30.

Ashton, Nigel John, 'Harold Macmillan and the "Golden Days" of Anglo-American relations revisited', *Diplomatic History*, 2005, 29(4):691–723.

Ball, S.J., 'Military Nuclear Relations between the United States and Great Britain under the Terms of the McMahon Act, 1946–1958', *Historical Journal*, June 1995, 38(2):439–54.

Baylis, John, 'The 1958 Anglo-American Mutual Defence Agreement: The Search for Nuclear Interdependence', *Journal of Strategic Studies*, 2008, 31(3):425–66.

Baylis, John & Alan Macmillan, 'The British Global Strategy Paper of 1952', *Journal of Strategic Studies*, 1993, 16(2):200–26.

Brinkworth, Brian, 'The Planning of British Aircraft Production for the Second World War', *Journal of Aeronautical History*, Paper 2018/09.

Brinkworth, Brian, 'The Anatomy of Deterrence', RAND, 23 July 1958.

Brodie, Bernard, 'Nuclear Weapons and Changing Strategic Outlooks', *Bulletin of the Atomic Scientists*, February 1957. Available at: https://www.rand.org/pubs/papers/P0811.htm (accessed 16 September 2021).

Buckley, John, 'Air Power and the Battle of the Atlantic', *Journal of Contemporary History*, January 1993, 28(1):146.

Buzzard, Anthony, John Slessor and Richard Lowenthal, 'The H-bomb: Massive Retaliation or Graduated Response?' *International Affairs*, July 1956, 32(2):148–65.

Byford, Group Captain Alistair, 'The Battle of France, May 1940: Enduring, combined and joint lessons', *Air Power Review*, Autumn/Winter 2011, 14(3):69–70.

Carter, John D., 'The Air Corps Ferrying Command', in W.F. Craven & J.L. Cate (eds), *The Army Air Forces in World War II, Vol. 1: Plans and Early Operations, January 1939–August 1942* (University of Chicago Press, 1948), ch. 9, p. 313.

Crampton, Squadron Leader John, RAF (ret'd), 'RB-45 Operations'. Air Intelligence Symposium Publication No. 7 *Royal Air Force Historical Society Journal* (1997), 124–32.

Davis, Jeffrey, 'Atfero: The Atlantic Ferry Organisation', *Journal of Contemporary History*, January 1985, 20(1):76 and 91.

Dulles, John Foster, 'Policy for Security and Peace', *Foreign Affairs*, April 1954, 32(3):353–64.

Edgerton, David, 'War, Reconstruction and the Nationalization of Britain, 1939–1951', *Past & Present*, 2011, 210(6):29–46.

Fairclough, Bob, 'Origins of the Project: The Canberra in the RAF', *Royal Air Force Historical Society Journal*, 2009, 43a:9–17.

Freedman, Sir Lawrence, 'The Origins and Development of the British Nuclear Deterrent Forces, 1945–1950'. Concluding review. *Royal Air Force History Society Journal*, 1990, 7:51–7.

Goldberg, Alfred, 'The Atomic Origins of the British Nuclear Deterrent', *International Affairs*, July 1964, 40(3):409–29.

Goldberg, Alfred, 'The Military Origins of the British Nuclear Deterrent', *International Affairs*, October 1964, 40(4):600–18.

Gott, Richard, 'The Evolution of the Independent British Deterrent', *International Affairs*, April 1963, 39(2):238–52.

Graham, Paul, 'RAF Nuclear Deterrence in the Cold War', *Royal Air Force Air Power Review*, Spring 2007, 10(1):50–75.

Howard, Sir Michael, 'Sir John Slessor: The Prevention of War', *Royal Air Force Historical Society Journal*, 1999, 19:127–39.

Jackson, Robert, 'Strategic Air Intelligence: Post-War', Air Intelligence Symposium No. 7. *Royal Air Force Historical Society Journal*, 1997, 116–23.

Johnston, Andrew M., 'Mr Slessor goes to Washington: The Influence of the British Global Strategy Paper in the Eisenhower "New Look"', *Diplomatic History*, July 1998, 22(3):361–97.

Lowe, Peter, 'An Ally and a Recalcitrant General: Great Britain, Douglas MacArthur and the Korean War, 1950–1', *English Historical Review*, July 1990, 105(416):624–53.

Lowenthal, Mark M., 'Roosevelt and the Coming of War: The Search for United States Policy, 1937–1942', *Journal of Contemporary History*, July 1981, 16(3).

Meilinger, Phillip, 'The Historiography of Air Power: Theory and Doctrine', *Journal of Military History*, April 2000, 64(2):467–501.

Millen, R., 'Eisenhower and US Grand Strategy', *Parameters*, Summer 2014, 44(2):35–47.

Pedlow, Gregory W. & Donald E. Welzenbach, 'The U-2 and Oxcart Programmes, 1954–1974'. CIA report originally published 1998 (declassified/released into the public domain 25 June 2013). Available at: https://www.cia.gov/library/center-for-the-study-of-intelligence/csi-publications/books-and-monographs/the-cia-and-the-u-2-program-1954-1974/u2.pdf (accessed 20 May 2015).

Reynolds, David, 'A "Special Relationship?", America, Britain and the International Order since the Second World War", *International Affairs*, 1985, 62(1):1–20.

Reynolds, David, 'Lord Lothian and the Anglo-American Relationship, 1939–1940', *Transactions of the American Philosophical Society*, 1983, 73(2):1–65.

Sallagar, F.M., 'Operation STRANGLE (Italy, Spring 1944): A Case Study of Tactical Air Interdiction', RAND CORPORATION, February 1972. Available at: https://www.rand.org/pubs/reports/R0851.html.

Shaw, Alexander, 'We have just about had it: Jack Slessor, the Foreign Office, and the Anglo-American Strategic Debate over Escalation of the Korean War, 1950–51', *Yonsei Journal of Modern Conflicts* [Korea], Winter 2014, 6(2):292–315.

Smalley, Edward, 'Qualified but unprepared: Training for War at the Staff College in the 1930s', *British Journal for Military History*, November 2015, 2(1).

Smith, Malcolm, The Royal Air Force, Air Power and British Foreign Policy, 1932–1937', *Journal of Contemporary History*, January 1977, 12(1):153–74.

Wallace, William & Christopher Phillips, 'Reassessing the special relationship', *International Affairs*, 2009, 85(2):263–84.

Warner, Michael, 'The Collapse of Intelligence Support for Air Power, 1944–52: Two Steps Backward' (Washington DC: CIA, 2007), 3. Available at: https://www.cia.gov/library/center-for-the-study-of-intelligence/csi (accessed 9 December 2015).

Welzenbach, Donald E., 'The Anglo-American Origins of Overflying the Soviet Union: The Case of "Invisible" Aircraft', in Roger D. Miller (ed.), *Seeing off the Bear* (Washington DC: Air Force and Museums Program, 1995), pp. 191–207.

Young, Ken, 'A Most Special Relationship: the Origins of Anglo-American Strike Planning', *Journal of Cold War Studies*, Spring 2007, 9(2):5–31.

Young, Ken, 'No Blank Cheque: Anglo-American (Mis)Understandings and the Use of the English Airbases', *Journal of Military History*, October 2007, 71(4):1133–67.

Young, Ken, 'US Atomic Capability and the British Forward bases in the early Cold War', *Journal of Contemporary History*, 2007, 28(4):117–36.

Young, Ken, 'Revisiting NSC-68', *Journal of Cold War Studies*, Winter 2013, 15(1):3–33.

Young, Ken, 'Cold War Insecurities and the Curious Case of John Strachey', *Intelligence and National Security*, 2014, 29(6):901–25.

Zeitlin, Jonathan, 'Flexibility and Mass Production at War: Aircraft Manufacture in Britain, the United States and Germany, 1939–1945', *Technology and Culture*, January 1995, 36(1).

Unpublished PhD Theses

Connolly, Major Corvin J., USAF, 'Marshal of the Royal Air Force Sir John Cotesworth Slessor and the Anglo-American Air Power Alliance, 1940–1945', PhD Texas A&M University, 2001. Available at: www.dtic.mil/cgi-bin/GetTRDoc?AD=ADA399435 (accessed 12 May 2016).

Index

Page numbers in **bold** refer to maps and those in *italic* denote tables.